Thinking History Globally

Thinking History Globally

Diego Olstein
*Associate Professor and Associate Director of World History Center,
University of Pittsburgh, USA*

© Diego Olstein 2015
Foreword © Yuval Noah Harari 2015
Foreword © Patrick Manning 2015

All rights reserved. No reproduction, copy or transmission of this publication may be made without written permission.

No portion of this publication may be reproduced, copied or transmitted save with written permission or in accordance with the provisions of the Copyright, Designs and Patents Act 1988, or under the terms of any licence permitting limited copying issued by the Copyright Licensing Agency, Saffron House, 6–10 Kirby Street, London EC1N 8TS.

Any person who does any unauthorized act in relation to this publication may be liable to criminal prosecution and civil claims for damages.

The author has asserted his right to be identified as the author of this work in accordance with the Copyright, Designs and Patents Act 1988.

First published 2015 by
PALGRAVE MACMILLAN

Palgrave Macmillan in the UK is an imprint of Macmillan Publishers Limited, registered in England, company number 785998, of Houndmills, Basingstoke, Hampshire RG21 6XS.

Palgrave Macmillan in the US is a division of St Martin's Press LLC,
175 Fifth Avenue, New York, NY 10010.

Palgrave Macmillan is the global academic imprint of the above companies and has companies and representatives throughout the world.

Palgrave® and Macmillan® are registered trademarks in the United States, the United Kingdom, Europe and other countries.

ISBN 978–0–230–36102–7 hardback
ISBN 978–1–137–47338–7 paperback

This book is printed on paper suitable for recycling and made from fully managed and sustained forest sources. Logging, pulping and manufacturing processes are expected to conform to the environmental regulations of the country of origin.

A catalogue record for this book is available from the British Library.

Library of Congress Cataloging-in-Publication Data
Olstein, Diego Adrian.
  Thinking history globally / Diego Olstein (associate professor and
  associate director of World History Center, University of Pittsburgh, USA).
       pages   cm
  Summary: "Thinking History Globally means thinking about the past and the present beyond national borders, language barriers, and enclosed regions. There are four thinking strategies to gain global perspectives: comparing, connecting, conceptualizing, and contextualizing. Comparing is about contrasting between several cases and drawing new conclusions. Connecting is tracking the interdependences between cases and assessing their importance. Conceptualizing is recognizing that developments in one or several cases belong within a larger recurring pattern. Contextualizing is making sense of one case amidst developments world-wide. This book offers a practical guide into these strategies of thinking by applying them to multiple historical cases, ranging from the first civilizations and up to the First World War. While doing that, Olstein also presents the twelve branches of history that outstand in the application of these four strategies and in thinking history globally: comparative, relational, international, transnational, oceanic, global, world, and big histories, historical sociology, civilizational analysis, world-system approach, and history of globalization" — Provided by publisher.
  Includes bibliographical references.
  ISBN 978–0–230–36102–7 (hardback) — ISBN 978–1–137–47338–7 (paperback)
  1. History—Philosophy.   2. Historiography—Philosophy.   3. History—Methodology.   4. Historiography—Methodology.   5. Globalization.
  6. World history.   I. Title.
  D16.8.O556 2014
  901—dc23   2014026282

*A mis padres, Susana Ejdem y Félix Olstein,
por sus esfuerzos sostenidos, su amor y dedicación*

Contents

List of Tables and Figures	viii
Foreword by Yuval Noah Harari	x
Foreword by Patrick Manning	xii
Acknowledgments	xiv
Introduction	1
1 Thinking History Globally: Theory in Practice. Argentina under Perón (1946–1955), Thinking Globally a National History	9
2 Thinking History Globally: 12 Branches in Their Singularities, Overlaps, and Clusters	33
3 Thinking History Globally: Comparing or Connecting	59
4 Thinking History Globally: Comparing and Connecting	82
5 Thinking History Globally: Varieties of Connections	98
6 Thinking History Globally: Conceptualizing through Social Sciences	113
7 Thinking History Globally, Thinking Globalization Historically	125
8 Thinking History Globally: Contextualizing on a Bigger Scale	140
9 All Together Now, a Last Rehearsal: Thinking Globally on Border Crossing Phenomena, the First World War	157
Notes	184
Analytic Bibliography	194
Index	219

Tables and Figures

Tables

1.1	Concomitant variations of anti-hegemonic party states	24
2.1	Thinking history globally: Categories and networks	47
2.2	The units of analysis	50
2.3	Categories clustered by scale of unit of analysis	52
2.4	Time scope	53
2.5	Clusters by time scope	53
2.6	Clusters by discipline, approach, and sources	54
2.7	Twelve branches in their singularities and overlaps	56
2.8	Clustering the 12 branches by five parameters	57
2.9	Clustering the 12 branches by the four big Cs	58
3.1	Ways of crossing borders	60
3.2	Thinking history globally: The comparative–connective divide	68
3.3	Comparison typologies reconciled	73
3.4	How to connect? A typology of connections as method	76
5.1	Unity and variety in the enlarged relational family	100
5.2	Oceanic histories	112
6.1	The world that the *world-system approach* has created	121
7.1	Approaches to the history of globalization: Three main analytical categories	133
7.2	Histories of globalization classified chronologically and comparatively	137
8.1	Harari's "Imperial Wheel" throughout world history	143
8.2	Abernethy's pulses of "power-profit-proselytization" in global history	144
8.3	World history in a nutshell: Major transformations by variables	148
8.4	World history overlaps with all other branches	155
9.1	First and last chapters contrasted: Singularities and clusters assessed (Compare with Table 2.8)	182

Figures

I.1	The Roman Empire: Border closed	2
I.2	Eurasian empires: Border crossed	3
5.1	"Gestaltic" terrestrial and oceanic world maps	107
5.2	"Gestaltic" terrestrial and oceanic world maps	108

5.3	Silk and Spice roads	109
6.1	Core, semi-peripheral, and peripheral states	122
9.1	The Western and Eastern Fronts compared	178

Foreword

Yuval Noah Harari

Historians think that the present is the product of the past. But when it comes to thinking about history, the past is often the product of the present, that is present day conditions and concerns color our understanding of past events. When in the late nineteenth century and early twentieth century nation-states were the most powerful actors in the world, historians thought about the entire course of history in terms of nations and states. When class warfare dominated politics, historians saw class warfare everywhere they looked in the past. When gender became a major political and social issue, medievalists and Egyptologists began to think about medieval Scotland and Pharaohnic Egypt in terms of gender.

It is not surprising, then, that in the early twenty-first century historians are increasingly adopting a global approach to the past. The world of today is a single unit. It is impossible to understand the economy, politics or culture of a particular country without taking into account events and processes in distant lands. The major problems facing the world—whether ecological, economical or epidemiological—are global in nature and cannot be solved except by global efforts. Though there are still distinct cultures, religions and identities in the world, for the first time in history almost all people share at least some basic perceptions. If you go to Buenos Aires, Tel Aviv, Tehran or Beijing, you will find that most business people think about the economy in capitalist terms; that most legal experts speak the peculiar language of rights; and that most doctors share the same views of the human body and of the natural world. If you have a heart attack and are rushed to hospital, an Iranian doctor and an Israeli doctor are likely to follow identical procedures and give you an identical treatment. Historians are faced with the double task of understanding how we got here, and of rewriting the narrative of the past from a fresh global perspective. Just as the citizens of twentieth-century nation-states needed a national history, so the travelers of spaceship Earth now need a global history.

But how do you adopt a "global" approach to the past? Over the last few decades, scholars have answered this question in a bewildering number of ways. Almost everybody agrees that we need to start thinking history globally, but it is far from obvious what that means. *Thinking History Globally* brings order to this chaos. It maps all the various ways in which scholars have tried to think globally about the past, dividing them into 12 distinct categories, and highlighting four main strategies: comparing, connecting, conceptualizing and contextualizing.

Yet in the process of mapping and cataloguing, the book does something far more ambitious and important. Its underlying argument is that the old way of thinking and doing history are obsolete. Thinking history globally means far more than just adjusting the focus of our lens. It is not enough to apply traditional tools and methods to bigger units of analysis. If we want to study planet Earth as a historical unit, we cannot simply take the old nation-state matrix, replace "France" or "Argentina" with "humankind" or "the world," and go on asking the same questions and answering them using the same methodology. We will have to start asking completely new questions and adopt completely new methods. *Thinking History Globally* examines the deep logic of historical thinking, and highlights what must be changed if we are to adopt a truly global outlook. Since nowadays it makes little sense to think about history except in global terms, what *Thinking History Globally* really seeks to do, is to redefine the historical discipline.

In the twentieth century, the guiding metaphor of historical disciplines was "the foreign country". First year undergraduates were told that the past is a foreign country, and the task of historians was to lay aside their prejudices and preconceptions, learn the foreign language of primary sources, and use that to understand the strange practices of that foreign country. But in the twenty-first century, there are no longer foreign countries. Wherever you go, there are Google, McDonalds, alienating airport terminals, and the invisible hand of global capital. True, it is unlikely that archeologists will start finding ruins of ancient McDonald restaurants in medieval Scotland or Pharaohnic Egypt. But twenty-first century students and scholars will no longer have the mindset of visiting a truly foreign country. For them, everything will be part of a single whole, and the past too will be another link in a global chain of supply, which cannot be understood "on its own terms," just as no present-day country can be understood in isolation.

Yuval Noah Harari
Jerusalem, July 2014
The Hebrew University of Jerusalem

Foreword

Patrick Manning

What is world history? What is global history? Why do historians ask such questions, and why do they give so many different answers? Here is a book-length response to the question of how to think globally about history. Diego Olstein answers that thinking globally about history can be orderly, but also that it requires flexibility. He argues that the truth about the past reveals itself through the interplay of different perspectives. Further, despite all the variations in outlook, he treats the multiple views of the past as more complementary than contradictory. His framework identifies four principal strategies for understanding of the past: comparison, connection, conceptualization, and contextualization. As he sees it, balancing these strategies enables us to find satisfactory answers to global historical questions, even complex ones.

This book is one of those remarkable volumes that is, at once, a basic guide to undergraduate students and a sophisticated roadmap for leaders in the profession. The book demonstrates how far historical studies have moved away from viewing "history" as an essential and true narrative of the past—and toward treating history as an overlapping array of evidence and interpretations. Professor Olstein did not create this new situation, but his book brings an important advance in learning to live with it. Thus, his Bibliography—classifying books by approach rather than by subject matter—shows how to read history by interpretive approach and not just by the facts of time and place.

Olstein developed his understanding of multiple perspectives in history not only through the strength of his intellect but also through his various experiences around the world. His insights came out of his Argentine homeland, his education and teaching in Israel, his years of research in Spain, his current academic position in the United States, and even his teaching experience in China—they all contribute to his outlook. I believe that the result enables him to assist readers in sorting out the dilemma of multiple perspectives in global history. His skill in proposing clear historical generalizations makes it possible for readers to join him in apprehending the order that accompanies the complexity of the world's detail.

While history has been written for thousands of years, historical studies have experienced enormous transformations during the past half-century. History now reaches beyond politics to every arena of culture and technology, to every continent, to the oceans—and, in partnership with other disciplines, to the depths of our psyche and to the earliest days of humanity.

Historians now study new types of data in climate, health, genetics, artistic creation, and psychology—as well economic, social, and political change among people previously neglected. Each new type of historical knowledge brings an additional type of perspective.

Olstein's wide-ranging reading traces many authors and the arguments they have developed—arguments intended to explain processes of social change. Further, recent globalization has accelerated the innovative arguments of historians, as they seek to explain the growth in global complexity. Various historians, seizing on different aspects of history, developed and named approaches that they labeled as "international," "transnational," "entangled," "deep," and "new global," as well as the better-known "world" and "global." Does labeling an approach as "global" guarantee that those who adopt the label will follow a common set of precepts? Are all the practitioners of a given genre expected to analyze in one way rather than another? These are problems currently under debate in world-historical studies. Olstein sets these interpretive approaches alongside each other, making the case that all are logical if partial approaches, and that something is gained by considering them all. This book discusses how to accommodate global complexity through new interpretations of history.

The book focuses on the twentieth-century era of nations, notably through Peron's Argentina and the clash of nations and empires in World War I. Do we think of the past century as a unique moment in history? Or do we see it as representative of processes in the deeper history of mankind? With attention to the author's treatment of historical scales, we can see ways in which we can say that the answer is "both." At its core, this book is designed to help readers in thinking globally about the history of any era.

Understanding history, Olstein shows us, relies on reasoning, not just facts. He invites readers to join in tracing how authors have developed different logics of past change, responding to the arguments of other authors and the recent proliferation of historical topics. Olstein's logical thinking is straightforward, when considered one step at a time. He considers as many as 12 "branches" or steps for crossing historical boundaries. He moves by steps from comparison to connection, then moves to a larger scale for steps in conceptualization and contextualization. Such a combination of simple steps, if one can keep them in mind, builds a powerful set of tools for looking at the complexity of history, as if through the facets of a prism.

Patrick Manning
Pittsburgh, August 2014
University of Pittsburgh

Acknowledgments

This book was written while working at four institutions: the Hebrew University of Jerusalem, my alma mater; the University of Wisconsin-Madison, where I spent my first sabbatical year; the University of Pittsburgh, my new academic home; and Jacobs University, which hosted me last summer. I am indebted to all four and to many colleagues from these institutions that collaborated with me and on this project.

Benjamin Kedar, my teacher and mentor, introduced me to the field of comparative history and entrusted me with the establishment of a world history program at the Hebrew University. Moshe Zimmerman was by my side from very early on and throughout my career in the history of historiography. My close friend and former colleague Yuval Noah Harari sustains with me a lifelong and thorough exchange of ideas on the subjects of this book and beyond. He also commented extensively on this manuscript and significantly improved it. In addition, throughout all my years at the Department of History in Jerusalem, Sara Parnasa cared for all my administrative needs on campus.

The George Mosse Program hosted me at the University of Wisconsin-Madison from 2009 to 2010. John Tortorice received me wonderfully upon my arrival and facilitated my work throughout the year in many respects. Stanley Payne was my main collocutor while there and strongly encouraged me at the earliest stages of this project. Also, David Sorkin and Jeremy Suri showed their interest in my work and trajectory, pointing very wisely toward several courses of action.

The World History Center and the Department of History at the University of Pittsburgh welcomed me since my first visit in 2009, throughout my incorporation in 2011, and since. Fortunately, after being a source of inspiration for years beforehand and from a geographic distance, Pat Manning became a close colleague. I had the honor and pleasure to discuss with him our ideas on the subjects of this book. He also thoroughly read and commented on its several drafts. Many other affiliates to the World History Center and members of the Department of History at Pitt provided me with valuable comments, corrections, and suggestions for this work, including John Markoff, Molly Warsh, Reid Andrews, Bill Chase, Vincent Leung, John Galante, Justin Classen, Pedro Machado, and Torsten Feys. Katie Jones was extremely helpful with all administrative concerns at the World History Center. Grace Tomcho, besides caring for all regular administrative needs, took extraordinary good care of the multiple aspects of my transition to the United States, Pittsburgh, and Pitt. Also Derek Baran from the Office of International Services at Pitt was remarkably efficient in facilitating our transition. Alex Wolfe copyedited the final manuscript. The Richard D. and Mary Jane Edwards Endowed Publication Fund provided generous support for the publication of this book.

In an intensive seminar and research stay at Jacobs University last summer, Corinna Unger, Dominic Sachsenmaier, Marc Frey, and their graduate students raised challenging questions and inspiring suggestions, many of which found their way into this book. The Humboldt Foundation was very generous in providing this fruitful opportunity.

Besides these institutions, several networks provided an additional framework for evolving and presenting parts of this project as well as harvesting more challenges: Global History, Globally, organized by Harvard, Duke, and Humboldt-Universität zu Berlin, the European Network in Universal and Global History, the German-Israel Frontiers of Humanities Program, and the Latin American Network of Global History. Among the many colleagues that helped enrich my work within these networks, I would particularly like to mention Sven Beckert, Erez Manela, Matthias Middel, Gareth Austin, Michal Biran, Claudia Kedar, Sergio Serulnikov, Andrea Lluch, Sandra Kuntz Ficker, Hilda Sabato, and Silvana Ablin.

Alongside my colleagues, both graduate and undergraduate students in Jerusalem, Madison, Pittsburgh, Buenos Aires, Bahía Blanca, Wuhan, and Bremen provided me with important feedback from the intended targeted audiences for this book.

Many people beyond the academic world also enabled the writing of this book. Maureen States was extremely kind and helpful in getting me and my family settled in Pittsburgh. Dr. Gretchen Arendt, Dr. Vu Nuen, Dr. Sushil Beriwal, Dr. Stanley Marks, Dr. Esther Elyashiv, and their teams, as well as Etty Reut and Amanda Kalbaugh helped us overcome illness. Many, many people—family, friends, colleagues, acquaintances, and strangers—supported us in the process. Tica Hall, Judy Rosen, and Stefania Pianetti were at the forefront of that struggle, providing us with their support and guidance. Jaia Lerner overcame all impending obstacles to be with us.

Many friends, from within and outside of the history profession, have also brought their contributions to the manuscript and/or encouragement and assistance to its author: Assaf and Dana Meshulam, Elisa Heymann, Mike and Marion Taube, Lara Putnam, Michal Friedman, Paul Eiss, Roee Teper, Harel Schwartz, Maya Haber, Sean Guillory, Gregor Thum, Golan Barak, Laura Gotkowitz, and Michel Gobat. Ezequiel Lein, my lifelong friend, deserves a special mention not only for his friendship but also for his valuable comments on this text.

I encountered much encouragement, inspiration, and happiness, in my close relations with Betty Ejdem, David Rapaport, and four generations of Olsteins, Zaselskys, and Lerners. However, when it comes to driving forces, first place clearly belongs to Irit Lerner-Olstein, Racheli, Ariel, and Maya Holstein, my beloved family and global companions.

I am deeply thankful to all these institutions, networks, and individuals.

Introduction

Thinking within and beyond boundaries: Rome, open city

Legend has it that Romulus, the son of Rhea Silvia, was nourished by a female wolf and later founded a city on top of the Palatine Hill in 753 BCE. Romulus named the city after himself and became the first of its seven kings. In time Rome grew to encompass the entire Mediterranean Sea, becoming one of the largest and most powerful empires of the ancient world. By 27 BCE Augustus brought five centuries of republican regime to a close when he became the first Roman emperor. Five centuries later, on 4 September 476 BCE, the last Roman emperor in the West, Romulus Augustus, whose name combined both of the above-mentioned heroes, surrendered the imperial throne to Odoacer, a Germanic chieftain and Roman officer.

Few developments in history have been subjected to such scrutiny as the fall of the Roman Empire in the West. No less than 210 theories address the riddle of Roman collapse. Some of these theories point toward one major culprit, for example, the rise of Christianity, the invasion of Germanic peoples, the weakening of the Roman army. Other theories argue that there were multiple factors at play, such as climatic change, population decline, and inner-social conflict. Some theories depict a free fall collapse. Others, by contrast, describe a more gradual decline. There are explanations based on the fragility of the imperial economy. Alternatively, other explanations attribute the collapse to the decline of Roman values.

Whether the collapse of the Roman Empire was abrupt or gradual, due to a major single reason or many causes, and whether these causes were mainly material or ideal, in general the literature on the fall of Rome privileges internal explanations. The decline of slave manpower supply, the rise of Christianity, or lead poisoning due to contamination of water from lead pipelines are good examples of that. Alternatively, there are studies ready to cross the boundaries of the Roman Empire, the *limes*, and engage more cases of imperial collapse. From this wider perspective, the collapse of the Roman Empire is a particular

2 *Thinking History Globally*

case of overstretching, a pattern of imperial expansion beyond logistic capability identified in several empires. Moreover, by moving beyond the borders of the Roman Empire we become aware of the rather simultaneous and similar fates of other empires across Eurasia—that is, the Parthian, Kushan, and Han empires. This synchronicity stimulates thought about the underlying reasons for all of these collapses, such as climatic change, the impact of simultaneous nomadic invasions to imperial territories, and the diffusion of epidemics across Eurasia (Figures I.1 and I.2).

To us, citizens of a globalized world, this type of reasoning comes almost naturally. It is only lately that we tracked the global unfolding of the financial crisis. We also made sense of the Arab Spring as a domino effect. We spot the sequence of environmental disasters and connect the dots of climate change. We learn to be alert, finding the next butterfly's wings that can unleash a storm in our backyard. Thinking beyond fixed boundaries, thinking out of the box, thinking globally is an outgrowth of our contemporary global experience. This kind of global thinking can also be harnessed to make sense of the past in innovative ways. As historians usually confront the past with the concerns of the present, thinking globally about history is on the rise. In fact, it is one of the greatest innovations in the ways of researching, writing, and teaching history.

As you might recall from your history classes, reading, professors, and colleagues, most of the study of the past was circumscribed to a particular place

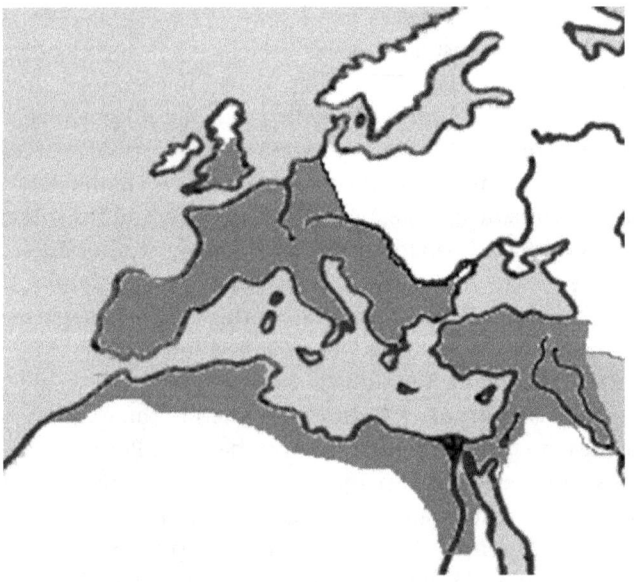

Figure I.1 The Roman Empire: Border closed

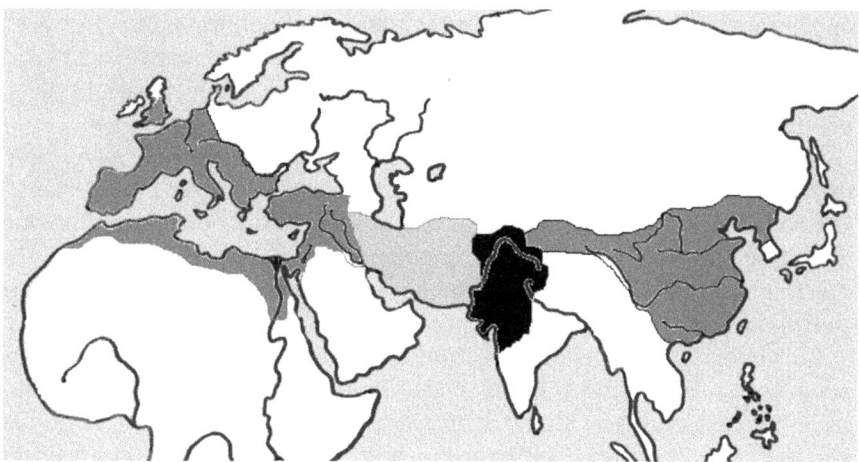

Figure I.2 Eurasian empires: Border crossed

delimited by its political boundaries and language barriers. But what if you need to think beyond these boundaries? What if you want to think of history outside of the box? That is, what if instead of writing another paper, thesis, dissertation, book, or syllabus framed within the boundaries of any country, you are asked to or proactively choose to move beyond boundaries and even reach a global perspective? Imagine any unit of analysis with which you are familiar, say Russia, Spain, China, Ethiopia, or the United States, how do their histories compare to others? How do their histories relate to others? What inroads have the histories of other places made into them? How do these histories fit within other generalized trends and patterns? How are these histories part of a larger story, that of an entire civilization, ocean basin, the globe, humankind, or even the universe? This book invites and guides you to think globally about the past and comes back to our global present historically informed.

Thinking within boundaries in the global village

We are now, and have been for the last several decades, citizens of a *global village*. That means, in a nutshell, that we live in an integrated and interdependent economy that works as a unit in real time on a planetary basis. This economy relies on information superhighways, communication, and transportation networks. These networks simultaneously contribute to enhancements of and reactions to a global culture. Moreover, these networks facilitate the articulation of a global civil society reflected by the blooming of thousands of international and transnational nongovernmental organizations. The political realm, however, lags behind this fast-forward compression of both the temporal and spatial dimensions. The nation-state persists as the central political entity. However, nation-states are deeply subsumed under the impact of the above-mentioned economic, cultural, and social globalizing effects. Moreover, regional and global political institutions have formed to coexist with them.

All of these circumstances stimulate global awareness. It is hardly surprising, then, that historical thinking and writing increasingly strives toward globalization too. Based on our experiences and perceptions of global lives, thinking globally about history enhances our understanding of the past. Conversely, discovering the global dimensions of our past expands our understanding of the globalized world in which we live.

And yet historical thinking grew strongly constrained by borders: the borders of nation-states (e.g., the Arab Republic of Egypt since 1953) or previous political entities (e.g., the New Kingdom of Egypt, circa 1550–1077 BCE), often times also associated with language barriers (e.g., the Arab language), and embedded in a region so defined (e.g., the Near or Middle East). That is the case because history as a profession and academic discipline emerged in the late nineteenth century and was closely related to the consolidation of the modern nation-state. Nation-states conditioned the research and writing of history by funding the departments of history and the training of professional historians as well as the national archives in which the national records were deposited.

The attached expectation of this arrangement was for historians to write the history of the nation and its origins. This was a task that many historians were willing to fulfill in the first place, as their thinking was shaped by nationalism, a predominant ideology at the time. The disciplinary imperative of language proficiency to properly scrutinize primary sources in their original form brought an additional limit. To a great extent, nation-states' borders and language barriers were mutually reinforcing in establishing historical thinking as a border-closed endeavor. Politically enclosed, primary source-based histories became the disciplinary norm known as "methodological nationalism."

Since this foundational period, historical thinking has evolved enormously. A broad range of dimensions, subjects, perspectives, and types of sources and methods have been cumulatively adopted. From the early twentieth century on, history has cumulatively incorporated economic, social, quantitative, intellectual, cultural, gender-centered, and postcolonial dimensions, establishing new branches of historical knowledge. However, by and large, the mutually reinforced principles of enclosed political borders and language barriers have remained in place. Historical thinking expanded the past enormously by studying phenomena other than the nation, its state, and origins. Nevertheless, as renovating as the new subjects and perspectives were, they were generally framed within the limits of an enclosed spatial unit, usually a state, of the 12 branches in their singularities, and second, it highlights how the 12 branches overlap on multiple dimensions, reflecting the connections and interrelations shared by their agendas, publications, and associations.

All in all, the first two chapters offer a comprehensive typology of the possibilities for thinking globally about history. This typology is not an ontological exercise in which each publication must necessarily fit into one and only one category. Rather this typology is envisioned as a functional tool to help visualize clearly the possible strategies and historiographies at hand when it comes to thinking history globally. Based on the conclusions drawn from this typology, chapters 3 through 8 are organized by the four strategies for thinking history globally—comparing, connecting, conceptualizing, and contextualizing—while presenting and exemplifying the 12 historical branches in their singularities.

Chapter 3 addresses the alternative paths offered by comparisons and connections as methods of thinking history globally. Through three major themes—"the eve of civilization," "imperial history," and "the American Divergence"—this chapter explains the aims, means, and results of each of these two first Cs of global thinking. Moreover, comparisons and connections are described, applied, and exemplified in their varieties. Finally, the comparative–connective rift allows for an additional way of clustering the 12 transboundary branches of history, a rift that confronts comparative and relational histories.

Chapter 4 takes a closer look into this rift by examining the criticism on comparative history and the comparative method as well as the alternatives advanced by relational histories through the study of connections. Moving beyond the exclusionary vision regarding these two methods, the chapter accentuates the possibilities for collaboration between them, their achievements, and prospects.

Chapter 5 expands the family of relational approaches to include new international, transnational, and oceanic histories. Through these three additional branches, the varieties of connections are further explored. Both comparisons and connections reemerge in the remaining chapters in tandem with the presentation of the remaining two big Cs: conceptualization and contextualization.

Chapter 6 presents conceptualization as the third strategy for thinking globally, as offered by historically oriented social sciences. Historical sociology, civilizational analysis, and the world-system approach are introduced as ways of thinking history globally while combining comparisons and connections with conceptualization.

Up to this point, globalization and the global consciousness that it brought were presented as major driving forces for thinking history globally. Chapter 7 turns the tables on the present as it analyzes globalization from a historical perspective. This chapter shows that thinking history globally is not only about what globalization can do for history but also what history can do for globalization. Moreover, the chapter serves as a necessary introduction for the remaining three branches of history and the strategy that they stand for, contextualization.

Chapter 8 presents three branches of history ready to encompass the globe and beyond: global, world, and big history. By adopting the largest possible contexts, either the planet or the cosmos, in order to make comparisons or track connections, these branches use contextualization as their prominent strategy for thinking history globally.

The ninth and final chapter offers a second experimental laboratory for the reader to think history globally, but this time readers will have insight about the four strategies and the individualized 12 branches. Also this second experiment presents a well-known and global phenomenon by definition: the First World War. The main considerations for thinking globally about history and thinking historically about the global village will be illuminated.

Finally, the book ends with a very helpful tool for readers: an analytical bibliography arranged by the four strategies and 12 branches. This bibliography provides a convenient guide to further reading to meet the specific interests and needs of readers.

1
Thinking History Globally: Theory in Practice. Argentina under Perón (1946–1955), Thinking Globally a National History

Globalization is all about transcending boundaries that are economic, political, linguistic, cultural, and regional, and in order to think globally about history, we need to move beyond these boundaries too. Contemporary historiography offers 12 distinct branches defined precisely by their particular transcendence of boundaries. The list of 12 branches can be collapsed into four main categories, each standing for the four main strategies for global thinking applied by these branches. By way of a concrete case study, this chapter defines and exemplifies each of these four main strategies for global thinking and the 12 branches subsumed by them. Argentina under Juan Domingo Perón (1946–1955) is a case study typically framed within the boundaries of national history; however, in the following thought experiment, this case provides a platform for exemplifying the strategies and branches for thinking history globally. Moreover, readers will see firsthand how global thinking brings history out of the national box.

On the eve of October 17, 1945, thousands of workers made their way, rather spontaneously, to the Plaza de Mayo in Buenos Aires. They came to demand the liberation of Colonel Juan Domingo Perón. For the last two years, in his capacity as the secretary of labor in a military government, Perón sanctioned a series of decrees on compensations, retirement, and working conditions that were favorable to the working class. Anxious due to the mutual empowerment of Perón and the labor organizations, the members of the military junta pressed Perón into resignation, which was then followed by his imprisonment. But this series of events was of no avail for the junta. In a week, the broad mobilization of the workers in the capital city and nearby locations resulted in the liberation of Perón and his overwhelming return to the political scene.

On February 24, 1946, Juan Domingo Perón obtained 56 percent of the popular vote and won the national elections in 22 of the 23 provinces.

His presidential mandate, prolonged by winning the subsequent election in 1952 and thereafter interrupted by a military coup in September 1955, profoundly transformed the history of Argentina. As such, Perón's regime captured great attention resulting in a wide historiography mostly framed within the Argentinean borders.

Argentina under Perón (1946–1955): Nation-state-based histories

Political historians wrote careful accounts of Perón's political party, regime, decision-making, constitutional reform, political struggles from within and without, and fluctuations in power. Similarly, they paid close attention to his "Third Position" (neither capitalist nor communist) in foreign policy and his relations with Cold War-age superpowers as well as neighboring states. Economic historians have studied the nationalization of foreign companies, his import substitution policies, the five-year programs envisioned to develop the national economy, and the shifting balance of power between capital and labor, favoring the latter.

Social and labor historians have addressed the emergence of a new working class resulting from the large migration from the provinces to the capital, the labor unions and federations, and Perón's social reforms. Gender-centered historiography has paid close attention to the figure of Evita, Perón's second wife, and an additional branch of the party called "The Feminine Section" in Perón's political party, and to women's changing status during these two consecutive mandates in which women gained legal and political equality, including the right to vote and be elected.

All of these transformations were also approached by intellectual historians who have searched for the ideological roots and underpinnings guiding and justifying all the above-mentioned transformations. Similarly, educational policies, the conflict with the Catholic Church, the emergence of a new popular culture, and the impact of Perón's regime on Argentinean literature, cinema, and architecture attracted the interest of cultural historians.

All of these historiographies were contested and enriched by decentralized views that preferred local perspectives and those from below. In this vein, later publications have described daily life, family life, private life, and urban life during the years of Perón's regime. Moreover, many studies have addressed how Perón's rise to power and his regime coalesced in the specific settings of individualized localities, including the rural domain, within particular Argentinean provinces. Some 20 years ago an international bibliography on the subject amounted to 3392 publications,[1] and several thousand more have accumulated since.[2] This entire range of nation-state-based historical research shed light on many dimensions of Perón's regime, a crucial period in the history of Argentina.

Thinking Argentina under Perón globally: Four strategies, 12 branches

And yet what would Perón's regime look like while thinking about it globally? Are there historical arguments to be made beyond the Argentinean borders in relation to Perón's regime? The following chapter addresses these two questions by drafting 12 cross-boundary sketches of alternative narratives. Each of these sketches is inspired by one of the 12 cross-boundary historical branches and their particular ways of applying the four major strategies to global thinking. Simultaneously, these 12 sketches also serve to define and provide examples of each of these branches' conceptual and methodological singularities. In short, by tackling a crucial development within a nation-state, which normally is framed as a national history, from a global perspective, the four strategies for thinking globally about history, the 12 branches that apply them, and their innovative contributions will be made clear and concrete.

Thinking history globally: Comparing and connecting

Comparing and connecting are two major strategies for thinking globally about history. Comparisons bring two or more units side by side in order to describe or analyze their similarities and differences. Connections bring two or more units together to assess their interdependence. Comparative history and relational histories are two historical branches based on these two strategies, respectively.

Comparative history

Comparative history seeks similarities and differences between two or more units for analytical or descriptive purposes.

Comparative history seeks similarities and differences between two or more units for analytical or descriptive purposes, and Perón's regime could act as the subject. For example, Perón's regime can be contrasted with Getulio Vargas's regime in Brazil. In 1945, while holding power during the days of his *Estado Novo* (New State, 1937–1945), Getulio Vargas created the Partido Trabalhista Brasileiro. This political party was bound to urban workers and was intended to provide Vargas with a broad basis of social support to transition out of his authoritarian regime. As Vargas got ready to test his party in democratic elections, the army overthrew him. It was only in 1950 that this electoral goal and the subsequent victory of the Partido Trabalhista Brasileiro were accomplished.

The resulting government was supported by a broad social coalition that included the working class as well as some sectors of the urban middle class. This regime combined an economic developmentalist policy that checked the elite's wealth accumulation and favored rights and social programs for the working class with a protectionist and nationalist stance. These twofold policies are expressed in the state management of natural resources, economic planning, and wealth distribution. Petroleum development and refining were nationalized in 1953. The nationalization of electric power utilities was also pursued, although without success. A national development bank was created in order to provide public loans to basic industry. Labor laws, social security, and welfare services were fostered. In 1954, under the threat of an imminent military coup, Vargas committed suicide.

A series of similarities stand out between the Perón and Vargas regimes. Both figures amassed political power in the framework of an authoritarian regime. Subsequently, both aimed to establish a broad social basis of support and gained legitimacy through democratic elections. In pursuing that, both were held back by military intervention. However, sooner or later both leaders achieved those goals. Once in power, both regimes attempted industrialization through the nationalization of resources and infrastructure as well as import substitution that aimed to transform the agro-exporting economies of their countries. This transformation occurred while protecting the interests of the working class by shifting the balance of power between capital and labor, favoring the latter. Finally, both the Perón and Vargas regimes were overthrown by the military or by military threat, resulting in military dictatorships for decades afterwards that brought these transformations to a halt and opened a political cycle of military dictatorship alternating with a low-efficiency democratic regime.

Comparative history can also take a different direction by matching Perón's Argentina with an almost unrelated state both geographically and, most crucially, chronologically. For instance, a comparison can be designed to contrast Perón's regime in Argentina and Colonel Gamal Abdel Nasser's regime in Egypt (1956–1970). In 1952 Nasser was also brought to power by a military coup. By 1956 his rule gained legitimacy by a public referendum that reflected his broad popular support. Even though social mobilization was not carried out by a very dynamic political party—as the Partido Justicialista had for Perón—national rallies fulfilled this function: First the Liberation Rally, then the National Unity, and finally the Arab Socialist Union. Moreover, social support was also achieved by a tightly controlled trade union, the Confederation of Egyptian Workers, and other professional associations under state control— similar to the role played by the labor federation, the Confederación General de los Trabajadores, in Argentina. Yet the concentration of power was mainly achieved by an impressive enlargement of the state apparatuses such as bureaucracy and security forces, which was reflected in the government's increased expenditures on the army and paramilitary police from 18.3 percent of the budget in 1954–1955 to 55.7 percent in 1970.

This combination of an enlarged state machinery backed by the mobilized social sectors was in charge of implementing a series of measures aimed at achieving economic development: a land reform (already started by 1952) that by 1961 expropriated a seventh of all cultivated land from large landowners and distributed it among small proprietors and landless peasants; the decision to build the Aswan High Dam in order to bring the large area between Cairo and Alexandria into cultivation; and the formation of the Helwan Iron and Steel Complex (1954). At the same time, the evacuation of British troops from the Suez Canal (1954) ended in the nationalization of the canal, while the Anglo-French-Israeli invasion (1956) resulted in the nationalization of foreign property. These initial steps developed by 1960 into a fully-fledged five-year plan (1960–1965), which included the nationalization of private banks, foreign investments, and factories.

A series of similarities and differences are easily recognizable in making the contrast between Perón's and Nasser's regimes. Both leaders gained power as colonels participating in a military coup. Both managed to become the most acclaimed figures of the regimes installed by these coups. Both gained legitimacy by popular suffrage. Once in power, they both launched similar economic and social policies—for example, nationalization, property reforms, and five-year programs—aiming to transform their countries by catching up with the industrialized world. On the other hand, Nasser relied first and foremost on the army that backed his regime all the way through to the Arab Spring in 2011. Perón, instead, based his support on a political party and was ousted from power by the army. The armies that challenged Nasser's regime were foreign—British, French, and Israeli—reflecting the difference between a country like Argentina, which experienced decolonization at the beginning of the nineteenth century, and a country like Egypt, where decolonization was still a work in progress by the 1950s. And yet amid these differences, it is very telling that Perón's Third Position (neither capitalist nor communist) foreign policy became a full-fledged political stance vis-à-vis the Cold War powers as Nasser and others established the Non-Aligned Movement by 1961.

Relational histories

Relational histories—including histoire croissé *or entangled history, connected histories, and shared histories—focus on the ways in which two or more units of research are entwined in such significant ways that only by addressing those entanglements or connections is it possible to make sense of the historical path of one or both units involved.*

Relational histories share the scale of comparative history but pursue an entirely different goal and perform an entirely different task. A relational history does not move between two surgically detached states and societies in the search for similarities and differences in the way that comparative history did for Perón's Argentina and Vargas's Brazil and Nasser's Egypt. Instead, relational histories are looking precisely for entwinements between societies, focusing on how they contributed to the mutual development of one or both societies.

In this regard a *histoire croisé* or entangled history of Perón's Argentina with Nasser's Egypt is impracticable.

We could, though, envision an entangled history of Perón's Argentina with Vargas's Brazil that looks at how these two regimes, states, and societies shaped one another. However, whereas the necessity of comparative history is to find comparable units in order to avoid comparing oranges and apples, as the old proverb goes, that is not the case for entangled history. What really matters for entangled history is the deep involvement of one society with the other. The main consideration, then, is the degree of entwinement not of similarity. Therefore, although an entangled history of Perón's Argentina with Vargas's Brazil is feasible, it would probably profit more from pairing Argentina with Great Britain rather than with Brazil. For entangled history, the choice of a pairing is about the search for the most relevant other.

An entangled history of Perón's Argentina and Great Britain would then focus on the ways in which the decline of the British Empire represented a blow for the Argentinean economic elite and how agro-business declined in tandem. Conversely, this dual decline abroad and at home in Argentina paved the way for new social and political forces to gain power and create an alternative political economy based on the nationalization of the economic infrastructure (transportation and communication), the development of the industrial sector and its protection, and the stimulation of the domestic market. That is in a nutshell what Perón's regime meant to Argentina. Moreover, as the nationalized infrastructure was British, the import substitution industry was protected from the British industry, and the domestic market was meant as an alternative to the British one, an entangled history of Argentina and Great Britain should also address the British receiving end of the Perón regime's policies as well despite the asymmetry of the magnitude of impact on these states.

Thinking history globally: Varieties of connections

Two or more units can be connected with one another by sharing the same space (for example, a region, an ocean basin, or a hemisphere) and/or by links that bring them together (for example, diplomatic relations, student exchange programs, trade). Moreover, connections can create units of their own (for example, the economic relations between the United States and China can be referred to as an economic unit, namely, "Chimerica"). Conversely, some units are established purposefully to create connections beyond existing frontiers, such as Médecins Sans Frontières (Doctors Without Borders). Others outgrow national boundaries and become likewise transnational organizations (for example, McDonalds or Walmart). These varieties of connections are reflected in their singularities by the next three branches of history: international history, transnational history, and oceanic histories.

New international history

New international history deals with the history of multilayered relations between nation-states and stresses the bidirectional interactions between inner-state developments and their imprint on foreign relations and/or the input that foreign relations have upon domestic developments.

New international history can be portrayed as a particular type of entanglement between two societies specifically conducted at the state level, using either diplomatic or violent means. Being a specific type of entanglement confined to the diplomatic domain, we can think of a diplomatic history that specifically addresses the interstate negotiations between Great Britain and Argentina, as the entanglements between these two entered a new phase under Perón's regime. Documentation coming from the embassies, the British Foreign Office and Argentinean Ministry of the Exterior, diaries of diplomats, and other diplomatic sources would enable this type of research, which far from being new is at the very core of history professions from their very beginnings.

However, by combining these diplomatic concerns with culture, ideology, race, class, and gender, new international history opened wide venues for researching interactions between states that are not necessarily official and are even informal, but yet help create bridges or enmities between states. These venues would allow for the review of, for example, the cultural affinity that evolved by the transmission of sports. Amid the bilateral relations at the state level, sports developed in England or adopted by the British made deep inroads in Argentina's culture and society and became fundamental components of it. Polo, a sport of Persian and Afghan origins adapted by the British in India, was warmly embraced by the Argentinean landed aristocracy. Tennis was adopted by the urban upper class, and, most prominently, soccer became the most popular sport following the encounters between British and Argentinean workers. The names of the first soccer clubs—Racing, River Plate, Boca Juniors, Old Boys—attest to their English legacy.

Under Perón's regime, the original Argentine Association Football League adopted its current name, the "Asociación del Fútbol Argentino" Perón entrusted this asociación with the arrangement of an official match against the English national team. Argentina was the first national team to play against England in London at Wembley Stadium in 1951. The Argentinean team led 1–0 up to the last seven minutes of the game. The final result, though, was 1–2 to England. Nevertheless, back home the Argentinean players were strongly acclaimed by the public upon their return. In 1953 a second game between these two national teams was played, this time in Buenos Aires at the River Plate stadium. The visitors scored first, but the locals won 3–1. That day, 14 May, has since become the day of the soccer player, "día del futbolista." The following day the defeat of the English team was equated to the rejection of the English invasions in 1806 and 1807 in a newspaper article. Another analogy entered the political discourse, stating that soccer has been nationalized now as the railways were nationalized shortly before.

All of the sudden, the long-lasting history of domination typical of the British-Argentinean foreign relations and their challenge by Perón's regime was channeled into a series of three games (the third was suspended due to bad weather). Moreover, the shape of these international relations and their transformation became far more visible to Argentinean society at large through these games than all previous diplomatic exchanges combined. Moving into these social and cultural dimensions of foreign relations is what makes new international history *new*. In fact, by pushing the boundaries of diplomacy into the domains of culture and society, new international history moves closer to *transnational history*, sharing interests in processes of transfer, appropriation, and hybridization and creating some overlaps between these two branches.

Transnational history

Transnational history focuses on either phenomena (for example, processes of cultural transfer) or entities (for example, transnational organizations) that transcend national states, that is, their boundaries and their institutions. The state as both the basic unit of analysis and the main agent is replaced by intergovernmental institutions (for example, the United Nations (UN) or World Trade Organization (WTO)), nongovernmental organizations (for example, the Red Cross or Green Peace), and transnational non-state actors (for example, transnational companies).

Transnational history focuses on transnational phenomena, either processes of cultural transfer or transnational organizations. Overlaps with new international history may emerge then with the first component of transnational history's focus. However, there is an important distinction even within this thematic overlap. The interest of new international history in cultural transfers and social relations is associated with the foreign relations between the states involved in the transfer. Transnational history, instead, concentrates on cultural transfers without necessarily paying attention to diplomatic relations. Perón's regime illustrates this aspect of transnational history. Furthermore, transnational history breaks new ground in the study of Perón's regime and policies because they involved a wide series of transfers covering political, economic, and ideological realms, independent of Argentina's international history.

On a political level, the party structure and the combination and intertwinement of party and state apparatuses into a particular structure of power concentration stands out. Certainly, the inspiration for this type of political organization and the ways in which it arrived and was adapted to Argentina's politics is a transnational history project to be pursued. On an economic level, central planning, nationalization, protectionism, and import substitution are among the most prominent features of Argentina's development. These features can be further granulated into much more specific economic policies such as five-year programs and property reforms that did not originate in Argentina but were applied in several places in the world. Once again a transnational history project would follow the flow of those ideas, policies, and institutions as well as their appropriation and hybridization by Perón's regime. Similar projects can be pursued on an ideological level by focusing on concepts such as development, industrialization, modernization, nationalization, "catching up," and convergence, which structured the discourses that oriented and legitimized the practices of Perón's regime.

All of these possibilities opened up by the writing of transnational histories of Perón's Argentina would result in a mostly national history, instead of the interaction and accommodation between local conditions, sources, and constraints and the flow of policies, institutions, and ideas from the outside. The study of these processes of diffusion, adaptation, and hybridization would contribute to explaining the transnational dimensions of national developments.

Moreover, transnational history also focuses on transnational organizations as units of analysis. Therefore, an additional transnational path of inquiry would question the involvement of transnational organizations with Perón's regime. Several such organizations come to mind. Among intergovernmental institutions, a transnational history of Perón's regime can track the record of Argentina's performance at the UN and what type of impact the UN had upon Argentina during Perón's years. The Organization of American States, the International Monetary Fund, and the World Bank are additional possibilities of inquiry in the intergovernmental transnational path. The fate of transnational companies that operated in Argentina during the 1940s and 1950s provides additional venues for transnational histories of Perón's Argentina.

In regard to nongovernmental organizations, what made Perón's regime particularly notorious was its relationship with the Red Cross and the "cardinal's network" or "network of the convents." This last entity was a network articulated by Antonio Caggiano, cardinal of the Catholic Church in Argentina in partnership with the Catholic Church at its highest international hierarchical level. The aim of this collaboration was to provide safe-conduct to Nazis, Fascists, and Ustashas. Up to 1950, around 6000–8000 war criminals entered the country as a result of this collaboration.

On a different note, another transnational network worthy of attention evolved out of the Eva Perón Foundation (Fundación Eva Perón). This foundation was a charity created in 1948 and directed by the first lady, Evita, until her death in 1952. The foundation built houses, schools, orphanages, asylums for the elderly, and so on, and distributed food, clothing, shoes, books, toys, and home equipment, among other things. Although the foundation started as a domestic enterprise, it has gone transnational by addressing requests and reaching out to about 80 countries throughout the world. Most prominently in the list appear Ecuador, Bolivia, Chile, Turkey, Italy, Czechoslovakia, and the United States. In 1949, Reverend Ralph Faywatters, president of the Children's Aid Society, requested the support of the Eva Perón Foundation. The foundation granted the request and infuriated the American administration, which demanded an explanation from the Argentinean embassy. This tense situation between the two states was brought about by nongovernmental organizations that had gone transnational.

Oceanic histories

Oceanic histories look at the activities of and connections between human societies in and through bodies of waters, reaching into terrestrial domains frequently distant and apart but for the transportation allowed by liquid roads represented by lakes, rivers, seas, and oceans.

An oceanic perspective on the emergence of Perón's regime offers a vantage point from the sea. Since the nineteenth century, most Argentinean exports and imports were transported by foreign carriers. Half of Argentina's production, especially beef and cereals, were purchased by Great Britain, which was in possession of the largest commercial fleet in the world. In this context, transportation, storage, distribution, prices, wages, and working conditions were out of the reach of the Argentinean government. However, this highly profitable agro-exporting model suited the local economic elite that was fully invested. The outbreak of the Second World War, however, divested the international merchant floats from the South Atlantic. The services of British, American, Spanish, and Swedish companies sharply declined. Those of German, Italian, and Japanese companies were banished altogether.

These new circumstances encouraged and even demanded both the development of local industries in order to replace the lost imports and the construction of an Argentinean merchant fleet to give exports an outlet. These are the seaborne origins of a regime committed to import substitution and national sovereignty rhetoric and practice as represented by the claim to the sea as well as the terms of transportation and trade.

The build-up of a merchant fleet began with purchasing Italian, German, Swedish, and French ships beached in Argentinean ports during the Second World War. However, the naval policy of Perón's regime aimed to control transportation as well as the shipping industry. This dual goal was reflected by the attempt to transport 50 percent of all fringes by Argentinean-made ships. Although this goal was not achieved, only 20 percent of all fringes were effectively carried by Argentinean-made ships during Perón's regime, and the total dependency on foreign transportation companies was brought to an end. The Argentinean nationalized fleet covered the oceans, with a special focus on the Atlantic and the Mediterranean Sea.

Besides trade, the nationalized merchant navy became the leading carrier of around 400,000 European immigrants to Argentina. Moreover, the development of the shipping industry is also tightly connected with the nationalization and fostering of the oil industry. Finally, another related implication of Perón's naval policy was the strengthening of the Argentinean naval forces. Paradoxically, however, the navy led the military coup that ousted Perón in 1955. By that time, Perón's regime was already at advanced stages of negotiation with several foreign companies, such as Kaiser, Mitsubishi, Nippon Kokan, and Sasabo, aiming to empower the Argentinean fleet even further. Instead, soon after the military coup the naval sector entered a long-lasting period of decline.

In short, the emergence of Perón's regime is closely associated with crucial developments at sea. His naval policy emerged as a response to constraints posed by both maritime dynamics in the Atlantic Basin and the oceans globally. These policies substantially modified the integration of Argentina in maritime traffic, as the Argentinean fleet became the 14th largest globally in carrying capacity. These are but a few examples of the kinds of concerns at the core of an oceanic history perspective. Many others, such as the exploitation of fisheries with the concomitant international rush and its consequences for the South Atlantic environment or the scientific explorations into Antarctica and the resulting diplomatic missions, indicate additional possibilities in entirely different directions.

Thinking history globally: Conceptualizing through social sciences

Sustained engagements with comparisons and connections combined with social scientific thinking allow for conceptualization, a third strategy for thinking history globally. Conceptualization brings the cumulative conclusions of comparisons and connections about a particular phenomenon into a level of abstraction represented by a concept. This concept defines the phenomenon under scrutiny and makes explicit the necessary and sufficient conditions for it to take place. Besides encompassing the studied phenomenon with a concept and a list of the necessary and sufficient conditions for its existence, conceptualization can also formulate explicit models that formalize the ways in which a phenomenon operates and unfolds. The definition of the concept civilization, the formalization of conditions for sociopolitical phenomena such as revolutions, and the explicit model of the world-system are three central examples provided by civilizational analysis, historical sociology, and the world-system approach, respectively.

Civilizational analysis

Civilizational analysis embraces several societies with shared cultural, economic, and/or geographical features within larger units of analysis defined as civilizations.

The study of the singularities of each civilization, the contrasts between them, and their interactions are its main subjects of study.

Based on the above definition, from a civilizational analysis point of view, the singularity of Perón's regime in Argentina would be contextualized in a broader framework than the Argentinean state, namely, Latin American civilization. The comparison made above between Perón's Argentina and Vargas's Brazil represents just one step in this direction. The incorporation of additional comparable Latin American case studies, such as Lázaro Cardenas's rule in Mexico (1934–1940), Rómulo Betancourt in Venezuela (1945–1948, 1959–1964), Arnulfo Arias in Panamá (1940–1941, 1949–1951), and José María Velasco Ibarra in Ecuador (who was in power five times between 1934 and 1972) among others, would pave the way to a study framed as civilizational analysis. In such a study, Perón's regime would be portrayed as an overall phase in Latin American political history, running through the 1940s and 1950s.

This phase is depicted as one in which the government was in the hands of a charismatic leader supported by a wide social coalition. This type of political regime would be defined as Latin American Populism. Besides their basic political structures, these Populist regimes shared significant attempts at social reforms by political intervention, economic regulation, increased spending, and public ownership, aiming to catch up with the industrialized world.

Moreover, civilizational analysis would trace the historical roots and cultural commonalities that lead to the outburst of Populists regimes throughout Latin America. Several colonial legacies would be identified as the sources of Populist features. For example, the political legacy of *caudillismo*, the prominence of powerful charismatic leaders in the wake of the political vacuum opened by the collapse of colonial empires, could be associated with the appearance of populist leaders in the wake of waning British imperialism. Similarly, the social legacy of patronage, the quid pro quo mechanism of distributing favor for political support, enrooted since colonial times, could be identified as the source of reminiscent practices by Populist regimes. Finally, the colonial economic legacy of the agro-exporting model perpetuated the rule of the landed aristocracy at home and the supply of raw materials abroad. It was against these social and economic legacies that Populist regimes like Perón's Argentina struggled.

The much closer similarity between Perón's and Vargas's regimes as opposed to the mixed bag of commonalities and differences between Perón's and Nasser's regimes strengthens the points made by civilizational analysis. However, at the same time, a comparison beyond civilizational boundaries like that with Nasser's regimes and several additional plausible cases—such as Nehru's India, Sukarno's Indonesia, and Nkrumah's Ghana—can indicate that the synergy between a charismatic leader and a wide constituency, made up of a broad social coalition aiming to transform society, goes significantly well beyond the singularity of the Latin American civilization and represents a larger phenomenon in need of wider conceptualization. Such is the task of historical sociology.

Historical sociology

Historical sociology offers a sociological perspective of history by searching for recurrent structures and sequences of processes across time and space in order to determine necessary and sufficient conditions for a given phenomenon.

From a historical sociological perspective, Perón's regime and comparable cases would be scrutinized in the hope of identifying a unified social phenomenon. Eventually, such a study could recognize an underlying social phenomenon shared by several societies: the application of a political strategy, based on a twofold reliance on state institutions and party apparatuses, combined with the mobilization of a society lead by a collectivist ideology aiming for the transformation of the society it rules.

Based on these features, the phenomenon in question can be labeled as a "transformative mobilizational party state." The necessary and sufficient conditions for them coming into being are:

1. The enhancement of state power by harnessing the combined mechanisms of state apparatuses and a leading political party.
2. The mobilization of society and economy through these mechanisms and guided by a collectivist ideology.
3. The attempt to transform the economy and society in order to catch up with the industrialized world.

To the extent that in a given society a political regime is fulfilling these three conditions, it can be determined that a transformative mobilizational party state is in place. In the case of Perón's Argentina, arguably all three conditions were met, and, therefore, a historical sociological take on Perón's Argentina would conclude that Perón's regime was a transformative mobilizational party state. There is clearly no intrinsic value in mere labeling, rather the value is located in the identification of the fundamental phenomenon referred by it. It is through this recognition that Perón's regime can be reinterpreted once contextualized amid other regimes belonging to the same category.

Based on such a category, some general features could be recognized. For example, an evolutionary perspective of this social phenomenon, which has as its starting point a political force placed in the antipodes of a prevailing political regime. Nevertheless, at some point in its development, this political force becomes a well-organized party, a mass movement, and the head of the state (although not necessarily in this order). Once holding state power, the party goes through a process of adaptation to the transition from the antipodes of the political regime to the centers of power, surviving this transformation.

Once in power, the resulting regime accumulates and concentrates power by the apparatuses of the state and the party organizations that impose internal unity. One type of means for this purpose is the application of conciliatory policies between social classes in order to form a broad social coalition. Another is a thorough repression of dissidents in order to eliminate opposition. These measures are derived from and/or justified by a collectivist ideology. From this collectivist ideology the economic and social policies are also derived, with the ultimate goal of catching up with the industrialized world.

Bringing this category of transformative mobilizational party state in conversation with the wider world from a historical sociological perspective means moving from one country to another with the three necessary and sufficient conditions at hand. Not only would Perón's Argentina and other Latin American Populist regimes make up the list but also present would be Nasser's Egypt, Nehru's India, Sukarno's Indonesia, and Nkrumah's Ghana, among many others.

Bringing this category of transformative mobilizational party state into conversation with the wider world from the perspective offered by the world-system approach will result in the combination of these same domestic features with determining exogenous factors.

The world-system approach

The world-system approach contextualizes every historical phenomenon within the hierarchical division of labor established between societies, a relationship that entangled them into a system composed by a dominant core, a dependent periphery, and a mediating semi-periphery.

The contextualization of the transformative mobilizational party state within the framework of the tripartite world—core, periphery, and semi-periphery—articulated by the world-system approach, with its world division of labor and hegemonic struggles, reveals that Perón's regime, as all others applying the same political strategy, represented an attempt at upward mobility within the world division of labor.

Upward mobility within the world-system for a semi-peripheral state like Perón's Argentina meant the achievement of economic independence by ending the cycle of unequal exchange through import-substitution industrialization. Upward mobility for peripheral states meant to consolidate the recently achieved political independence and subsequently to improve their economic situation by attempting to add value to their exports through some degree of industrialized processing (for example, Ghana's cocoa industry). Finally, for core countries that did not need to catch up with the industrialized world because they were an integral part of it, upward mobility meant openly attacking the hegemonic powers in order to gain their position at the very top of the world-system (for example, Nazi Germany).

In all cases, however, the application of the transformative mobilizational party state entails a contestation of the world division of labor, capital, and power as envisioned and designed by the hegemonic power in the world-system. In this regard, what the world-system approach is adding to the historical sociological perspective is attention to the exogenous dimension. In other words, the mobilization of a society from within by the apparatuses of state and party led by a collectivist ideology—as defined by historical sociology—is made in order to confront the hegemonic world order from without, with the ultimate goal being the improvement of the state's position in the world division of labor, wealth, and power. By adding the external dimension to the more inward-looking historical sociological perspective, the world-system approach can redefine the transformative mobilizational party state as the "anti-hegemonic party state." At this point, a forth necessary condition should be added:

4. The confrontation of the world order in order to improve the state and its society's position in the world division of wealth and power.

Again, the tripartite world—core, periphery, and semi-periphery—articulated by the world-system approach is instrumental in delineating the variation of anti-hegemonic party states. The capacity to mobilize society by harnessing the combined mechanisms of state and party varies concomitantly according to the scale, wealth, and power of each state as schematized by this tripartite world. That is, core states are more able to achieve a massive mobilization of society. The degree of mobilization of society decreases through semi-peripheral and peripheral nation-states. Also the configuration of the social coalition representing the constituency of each political regime applying the anti-hegemonic party state strategy is conditioned by the tripartite world. In core societies, anti-hegemonic party states count on the support of the capitalist class; in semi-peripheral countries, the support of the urban working class is key; while in peripheral countries the backbone of the party state is the peasantry.

Finally, the aims of upgrading the position of a particular state and the range of policies challenging the hegemonic power within the world order vary concomitantly with the tripartite world scheme. The anti-hegemonic party state strategy in core states able to thoroughly mobilize society leads to the open attack of hegemonic powers in order to gain their position. The anti-hegemonic party state strategy applied in the semi-periphery appears as a struggle to achieve economic independence. And the anti-hegemonic party state strategy in the periphery represents a struggle initially to consolidate political independence and subsequently to improve an economic situation.

As important as these distinctions are, there is substantial common ground for all anti-hegemonic party states: the mobilization of society from within

Table 1.1 Concomitant variations of anti-hegemonic party states

Position in world-system	Core	Semi-periphery	Periphery
Degree of mass mobilization	Major	Lesser	Minor
Aims at challenging the hegemonic world order	Open attack on hegemony	Redefinition of economic relations	Political independence, consolidation

through the parallel mechanisms of party and state, guided or justified by a collectivist ideology, in order to modify the position of this state and society in the world division of labor and to confront the hegemonic order outside.

The global scope in the spread of anti-hegemonic party states can place the history of Perón's Argentina genuinely within a worldwide context. However, so far, this world was but a theoretical one. Now it remains to be seen how it would appear in the historical worlds of global history, the history of globalization, world history, and big history.

Thinking history globally: Contextualizing on a bigger scale

Contextualization is about bringing the issue at hand under scrutiny within a particular framework, as Perón's Argentina was brought side by side with Brazil and Egypt, the Atlantic Ocean Basin, and the anti-hegemonic party states. Contextualizing on a bigger scale as a strategy for thinking globally is about providing a framework, potentially as large as the world or even the universe, and as long lasting as the existence of humankind or even that of the entire cosmos, for any case or cases in point. Embedded within such frameworks, a scrutinized case or cases acquire new meanings, understandings, and insights.

Global history

Global history adopts the interconnected world created by the process of globalization as its larger unit of analysis, providing the ultimate context for the analysis of any historical entity, phenomenon, or process.

For global history, the world is a functionally articulated unit created by the establishment of long-lasting relationships between human societies all over the planet; therefore, when analyzing Perón's Argentina from the perspective of global history, the challenge is to write that history as not only emerging out of the secretary of labor in a military junta and the wide support of the newly emerging working class but also as an outcome of the interconnected world created by the process of globalization.

The First World War was the first trigger for the emergence of anti-hegemonic party states. The attempt by Central Powers to modify the British hegemonic world order during the First World War failed. However, the First World War has shown the tremendous power that states can obtain by a massive mobilization of their societies. This scale of mobilization was harnessed by a new regime that emerged as an additional result of the First World War: the Soviet Union. Its goal of a world Communist revolution was contained in multiple failed attempts. However, certain organizational features rather than ideological and political goals were exported worldwide. The mobilization of society by state and party apparatuses, aiming for social transformation, evolved in Communist Mongolia (1921), Fascist Italy (1922), Republican China under Sun Yat-Sen (since 1928), Nazi Germany (1933), and México under Lázaro Cárdenas (1934). This first wave came to a halt amid the Second World War.

The immediate consequence of the Second World War was the overall decline of all the above-mentioned regimes except the Soviet Union. However, a second wave of similar regimes emerged in the wake of the Second World War; regimes that were informed both by the model provided by those of the first wave and the profound shocks and lasting effects of the Great Depression of 1929. The Great Depression brought the first wave of those regimes into fruition and also planted the seeds of the second wave. While the emergence of these regimes was limited to nation-states directly implicated either in the First World War (that is, Russia, Italy, and Germany) or inspired by the Soviet Union (that is, Mongolia, China, México), the Great Depression contributed to the emergence of similar regimes worldwide and in diverse ways.

Within each of the above-mentioned societies, the crush of the world economy produced social and political forces opposed to their placement within the world economic structure, which presented these forces with a golden opportunity to gain power. Conversely, the social and political forces that benefited from the position of their countries in the world economy either succumbed politically or joined their opponents. Moreover, this swing in the balance of intrasocietal power from the social and political forces associated with the world economy toward those against it coincided with the emergence of mass society and mass media that enabled the politicized oppositions to spread their messages among their fellow compatriots. Finally, as the global crisis unfolded, the first state to adopt this type of regime, the Soviet Union, not only appeared to be immune to the damage of the crisis but also, from 1929 to 1940, its industrial production tripled, at the very least.[3]

For states and societies worldwide, it was clear that since the economic threat came from outside, there was an impending need to protect their economies and societies from the outside world. As the prices of commodities collapsed, markets shrunk, and foreign investment ceased, national economies redirected their efforts toward the local market, import-substitution industrialization, and nationalization.

The development of a second wave of regimes applying these policies became evident in Latin America soon after the Second World War. There, unfulfilled expectations of social transformation, the decline of British hegemony, the challenge posed to the hegemonic coalition during the Second World War, and the inspiration of and relationships with the Soviet Union enabled the global emergence of this type of regime from the mid-1940s up to the mid-1970s.[4] It is within this global context that the emergence of Perón's regime in Argentina could be reinterpreted from the breath of global history.

History of globalization

The history of globalization tracks the processes that transformed the globe into a single interconnected unit in which external contacts, flows, and networks have a predominant impact on world societies in relation to their own internal developments.

The application of the perspectives provided by global history and transnational history as suggested above addressed the challenge of shedding light on the global dimensions of the emergence of Perón's Argentina. However, an additional challenge is to consider the global impact of the transformations that Perón's regime brought to Argentina's economy, society, gender roles, and culture. This challenge can be met by the history of globalization.

The prevalent narrative of the history of globalization portrays globalization as a U-shaped scheme representing one peak of globalization during 1850–1914, called "the first globalization," and a second one from 1973 until today, known as "today's globalization." Between these two peaks lies an understudied deep valley of de-globalization. Looking from this perspective at Perón's Argentina—with its nationalizations, import-substitution industrialization, and protectionist policies—there should be no wonder that the world economy became de-globalized. Global history taught us how globally widespread political strategies similar to those of Perón's were since 1917. The history of globalization can teach us that such a global spread of political strategies akin to those of Perón were negatively correlated with the decline of globalization. That is, the more states applied nationalizations, import-substitution industrialization, and protectionist policies, the more dismantled the globalized economy became. Conversely, the less these policies were applied, for instance, because the regimes applying them were removed—as Perón was removed in 1955 by a military coup—the more integrated the global economy became.

The history of globalization provides an additional and wider context to make sense of a national development. Simultaneously, the history of globalization profits from the realization that the U-shaped valley of economic de-globalization is inversely correlated with a very significant global process:

the worldwide application of a set of political strategies from 1917 up to the mid-1970s.

World history

World history adopts the world as its ultimate unit of analysis and looks for phenomena that had an impact on humanity as a whole (for example, climate changes, environmental issues, plagues) or processes that brought different societies into contact (for example, trade, migration, conquests, cultural diffusion), even before the entire world became interconnected through the process of globalization.

World history subtlety differs from global history in that its world, the largest unit of analysis, is the world before it was encompassed and articulated by the processes of globalization. This subtle distinction becomes more apparent while focusing on the huge chronological gap resulting from it: while global history deals with the last 500 years, world history covers the last 2.5 million years. This drastic departure steams out from the primary feature of world history as a teaching field. Framing Perón's Argentina within world history can take two basic forms.

First, as a typical cross-section theme approach, a world historical history would identify the most fundamental features underlying this political regime in order to track them throughout a chronological span that predates the twentieth century—as all previous macrohistories did—and even the modern period—as civilizational analysis did. Second, as primarily a teaching field, world history would minimize the details on Perón's Argentina while highlighting the perspectives and proportions distilled from it in order to articulate a grand narrative.

Perón started his political carrier as a colonel in a military junta that protected the interests of the Argentinean landed oligarchy. Perón was catapulted to power by establishing an alternative and antagonistic coalition: he reached out to the working class and labor unions. That move resulted in a long-lasting conflict between the two coalitions. Perón's coalition with the working class triumphed in 1945; the landed oligarchy and the military defeated them in 1955. One way to frame the most basic pattern underlying this story, then, is to focus on how a leader from the margins of the ruling elite managed to displace it and take its place by gathering forces with the popular classes.

That is the case, for example, of the tyrants coming from within the oligarchy in Ancient Greece (ca. 750–500 BCE). They confronted the old landowning aristocracy by establishing a coalition with the artisans and peasants to whom the tyrant accorded favorable treatment. The succession of materializations of this pattern across time and place would provide a world historical work. The first step in its formulation is the identification of the basic pattern or theme. The second step consists of tracking the entire human record, or a significant portion of it, in order to find instances in which the pattern materialized in times other than the twentieth century or the modern world and in places other than Latin America.

When searching for a grand narrative for Perón's Argentina, we arrive at its thriving for convergence with the industrialized world. In this context, the long nineteenth century (1789–1914) can be portrayed as the century of the "Great Divergence," in which the North Atlantic World moved forward into political democratization and economic industrialization, gaining global power under British hegemony. The short twentieth century (1914–1989) can be portrayed as a global effort to get rid of North Atlantic Power under British and later American hegemonies by adopting mass politics and industrialization globally. Perón's Argentina exemplifies and assesses this narrative as much as this narrative provides the widest possible context for it.

Big history

Big history is a multidisciplinary approach that studies the histories of the universe, planet Earth, life, and human societies from the beginning of time up to the present as a unified story of growing complexity.

Big history is the widest possible context that any macrohistory can provide. Its uniqueness lies in a multi-scalar 13.7-billion-year chronology associated with its multi-disciplinarity. From this big history perspective, by the time that Perón reached power in Argentina, all eight thresholds (the Big Bang and the creation of the universe; the creation of the first stars; the creation of chemical elements inside dying stars that served as the catalysts for more chemically complex objects, including plants and animals; the formation of planets; the creation and evolution of life; the development of *Homo sapiens*; the genesis of agriculture; and the modern revolution) were trespassed. The last one, the emergence of the modern world, gets started around five centuries before Perón. Another way to phrase it is that by converting the approximately 13 billion years of the history of the universe into 13 years, the history of the twentieth century lasted about two seconds! Concomitantly, Perón's regime would probably pass unmentioned in any big history publication.

And yet, from this tour of our horizon, big history highlights the twentieth century as a period of deep transformation of government due to state-driven industrialization, mass politics, and involvement in economic planning, education, public health, and policing, with all those framed by nationalism as a worldview. From the heights of a cosmological scope, this overall distilled trend quite catches the essence of Perón's regime. Moreover, big history argues that there are patterns that recur on all different scales. The most prominent among those is the pattern of chaos and order. Pursuing its identification or that of another multi-scalar pattern would be the specific way that big history makes sense of Perón's Argentina. Although, most probably, Perón's Argentina would fall off of big history's radar.

Preliminary conclusions

These short sketches above hint at several possible contributions to the study of a subject usually envisioned, framed, and approached as merely national history once we are ready to go beyond boundaries and think history globally. Unique and similar aspects can be revealed by *comparisons* as *comparative history* does. It is only by the use of this first strategy that claims of uniqueness can be made. As for the similarities revealed by comparisons, those can be interpreted and attributed to different, broader social contexts and can be conceptualized in many ways. One such context could be a cluster of societies geographically, historically, and culturally related conceptualized as civilization and offered by civilizational analysis. An alternative context, advanced by historical sociology, could be even broader and include societies that, regardless of a shared geography, history, and culture, are structurally similar or underwent a comparable process.

Along these two different contexts, Perón's Argentina emerged as part of broader phenomena. By way of *conceptualization*, the third strategy, these broader phenomena can be defined as either the Populist regimes of Latin America in the 1940s and 1950s or the transformative mobilizational party state of the short twentieth century worldwide. Moreover, by conceptualizing the world as a hierarchical tripartite (core, periphery, and semi-periphery) system immersed in hegemonic struggles, as the world-system approach does, Perón's regime emerges as another anti-hegemonic party state. The concepts of Populist regimes, transformative mobilizational party state, and anti-hegemonic party state advanced by *civilizational analysis*, *historical sociology*, and the *world-system approach*, respectively, revealed the global dimensions of Perón's Argentina. Conversely, its local uniqueness can be better assessed precisely by a systematic contrast with those regimes belonging within these three concepts.

Moreover, a myriad of *connections* between Perón's Argentina and several states and non-state entities can be pursued on many levels. By tracking these connections, a series of entanglements, transfers, conditionings, and influences that molded the emergence and unfolding of Perón's Argentina would surface. Most prominent is the presence of the informal British Empire in the forging of Argentina and Perón's rejection of it as portrayed by *relational histories*.

This rejection, coincidental with the final demise of British global hegemony in the wake of the Second World War and amply studied by the *new international history*, was facilitated by the transnational flow of ideas, technology, and institutions chartered by *transnational history*. Among these transfers there are central planning, five-year programs, industrialization, Taylorism (scientific management), the development of mass party support, and many more, coming from such diverse places as the Communist Soviet Union, capitalist United States, and Fascist Italy. This rejection also has its origins in the temporal vacuum created by the Second World War in the South Atlantic Ocean, addressed by *oceanic histories* that encouraged and allowed Argentina to develop its own merchant fleet. By gaining command of its trade to some extent, Perón's Argentina fostered industrialization and the growth of a domestic market. Finally, in detaching Argentina from Great Britain, Perón attempted to establish alternative relations with *transnational* institutions such as the International Monetary Fund and the World Bank as potential creditors. All of these connections coming outside-in and inside-out exemplified how thinking globally through connections brought Perón's Argentina out of the national box.

Also *contextualization* already played an important role in thinking Perón's Argentina globally. The Latin American civilization, the world-system, the British Empire, the South Atlantic Ocean, and the Second World War were all important contexts that allowed for interpretations of and insights into Perón's regime. The application of this fourth strategy, though, can be brought to its most encompassing stage by moving into the *bigger scales* of the entire globe, humanity's whole past, and even beyond. Looked at in bigger contexts such as the globalized world of *global history*, Perón's regime can be understood as a local ramification of a global trend that unfolded throughout the short twentieth century, namely, the global rise and demise of anti-hegemonic party states.

Moreover, this global trend in which Perón's regime belongs is correlated with the *history of globalization*. The sharp decline of the global economy that had emerged in the nineteenth century coincides with the global rise of anti-hegemonic party states as much as their global demise coincides with the takeoff of current globalization. In this big context, Perón's regime is one additional instance in the resistance of the first wave of globalization and fostering an alternative to it. In the bigger context of *world history*, the first globalization fades away. It is displaced by a more fundamental and recurring pattern in human societies: the resolution of internal political struggles within the ruling elite as one camp manages to recruit the bulk of the population by having it vested within the resulting regime. As contexts grow even bigger still, as *big history* does, the chances are that the case in point—Peron's regime in the above experimental thought—would fade away.

Comparisons, connections, conceptualizations, and contextualizations shed new light on a national case study, making it truly global. At the same time, by studying Perón's Argentina globally, an awareness of global processes was also stimulated. The conceptualization of anti-hegemonic party states is a case in point. Political regimes are regularly differentiated as Democratic, Communist, Fascist, Populist, one-party states, and national liberation movement regimes. The origins of these regimes are found in democratic elections, revolutions, military coups, or wars of independence. Because of this wide range of political regimes, with their singular ways of emerging, any global trend unifying all of them was overlooked.

However, for all of their differences and besides their internal variety, anti-hegemonic party states appear to be a unified political strategy: mobilization from within by state and party and challenges from outside. That was the case for Perón's Argentina and for the comparative cases brought about by comparative history, civilizational analysis, and historical sociology. Moreover, as the outlines of the world-system approach and global history have shown, the application of this political strategy on a global scale is an outstanding feature of the short twentieth century. Similarly, the global demise of anti-hegemonic party states is a crucial phenomenon in the history of current globalization—the globalization in which we live today.

As a whole, these short sketches provided hands-on introductions to the four big Cs for thinking history globally as well as for the 12 branches of history that deploy them. The definitions and applications of these 12 branches aimed to present the readers from the very outset of this book with the manifold possibilities at their disposal while thinking history globally. The ultimate test for this book is the readers' capabilities in applying them.

Twelve history branches and four major strategies of thinking make an interesting balance of singularity and clustering. To begin with, all 12 branches can be grouped according to their way of transcending national boundaries or political frontiers: by way of *comparison* or by way of *connection*. The roads to Argentina's Perón were entirely different as made by *comparative* and *relational histories*: it would be meaningless to compare Argentina with Great Britain and entangle Perón's Argentina with Nasser's Egypt, but it was meaningful to do that the other way around.

Again, matching Perón's Argentina with Nasser's Egypt would be of no use from a *civilizational analysis* perspective but was very important from the historical sociological approach. *Historical sociology* came to the realization of a common political pattern while keeping each society enclosed. Different contextualizations lead to different comparisons that resulted in turn in different conceptualizations. The *world-system approach* departed altogether from comparing enclosed states, focusing instead on the ways in which societies are connected to one another in an overall system. From this perspective another original conceptualization emerged for the common political pattern observed.

Connections were also the points of departure for the projects of *international, transnational, oceanic,* and *global histories* and the *history of globalization*. *Global history* and the *history of globalization*, and even more so *world* and *big histories*, provided the largest *contexts* against which Perón's Argentina could be interpreted.

Moreover, branches and strategies not only live in a good balance of singularity and clustering but also in fruitful collaboration. In this particular thought experiment, *comparative history* led toward *civilizational analysis* and *historical sociology*, bringing *comparisons, contexts,* and *conceptualization* into collaboration. The introduction of the exogenous dimension to the historical sociological analysis by the world-system approach—how any particular society relates to the wider world—opened up a new *conceptualization* enabled by searching for *connections* instead of comparisons. Conversely, this *conceptualization* facilitated revealing *connections* pursued by transnational history, global history, and the history of globalization.

Taken as a whole, the transition from nation-state-based histories to a global scope was made here through comparative history, which earned a pivotal role in the transition from nation-based to cross-boundary historiography. However, the trajectory of collaborations followed in this particular example is just one of very many possibilities. The four strategies for global thinking and the 12 cross-boundary branches are neither incompatible with one another nor with nationally based histories. To the contrary, these branches and their four embedded strategies for thinking history globally are inclusive and their use enhances historical thinking and research of all sorts and at all levels. Once these four strategies and 12 paths are clearly delineated, they add a valuable supplementary toolbox to the history profession.

This exercise has transformed the invitation in the introduction to think history globally into a very concrete one. The invitation extends to all those willing to incorporate a global dimension into their historical nation-based research, including those willing to embrace global thinking as their main way of research and writing history and those aiming to gain historical depth in their dealings with our contemporary globalized world. The path suggested by this thought experiment is clear: whatever the case study in question, it can be enriched by thinking it through four strategies and 12 alternative paths of inquiry as well as the manifold combinations between them. Whatever the case study in question and whatever the format of the piece to be written, studied, or analyzed—a paper, a thesis, a dissertation, a course, or a book—this book challenges the reader to sketch their history 12 times to realize the potentials of the horizons opened up by thinking history globally before pursuing the most suitable or affordable project.

In order to facilitate that goal, the book presents several historiographical considerations and methodological tools. Historiographically speaking, the book presents the intellectual and institutional trajectories of each of the 12 cross-boundary branches, their programmatic agendas, and examples of their literatures. Methodologically, the book presents the four big Cs throughout different methods and designs, fully exemplifying, for the sake of teaching, how to think history globally in an applied way. The next seven chapters should train readers well enough so that we can reconvene eight chapters from now in order to run a second thought experiment that aims to articulate 12 alternative sketches of global narratives on the history of the First World War.

2
Thinking History Globally: 12 Branches in Their Singularities, Overlaps, and Clusters

The Roman monarchy established by Romulus was overthrown by a revolution in 509 BCE. The ensuing Roman republic witnessed subsequent quarrels between patricians and plebeians. The strife came to a pause 60 years later as the Roman constitution offered a compromise. The laws were carved on 12 bronze tables. The Law of the 12 Tables, representing the core of the *mos maiorum*, or way of the elders, was posted in the Roman Forum for all to know.

The number 12 is important to us here and now too, as there are 12 cross-boundary branches of history that help us to think history globally. These 12 branches, however, are not set in bronze or even in stone. In fact, and to begin with, how can we know that there are 12 distinct branches anyway? Answering this question requires some preliminary considerations of the history profession before proceeding to the actual accounting of the branches.

One of the many ways to look at the history profession from a sociological perspective is by applying Harrison White's concepts of *categories* and *networks*.[1] A population becomes a *category* when its members share a distinctive feature. Thus, by adopting a distinctive feature such as a particular period, region, dimension, subject, or perspective of specialization, historians can be arranged into categories. For instance, historians dealing with the European Middle Ages constitute the category of medievalists; historians dealing with the history of Africa represent the category of Africanists; historians concerned with economics belong to the category of economic historians; historians dealing with rural settlements constitute the category of rural historians; and historians approaching either medieval Europe, Africa, economics, or rural settlements from a Marxist perspective make up the category of Marxist historians.

A population constitutes a *network* when its members socially relate to each other. These social relations are sometimes straightforward and personal and sometimes mediated and impersonal. Historians active in the same professional association exemplify a network of the first type; historians subscribed to a

33

ir journal illustrate a mediated network. Finally, there is a relationship
categories and networks. Many times, a category elucidated abstractly
does exist as a real articulated network. This entwinement of category and network, a *category-network* or *cat-net*, is embodied for instance in the Medieval Academy of America: its members belong within the category of medievalists, some of them have direct social interaction in their meetings, and many more interact indirectly through its journal *Speculum*.

Not a single category-network is sufficient to describe the activity of a historian. Historians usually belong within several categories and take part in a number of networks. Nevertheless, the total sum of categories, networks, or cat-nets can be arranged as a taxonomy of historiography and the community of historians as a whole. These are the two preliminary conclusions that inform the 12 cross-boundary branches of history.

The 12 branches, which were defined and exemplified in the first chapter, are articulated by historians and groups of historians. By sharing similar ideas on how to cross boundaries while writing history, formulating research and writing agendas with similar goals, priorities, and methods, and pursuing them in their scholarly work, these practitioners constitute a particular category of historical writing. By interacting regularly, practitioners of the same category create networks that foster their category further by deepening their conceptualization, expanding and spreading their research, writing, and teaching.

Again, historians willing to cross boundaries probably belong in more than one category and take part in several networks. And yet the existing categories and networks offer a useful typology to clarify what are the options at our disposal while thinking globally about history. The following pages present the trajectories of the 12 cross-boundary branches, showing that they not only exist as perspectives on the past moving beyond enclosed units, as presented in the first chapter, but also as professional networks.

Thinking history globally: Comparing and connecting

Comparative history

Comparative history represents one of the earliest attempts to transcend enclosed units of analysis,[2] as Charles-Victor Langlois's precursor article "The Comparative History of England and France during the Middle Ages" exemplifies.[3] But it was only after the First World War that comparative history drew more attention. At the Fifth International Congress of Historical Sciences (1923), Henri Pirenne denounced the limitation of historical research to national boundaries and asserted that it is the comparative method that paves the way toward a universal, instead of a nationalistic, perspective on history. In the following International Congress of Historical Sciences (1928), it was Marc Bloch who raised his voice in a plea for comparative history.

Finally, by 1935 the first association for the study of comparative history, La Société Jean Bodin pour l'histoire comparative des institutions, was founded. The First World War was a major shock and strengthened the case for comparative history, and the Second World War had a similar effect. Following the Second World War, La Société Jean Bodin resumed publication of its *Recueils* in 1949 comparing institutions (for example, servitude, market, rural communities) along several civilizations. Later on in 1958, the journal *Comparative Studies in Society and History* was launched and, according to the editor Sylvia Thrupp, "forced on us by the times." It seems that once again this "forcefulness of the times" provides the increasingly global conditions that seem to enhance the interest and receptivity of comparative history.

By 1986, a new editor of *Comparative Studies in Society and History*, Raymon Grew, claimed that comparative history had become fashionable and respectable among historians, a view shared by other comparative historians.[4] By 1991, John H. Elliott claimed that at Oxford comparative history remedies the dangers of national history's provincialism. In this way he raised once again the idea that Langlois had advanced in his article a century before. The harvest of comparative history are works that highlight differences between compared units rather than studies of regularities based on tracking similarities between units.[5] The search for uniqueness remains predominant. Nevertheless, this idea of transcending national boundaries in order to gain larger and more insightful perspectives gained momentum as global developments unfolded in the twentieth century.

Relational histories

It is precisely the growing interconnections worldwide that brought comparative history and the comparative method into the spotlight. Comparing between units means, in general, to treat each of them in isolation regardless of the links between them. Relational histories (*histoire croisée*, or entangled history, *historia crocciata*, or connected histories, and shared histories) emerged as a critique of the comparative method by defining their mission as the study of the entanglements, interconnectedness, and entwinements between units as opposed to their isolation, compartmentalization, and enclosure for contrastive aims.

In a series of programmatic articles, Michael Werner and Bénédicte Zimmermann launched the histoire croisée that was subsequently applied in manifold studies.[6] Other scholars apply a very similar approach, although under a different name. For example, Sanjay Subrahmanyam and Serge Gruzinski refer to "connected histories" when dealing with early modern Eurasia and the Spanish Empire, respectively. In postcolonial studies the use of "shared histories" is similar to that of entangled histories too, except that the former concentrates on shared histories of different ethnic and gender groups instead on the entanglements between societies.

However, for all its conceptual clarity, programmatic writings, and several studies along the lines of these writings, relational histories did not yet evolve into an institutionalized historical branch with its own professional association and serial publications. The search for connections, however, is at the core of many of the branches moving beyond borders.

Thinking history globally: Varieties of connections

New international history

The origins of international history are closely associated with the emergence of history as an academic discipline. Interstate relations were one of the leading subjects of historical study from the very beginnings of academic history. Foreign policy, diplomacy, and war are all dimensions that, by definition, go beyond national boundaries. However, these key aspects of international history were pursued for the sake of informing what was considered the core of history: statecraft and nation building. It is because of these origins and this concentration on the political dimension that international history was considered "one of the most conservative discourses within [a] conservative discipline."[7]

However, the same forces of globalization that triggered the third wave of writing beyond borders since the 1990s also fostered the renovation of international history, attuning it to concerns wider than diplomacy that include social and cultural dimensions of interstate relations. This renovation is referred to as the "culturalist turn" that led to the understanding that "international relations are also intercultural relations."[8] This culturalist turn widened the range of subjects and perspectives for international history, including culture, ideology, class, race, gender, language, and emotion. The insights of critical theory, cultural studies, and postmodernism provided new viewpoints. From a methodological perspective, these perspectival changes and transformations were complemented by introducing multi-national archival research instead of relying mainly on sources from only one country's archives.[9]

These trends are visible in the journal *Diplomatic History*. Although since 1977 this journal has been dedicated to American international history and foreign relations, its articles and reviews increasingly show American relations in both global and comparative contexts. The second journal dedicated to international history, *The International History Review* (since 1979), is wider in both scales of time and space, as it deals with diplomacy and warfare since ancient times and throughout the world.

Transnational history

Current globalization brought to the forefront of world affairs transnational concerns that go beyond the realm and capacities of nation-states (for example, global warming, species extinction, and pandemics) that involve the movements of peoples, ideas, technologies, capital, production, institutions, and so forth across national boundaries, and that served as catalysts for the rapid growth and expansion of organizations associated with these concerns and movements (for example, international organizations, multinational corporations, and nongovernmental organizations). The historical branch focused on these concerns, movements, and organizations is transnational history.

In 1989, Akira Iriye was among the first to call for the study of transnational cultural history in the United States. Two years later, the *American Historical Review* published a forum on transnational history in the context of American history.[10] This seems to be the trigger in the growing number of publications and programs in the field in the United States. Rather simultaneously in Europe, Michelle Espagne started publishing his works on cultural transfers, mainly between France and Germany. The collaboration between Espagne's research group at the Centre National de la Recherche Scientifique in Paris and the Center for Global and European Studies at the University of Leipzig resulted in the creation of geschichte.transnational.

Since 2004, geschichte.transnational administers a forum on the web offering reviews of books, discussions, and announcements on conferences and research projects. The pivotal role of the University of Leipzig in articulating global history and transnational history reflects the proximity between these two branches. The same is true for the leadership of Akira Iriye in both transnational history and the "new global history" in the United States.

If transnational history focused on concerns and movements beyond frontiers before the emergence of nation-states, then several historiographical traditions could be presented as antecedents. Cross-boundary subjects such as migration, trade, technological transfers, circulation of texts, introduction of crops, and many others have been studied by historians for a long time. However, transnational historians deliberately adopted the transnational concept, and as such, the branch mostly deals with contemporary history. Moreover, the international and transnational organizations that generate or confront the concerns and movements that transnational history is interested in originated during the twentieth century. It is the archives of these organizations that provide transnational historians with their primary sources for research. Also in this sense transnational history stands out in comparison to previous historiographies concerned with movements across borders.

Oceanic history

The development of oceanic history is closely associated with the inspirational force of the Annales School and Fernand Braudel in particular. Braudel's book *The Mediterranean and the Mediterranean World in the Age of Philip II* represents a significant benchmark in the articulation of this branch of history. Focusing on movements and connections across and around the Mediterranean basin, the book presents a convergence of three continental areas—Europe, Africa, and Asia—integrated by a sea. This basic principle, focusing on the transformative relations between distant societies facilitated by movements across bodies of water, was subsequently applied on the larger scales of the Atlantic, Indian, and Pacific Oceans. Very tellingly, two of Braudel's followers, Pierre Chaunu and Kirti N. Chauduri, pioneered oceanic histories in the Atlantic and Indian Ocean basins, respectively.

With Chaunu, the opening of the Atlantic as a framework for historical analysis came from an Iberian angle. This perspective was prolonged by the works of Vitorino Magalhães Godinho, Frédéric Mauro, and Alberto Tenenti. Subsequently, multiple themes, such as the Atlantic slave trade, colonialism, empire building, and decolonization, widened the Atlantic horizons and facilitated the integration of the histories of the Americas, Europe, and Africa. The launching of the Johns Hopkins Studies in Atlantic History and Culture book series during the 1970s indicates the consolidation of the field as a network. Harvard University's International Seminar on the History of the Atlantic World, under the direction of Bernard Bailyn since the 1990s, reflects the growth and bolstering of the field. In 2004, the journal *Atlantic Studies* was launched.

By the time that Atlantic history was firmly established, Chaudhuri began writing about the unity of the Indian Ocean world, constituted by peoples from East Africa, the Middle East, China, Central Asia, India, and Europe, even if they did not share a common fate. This theme of unity and diversity was echoed in manifold studies on the Indian Ocean world that exploded soon after Chaudhuri's writings. Institutionally speaking, no specifically historical association or periodical publication was established. However, the Indian Ocean world exists not only as a category but also as a network reflected by the multiple conferences held by practitioners during the last decade and supported by institutions such as the Society for Indian Ocean Studies in India (1987), the Indian Ocean Rim Academic Group in Mauritius (1997), the Observatoire Québécois de l'Océan Indien in Canada (1997), the Indian Ocean Research Group in India and Australia (2002), the Indian Ocean Center Heidelberg in Germany (2003), and the Indian Ocean World Centre in Canada (2004).

In contrast to that, Pacific history was institutionalized remarkably early in time. The Pacific Coast branch was formed as a branch of the American Historical Association in 1903, publishing since 1933 the *Pacific Historical Review*. Later in 1949 and across the ocean, James Davidson was appointed the first chair of Pacific history at the Australian National University. The launching of the *Journal of Pacific History* and the establishment of the Pacific History Association followed suit in 1966 and 1972, respectively. However, the American network was mainly concerned with the history of the American West and its expansion to the Pacific, and the network in Oceania asserted the history of Pacific islanders, their societies, and cultures that resulted in a form of local histories. During the last three decades the interactions between peoples from Asia, the Americas, and Oceania became the focal point of interest for histories of the Pacific Rim. This shift is observable in the articles published in the long-established journals for the history of the Pacific Ocean as well as in books published during the same period.

Finally, besides and in addition to the articulation of the Atlantic Basin, the Indian Ocean world, and the Pacific Rim as cross-space categories (beyond political, linguistic, and cultural borders) and networks, maritime history also focuses on human societies at sea. Its major institutional benchmarks are the formation of the International Commission for Maritime History in 1960 and the establishment of the International Maritime Economic History Association followed by the launching of the *International Journal of Maritime History* in the late 1980s. Although typically absorbed within enclosed nation-based histories at first, maritime history moved beyond national frontiers and has the potential to move further, beyond ocean basins. That potential is tangible in latter publications such as *Maritime History as Global History*, edited by Daniel Finamore.

Thinking history globally: Conceptualizing through social sciences

Civilizational analysis

Civilizational analysis deals with units of a larger dimension and longer duration than the single societies they encompass. These units are defined as civilizations, the central organizing concept of the approach. Civilizations are based on a series of fundamental and comprehensive cultural patterns shared by several societies that appear as a "family of societies" or "hyper-social system of social systems."[11] Moreover, these same patterns appear sufficiently different from one group of societies or civilization to another as to define civilizations in the plural.

These larger units named civilizations were originally defined by the forerunners of this branch—Giambattista Vico, Montesquieu, and Johann Gottfried von Herder among others—before the advent of the nation-state that constrained the unit of analysis of disciplinary history. Latter on, the same global conditions that awakened comparative history, mainly the world wars, triggered a new wave of civilizational analysis of which Oswald Spengler's *Decline of the West* (1923), Arnold Toynbee's *Study of History* (1934–1961), and Franz Borkenau's posthumously published fragments (1981) are among its most outstanding examples. These works are based on uniform and consistent cyclical models (for example, trends of growth and decline; challenge–response chain reactions) applied rather rigidly from the top down. Nevertheless, since the 1960s a new wave of civilizational analysis developed around its singular unit of analysis while still carrying metahistorical baggage.

The foundational moment of civilizational analysis as a distinctive branch occurred in 1961 with the establishment of the International Society for the Comparative Study of Civilizations. Since 1979 this organization has published *Comparative Civilizations Review*. The several tasks put forward by civilizational analysis in this latter form are the classification of these units into typologies arranged according to different principles (for example, space location, stage of development), the study of their singular historical trajectories, the examination of the several kinds of inter-civilizational relations—that is, isolation, encounters, and conflicts—and their comparison.

Historical sociology

The comparative method was cherished not only by the analysts of civilizations and by comparative historians but also by the founding fathers of sociology—Karl Marx, Alexis de Tocqueville, Max Weber, and Émile Durkheim, the last of whom even dedicated a methodological treatise to it.[12] Moreover, sociology emerged not only as a comparative but also as a historically oriented discipline. The foundational issue for sociology was the rise of the modern capitalist society and industrial expansion. The implicit question was, "what accounted for the special dynamism of Europe compared to other civilizations"?[13] Based on such a point of departure, the historical and comparative dimensions of the discipline are evident. In this sense, sociology was from its very beginnings historical sociology.

Nevertheless, the generations of historians that followed the founding fathers generally concentrated on contemporary society and generally lost the historical perspective. The interest in history reemerged among a minority of sociologists since the 1950s. Key figures like Seymour Martin Lipset, Neil Smelser, and Reinhard Bendix among others led this reemergence. By the early 1980s, nearly a quarter of the articles in the main sociological journals had a historical dimension.

This renovated interest in the past was accompanied by the adoption, once again, of a comparative perspective. Indeed, historical sociologists affiliated with the American Sociological Association belong to the Comparative Historical Sociology section, one of the largest sections during the 1980s, the golden age of historical sociology. The launch of the *Journal of Historical Sociology* in 1988 represented another step toward the consolidation of this field. Throughout its development, historical sociology has become another influential enterprise going beyond boundaries. Its main concerns are deep processes that over considerable spans of time result in the build up of new social structures. The unfolding of these processes and the resulting social structures are tracked along several societies (for example, the emergence of absolutist states in Europe, the Middle East, and East Asia; revolutionary processes and revolutionary regimes in France, Russia, China, and Iran). Although the singularities of each compared unit are underlined, the regularities and generalized patterns are highlighted. Once identified, these patterns are conceptualized by formulating the necessary and sufficient conditions for their existence.

World-system approach

Formulated by Immanuel Wallesrtein in his *The Origins of the Capitalist World-System* (1974), the world-system approach started its project by accounting for the rise and spread of capitalism. The world-system is portrayed from a Marxist perspective as an exploitative one both within societies, that is, "surplus value" extracted from the working class by the capitalists, and between societies, as core capitalist ones take advantage of peripheral societies. In addition, the world-system approach is also indebted to the Annales School for the notion of "world-economy" (*économie-monde*) and its long cycles (fourteenth-century Italian city-states, seventeenth-century United Provinces, nineteenth-century Great Britain, and the twentieth-century United States) as described by Braudel.

But first and foremost, it seems that it is dependency theory that is the predominant substrate underlying the world-system approach. During the 1950s, the United Nations Economic Commission for Latin America was elaborating a conceptual framework for the understanding of the nature of the economic ties between the developed Western states and Latin America. These ties were defined by Raúl Prebisch as "unequal exchange," that is, trade conducted under relatively free market conditions between partners of different economic capacities. Economically stronger states, trading in relatively monopolized products, are able to obtain surplus value flowing to them from weaker states that trade with products of relatively low added value. These unequal exchanges resulted in an increasing polarization between core and peripheral states.

From these premises, the dependency approach confronted the then preponderant modernization theory that portrayed a normative pattern of transition from traditional to modern societies. According to modernization theory, a process of differentiation transformed traditional societies by creating new specialized institutions in the economic, political, cultural, and social areas. A series of preconditions in terms of values, institutions, and motivations were necessary for this transition to take place. Therefore, by meeting a set of preconditions and undergoing the process of differentiation, every society could move from the traditional stage toward modernization. Failure to complete this move resulted from a society's inability to meet the necessary conditions due to historical backwardness, in which case transference of technology, institutions, and values from modern (that is, Western) societies could put such a backward society on track toward modernization. In this way, modernization theory understood each society in an enclosed fashion with possible corrective inputs from the outside.

Dependency theory, and the world-system approach in its footsteps, confronts this assumption by understanding each society as shaped by the way in which it integrates into the whole system of societies, namely, the capitalist world-system. In other words, the state is replaced by a larger unit of analysis that historically had progressively encompassed the whole world. In this fundamental sense, the world-system approach diverges from comparative history and historical sociology as well as from civilizational analysis. For the first two, the enclosed state or society is the basic unit of reference. The latter embraces a larger unit encompassing several societies but still defines it by its internal singular patterns.

Since its formulation in 1974, the world-system approach developed as a significant sociological branch influencing the social sciences at large as well as informing historical writing. In fact, the world-system approach seeks to replace the compartmentalized way in which history and social sciences are arranged by crossing these disciplinary lines. The establishment of the Fernand Braudel Center at Binghamton University in 1976 together with the publication of its journal *Review* since 1977 represents the backbone of the institutionalization of this distinctive project. The newer electronic *Journal of World-System Research*, published since 1995, as well as the establishment of the Institute for Research of World-Systems at the University of California at Riverside in 2002, reflects the lasting dynamism of this enterprise.

Thinking history globally: Contextualizing on a bigger scale

Global history

Global history emerged almost simultaneously in several locations. In 1991, the Karl Lamprecht Gesellschaft institute at the University of Leipzig launched *Comparativ—Zeitschrift für Globalgeschichte und vergleichende Gesellschaftsforschung*. This journal opened a space for the publication of histories moving beyond national frontiers. The activities of this institute and the impact of its journal were a starting point in the development of the European Network in Universal and Global History (ENIUGH), which was formalized in 2005. A year after that the first issue of the *Journal of Global History* appeared.

Independently and as global history was in the making in Europe, in 1993 Bruce Mazlish edited a collected volume, *Conceptualizing Global History*, in which global history was envisioned as a subfield in history dedicated to the study of a new era: the "global epoch" or the "age of globalization," starting around the 1970s. The concept of global history, however, was subsequently embraced in the United States by historians willing to engage with a global scale of analysis but without this chronological limitation. Global historians concentrate on the modern and contemporary periods.

In 2008, the Network of Global and World History Organizations (NOGWHISTO) was formed. This association functions as a federation of regional associations. It brings together global and world historians from all across the world, regardless of whether their attention is an all-encompassing chronology since the dawn of mankind or a concentration of the last five centuries only. The collaboration was established by the World History Association and the ENIUGH. The Asian Association of World Historians was founded in 2008, and the African Network in Global History was established a year later.

In 2010, NOGWHISTO became a member of the Comité International des Sciences Historiques, the world association of historians. In January 2013, the first volume of the *Asian Review of World Histories* appeared. In August 2013, an inaugural conference held in Buenos Aires laid the basis for the development of a Latin American association of global historians, Red Latinoamericana de Historia Global. This newest network just launched its first series of publications in the e-journal *Nuevo Mundo Mundos Nuevos*.[14]

The history of globalization

The history of globalization emerged in close relations with the fields of global history and world history, although it is by far a much more focused and restricted enterprise. The history of globalization concentrates on the study of one major process only, a wide and crucial process, but one process nonetheless. The starting point of this field can be recognized in the attempt to provide a historical dimension to a concept widely defined, debated, and applied in the social sciences since the 1990s, the concept of globalization.

This aim was pioneered by Bruce Mazlish, as he introduced contemporary globalization into half a century of historical context under the label of global history. As this concept was appropriated by historians dealing with the interconnected world of the modern period and who were unwilling to identify themselves as world historians, Bruce Mazlish coined the term "new global history." This new global history concentrates on the study of the "global epoch" or the "age of globalization."[15]

Mazlish's project resulted in the articulation of a network represented by the journal *New Global Studies*. The editors made clear the singularity of their endeavor from the outset while establishing the aims and scope of the journal: "*New Global Studies* interprets globalization with a historical and sociological angle as opposed to history or sociology with a global angle."[16] On the one hand the historical angle differentiates it from purely contemporary dealings with globalization, as the journal *Globalizations* mostly does. On the other hand, the adoption of a historical view of globalization also differentiates *New Global Studies* from global history, which looks at modern and contemporary history at large from a global angle. Global history and the history of globalization are, therefore, clearly demarcated as two distinctive fields.

However, the size of the historical angle brought to globalization is really a matter of approach. As it turns out, in subsequent historiography the historical angle comes in many different degrees. When historians such as Kevin O'Rourke and Jeffrey Williamson; Dennis Flynn and Arturo Giraldez; Antony Hopkins et al.; Jürgen Osterhammel and Niels Petersson; Michael Bordo, Alan Taylor, and Jeffrey Williamson; and Barry Gills and William Thompson attempted to provide a historical dimension to the concept of globalization, their historical context was much wider than that originally allowed by Bruce Mazlish.

Globalization, as an exclusive research subject and approached from a wide historical angle, was undertaken mostly by collaborative publications in the form of collected volumes and coauthored articles. It did not lead, however, into the articulation of a professional association or journal. Perhaps, the history of globalization appears to be a formidable historical challenge that invites collaborative efforts but, so far, too narrow a field to evolve and sustain a fully fledged network with its own journal.

If the history of globalization could be agreed upon as a process, progressively expanding globally, initiated in the early modern period by Europeans, and the peoples they encountered and with whom they interacted, then *Itinerario: International Journal on the History of European Expansion and Global Interaction*, published since 1977, can be portrayed as the first network of historians devoted to the history of globalization. If so, the professional association linked to this journal, the Forum on European Expansion and Global Interaction (FEEGI), may represent the first direct network of the field. Although identifying itself as dedicated to the study of the expansion of Europe and the worldwide response to that expansion during the last half millennium, the FEEGI did not claim to be the network of historians of the history of globalization. Conversely, among historians of the history of globalization, several might be reluctant to be represented by an association placing Europe at the center of the history of globalization.

World history

The origins of world history can be tracked back to the seminal works of William H. McNeill, Leften Stavrianos, and Marshal G. S. Hodgson, the so-called "Chicago School." Writing during the 1960s, these authors emphasized interconnections between societies, such as processes of technological diffusion, adjustments to other cultures, societies, and polities, and the spread of ideas. Following these guidelines, world history had flourished during the last three decades following its institutionalization.

The institutionalization of world history is represented by the establishment of the World History Association founded in 1982 in the United States. From the very beginning, the development of world history was associated with the Advanced Placement World History course, a survey course offered in high school in the United States. Since 1983, the *World History Bulletin* offers articles on and resources for world history teaching. The launch of the *Journal of World History* in 1990 represents the growth of the field, which aimed to add a research profile. In 2003, an e-journal, *World History Connected*, was established and targeted educators in world history as a primary readership. Throughout this period, the world history survey became widely adopted in the American college system. Currently, the capability of teaching a world history survey has become a standard requirement for gaining a position in university and college history departments.

In their reconstruction of the history of historiography, world historians claim that history was written as world history from the very beginning. It was only the advent of history as an academic discipline that circumscribed historical writing to the borders of states. In this vein, Herodotus (484–424 BCE) and Sima Qian (ca. 145–87 BCE), the "fathers of history" in the Western and Chinese traditions, respectively, are portrayed as would-be world historians, as they did not constrain their writings by political boundaries. To the contrary, societies and cultures beyond their own and as far as their knowledge could possibly reach were part and parcel of their history writing.

From these foundational moments in the writing of history, chroniclers, thinkers, scientists, social scientists, and historians persisted in their efforts to grasp the history of humanity at large. For instance, within the Muslim world, Rashid al-din Fadl Allah (1247–1318) adopts for his *Compendium of Chronicles* (*Jāmi al-tawarīkh*) all of Eurasia as his unit of reference when writing about its peoples, ranging from the Franks to the Chinese. A century latter, Ibn Khaldun (1332–1406) in his *Prolegomena* (*Muqaddima*) offers a recurrent cyclical pattern of sociopolitical transformation linking the fates of nomadic societies and city dwellers. This attempt to establish an organizing principle according to which history evolves is recognizable in the Western tradition in a linear theological perspective. From Augustine's (354–430) *De civitate Dei* and up to Jacques Bénigne Bossuet's (1627–1704) *Discours sur l'histoire universelle*, history encompassed the fate of humankind at large arranged in successive stages leading to salvation.

Moreover, even if Voltaire (1694–1778) expelled divine intervention from history in his *La Philosophie de l'histoire*, the theological linear principle remained in place leading now toward progress, as presented by the Marquis de Condorcet (1743–1794) in his *Esquisse d'un tableau historique des progress de l'esprit humain*. This replacement of the final goal coincided with a renewed interest in societies and cultures as far away as in Voltaire's *Essai sur les moeurs et l'espirit des nations* and Georg Wilhelm Friedrich Hegel's (1770–1831) *Vorlesumgen über die Philosophie der Geschichte*. In this last work, indeed, the linear stages leading toward reason are entwined with cultures across space (that is, Eastern, Greek, Roman, and German).

It was only then that history started to emerge as an academic profession and historiography was framed within national boundaries. Viewed from this long-lasting perspective, academic history, with its national framed historiography, is a detour in the long-lasting tradition of thinking history globally. In fact, by connecting the long-lasting practice of historical writing beyond borders with the current wave of writing history globally, nationally framed historiography appears as a short-lived digression in the history of historiography.[17]

Big history

The most recent branch to emerge is big history. This branch and name appeared for the first time in the form of a college class at Macquarie University in 1989 taught by David Christian. Big history expanded first in the form of similar courses taught in Australia, the United States, and Europe, in all 32 institutions. The courses were followed by textbooks covering the entire chronological range since the Big Bang. In 2010, the International Big History Association was founded, aiming to enhance the teaching and research of this field.

Big historians trace back their origins to figures such as Alexander von Humboldt (1769–1859) and Robert Chambers (1802–1871). Humboldt's book *Cosmos*, an attempt to summarize all existing knowledge about nature and culture, is taken as a precedent to big history accounts. The same applies for Chambers's *Vestiges of the Natural History of Creation* that starts with the "fire mist" that started the universe and ends with the history of humankind. The specialization of science since the mid-nineteenth century corresponds with the decline of this type of *avant la lettre* big history synthesis.

Moreover, the crystallization of the historical discipline as a nation-state-based enterprise made big history or, for that matter, any cross-boundary branch rather unlikely. However, as the First World War triggered a reaction by some historians against the national base of the discipline—resulting in the very first wave of explicit attempts to move beyond borders during the twentieth century—a big history precedent also appeared. By combining the history of Earth, life, and humankind, H. G. Well's *The Outline of History* (1920) is reminiscent of the big history synthetic genre.

Half a century later and partially coincidental with the second wave of deliberate attempts to move beyond borders in the 1970s, a series of big history precedents came out as books, courses, and documentaries: for example, Robert Jastrow's book *Until the Sun Dies* (1977), Eric J. Chaisson's course on "cosmic evolution" at Harvard, and Carl Sagan's documentary *Cosmos*. Such are the traces of a self-portrayed genealogy of big history leading toward the recent formulation of the branch amid the third wave of writing beyond frontiers developing since the 1990s.[18]

Not set in stone: A typology

The trajectories above describe the emergence of 12 branches as discrete categories of historical writing and their articulation into professional networks amid a discipline dominated by enclosed units. Each of these 12 branches is embodied by its respective professional associations, or direct networks, as well as expressed through its professional journals. These 12 categories for the writing of history beyond borders, also discernible as social entities in the form of direct and indirect networks, are summarized in the table below.

Table 2.1 Thinking history globally: Categories and networks

Historical branch (category)	Professional association (direct network)	Professional journal (indirect network)
Comparative history	(1935) La Société Jean Bodin pour l'histoire comparative des institutions	(1935) *Recueils de la Société Jean Bodin pour l'histoire comparative des institutions* (reappeared in 1949)
		(1958) *Comparative Studies in Society and History*
Relational histories	None	None
New international history	(1967/72) Society for Historians of American Foreign Relations	(1977) *Diplomatic History*
		(1979) *The International History Review*
	International Studies Association	(2000) *Electronic Journal of International History*
Transnational history	(2004) Geschichte Transnational	None
Oceanic histories	(1903) Pacific Coast Branch of the American Historical Association	(1933) *Pacific Historical Review*
	(1960) International Commission for Maritime History	(1972) *Journal of Pacific History*
	Pacific History Association (1966)	(1988) *International Journal of Maritime History*
		(2004) *Atlantic Studies*
	(1988) International Maritime Economic History Association	

Table 2.1 (Continued)

Historical branch (category)	Professional association (direct network)	Professional journal (indirect network)
Historical sociology	(1980) Comparative Historical Sociology section within the American Sociological Association	(1988) *Journal of Historical Sociology*
Civilizational analysis	(1961) International Society for the Comparative Study of Civilizations	(1979) *Comparative Civilizations Review*
World-system approach	(1976) Ferdinand Braudel Center, Binghamton University (1978) Political Economy World-system section within the American Sociological Association (2002) Institute for Research of World-Systems, University of California at Riverside	(1977) *Review* (1995) *Journal of World-System Research* (e-journal)
Global history	(2005) European Network in Universal and Global History (2008) Network of Global and World History Organizations (2009) African Network of Global History (2013) Latin American Network of Global History	(1991) *Comparativ. Zeitschrift für Globalgeschichte und vergleichende Gesellschaftsforschung* (2006) *Journal of Global History*
History of globalization	(1996) The Forum on European Expansion and Global Interaction (FEEGI)	(1977) *Itinerario. International Journal on the History of European Expansion and Global Interaction* (2007) *New Global Studies*

World history	(1982) World History Association	(1983) *World History Bulletin*
	(2008) The Asian Association of World Historians	(1990) *Journal of World History*
		(2000) *Zeitschrift für weltgeschichte*
		(2003) *World History Connected* (e-journal)
		(2012) *Monde(s). Histoire, espaces, relations*
		(2013) *Asian Review of World Histories*
Big history	(2010) International Big History Association	None

The above table helps visualize the accounting of the 12 branches as categories figured by a unifying concept and research agenda as well as a professional network. Again, this account is not set in stone but provides a useful typology for mapping out the possibilities while thinking globally about history.

Up to this point and for the sake of clarity, the trajectories of these 12 branches were presented in a self-contained way. An analytical approach allowed mapping out parsimoniously the strategies for thinking globally about history and establishing a clear typology of the branches of history that apply them. In reality, however, there were and are many commonalities, influences, and interactions between these branches.

Twelve singular branches clustered by their overlaps

Inspired by the same conditions of our globalized present, the 12 branches are developing side by side and in communication with one another. Moreover, the same practitioners belong in many cases to more than one category and were or are active in several networks. Both the fluid communication between these branches and the multiple professional identities of practitioners challenge the parsimony of the typologies. Unsurprisingly, there are significant overlaps between these branches that seem to narrow their singularities, if not challenge them entirely.

These overlaps among the branches of history are expected because all of their definitions share the same constitutive components: time, space, discipline, and methods. Therefore, whenever the content of a particular component is shared by two or more definitions, an overlap happens. The more content that two definitions share in their component parts, the less exclusive they appear. Eventually, two or more branches sharing all or most of their defining component parts would lose their singularity altogether and collapse into one branch. However, overlaps between definitions represent not only a challenge for singularities but also the possibility of creating clusters of overlapping branches.

In order to track down these types of overlaps in a systematic way and to assess the singularity of each branch, a comparison of the components present in all definitions—space, time, discipline, sources, and methods—is required.

Singularities, overlaps, and clusters by space

The most prominent unit of analysis in history writing is a political entity. Depending on the time period in question, that entity could be a kingdom, an empire, or a nation-state. Despite the development of the historical discipline in so many thematic, conceptual, and methodological directions throughout the last century and a half, for the most part, political entities remained the most privileged units of analysis.

The 12 cross-boundary branches of history writing challenge this embedded assumption, known as "methodological nationalism," by configuring space differently and adopting alternative units of analysis. This shared defining feature is referred to as the "spatial turn," "new regimes of space," "global spatiality," or "global trend."[19] Different categories are recognizable by their particular "regime of space" as they privileged different units of analysis summarized in Table 2.2.

Table 2.2 makes it clear that there is something singular about civilizational analysis, transnational history, oceanic histories, and big history as far as the

Table 2.2 The units of analysis

Branch	Unit of analysis
Comparative history	Nation-states, empires, kingdoms
Historical sociology	Nation-states, empires
International history	Nation-states
Entangled history	Nation-states
Transnational history	Transnational entities and phenomena
Civilizational analysis	Civilizations
Oceanic histories	Ocean basin
World-system approach	World-systems
World history	World
Global history	World
History of globalization	World
Big history	Universe

unit of analysis is concerned. They are the only branches for which the main units of analysis are civilizations, transnational entities, ocean basins, and the universe, respectively. However, what stands out for the remaining eight categories—arranged in two pairs and a quartet—are their mutual overlaps in regard to their units of analysis.

Both comparative history and historical sociology deal with political entities as their primary units of analysis, which makes them indistinguishable in this regard. Their singularities then should be found in other defining components: discipline, aims, and methods as well as conceptualization. The same is true for new international and relational histories (particularly for entangled histories; connected histories deal with empires in the early modern era), as both deal for the most part with nation-states and the societies contained within them. It is the subjects that they focus upon in these interrelated units that make the difference: foreign relations for international history as opposed to the fabric of society, polity, and culture for entangled history.

A larger overlap occurs with the adoption of the world as the space component in defining world history, global history, the history of globalization, and the world-system approach. In this case, however, singularity resides with the meaning of the concept of world in each definition. The world of world history is a geographical entity. World history adopts planet Earth as the stage of humankind for telling its entire story, for surveying any aspect of human societies within this maximalist geographical context, or focusing on inter-societal contacts within it.

The world of global history is a historical entity. For global history, the world is a functionally articulated unit created by the establishment of long-lasting relationships between human societies all over the planet. The history of globalization is the story of the transformation of the world into an articulated functional unit: when, how, and why this articulated world came into being. Therefore, one way of formulating the difference between global history and the history of globalization is by pointing to the fact that the latter is basically about one big question—the coming into being of the articulated world—while the former deals with a plethora of developments, relations, and phenomena since this articulated world came into being.

Finally, the world of the world-system is a theoretical model. Although using world as the defining adjective, the world-system does not need to necessarily overlap with the entire world. Rather, it is a self-enclosed world occupying different extents of the globe depending on the period in question. Most crucially, whatever its physical extension, the world created by the world-system approach is a simplified abstraction, a parsimonious model that fits any particular society within one of three categories—core, periphery, semi-periphery—while the relationships between them are also reduced

Table 2.3 Categories clustered by scale of unit of analysis

Small	Organizations (e.g., states, NGOs)	Historical sociology, international history, transnational history, relational histories, comparative history
Medium	World region (i.e., oceans, civilizations)	Oceanic histories, civilizational analysis, relational histories
Large	World	World history, global history, the history of globalization, world-system approach
Huge	Universe	Big history

to a well-defined repertoire, including the world division of labor, unequal exchanges, hegemonic struggle, and antisystemic movements.

In short, the research and writing paths of four categories, civilizational analysis, transnational history, oceanic histories, and big history, are clearly singled out by their units of analysis. Four other categories, world history, global history, the history of globalization, and the world-system approach, can be individualized once the meanings of the world as a unit of analysis are clarified. Finally, for another four categories, comparative history, historical sociology, international history, and entangled history, singularity depends on other dimensions, as the core of their originality does not reside in their units of analysis but rather in the scale or size of their units of analysis: small, medium, large, and huge.

Singularities, overlaps, and clusters by time

The space dimension is of primary importance in defining the 12 branches because of their willingness to work with units other than the nation-state, its political predecessors, and the language barriers related to them. All of these branches are about dealing with history while engaging alternative regimes of space. And yet time rather than space is the crucial dimension for history at large. Also for the 12 branches of history, the time dimension is central and instrumental in accentuating singularities and overlaps between them.

From the outset, two branches can be clearly discerned from the others by their time scope: big history, with its 13.7 billion years, and world history, with its 2.5 million years. Both of these ranges are clearly different from all

Table 2.4 Time scope

Branch	Time scope
International history	Contemporary
Transnational history	Contemporary
Relational histories	Mostly modern and contemporary
Global history	Mostly modern and contemporary
History of globalization	Mostly modern and contemporary
Oceanic histories	Mostly modern
Historical sociology	Mostly modern and contemporary, up to 5000 years
World-system approach	Mostly modern and contemporary, up to 5000 years
Comparative history	Ancient to contemporary, up to 5000 years
Civilizational analysis	Up to 5000 years
World history	Up to 2.5 million years
Big history	Up to 14 billion years

Table 2.5 Clusters by time scope

Time scope	Categories
Contemporary	International history, transnational history
Modern onward	Global history, history of globalization, world-system, oceanic history, relational histories
Premodern onward	Historical sociology, civilizational analysis, comparative history
Prehistoric onward	World history
Cosmic	Big history

the others on the time dimension. Civilizational analysis, by definition, is limited to the existence of civilization, some 5000 years. Comparative history, historical sociology, and the world-system approach, although mostly modern and contemporary, can range up to 5000 years. That also applies to oceanic histories, although most of them are decidedly modern.

Instead, by dealing with a globalizing world, global history engages the last 500 years and, for the most part, that is also true for the history of globalization. The time span for relational histories encompasses in practice, although not necessarily in principle, the early modern and contemporary periods. Although diplomacy and warfare are as old as civilization, the time scope of international history, depending on the existence of nation-states, is 250 years. To the extent that transnational history depends on transnational entities, its time scope is around 130 years. Based on this chronological framework, clusters emerge, which are shown in Table 2.5.

Singularities, overlaps, and clusters by disciplines, methods, and sources

Another possible distinction within the 12 branches has to do with their disciplinary affiliation. Comparative, entangled, oceanic, global, and world histories, as well as the history of globalization, belong within the discipline of history. Historical sociology, civilization analysis, and the world-system approach fit better within the fields of sociology, political science, or political economy. International history and transnational history swing between history and international relations. Finally, big histories defy this duality between history and the social sciences by incorporating all domains of knowledge into a comprehensive multidisciplinary enterprise.

Two additional features substantially overlap with this clustering by discipline. Many of the categories coming from within a historical discipline are more prone to take an inductive approach, that is, bottom-up reasoning based on the analysis of information meticulously collected by a careful scrutiny of primary sources. Meanwhile, categories outside of the historical discipline usually make use of a much wider deductive approach, that is, top-down reasoning stemming from some premises in need of justification and assessed by information usually gathered from secondary sources.

Therefore, concomitantly to this inductive-deductive divide, there is another set of clusters within the 12 branches based on the type of sources privileged. The degree to which some of the branches use primary sources varies enormously, ranging from no use at all, by categories outside the historical discipline, up to heavy reliance, mainly by many categories from within the historical discipline. It is notable that the larger the scopes of space and

Table 2.6 Clusters by discipline, approach, and sources

Category	Discipline	Inductive/deductive	Core sources
Comparative history	History	Inductive	Primary/secondary
Relational histories	History	Inductive	Primary
International history	History, international relations	Inductive	Primary
Transnational history	History, international relations	Inductive	Primary
Oceanic history	History	Inductive	Primary
Global history	History	Deductive/inductive	Primary/secondary
History of globalization	History	Deductive/inductive	Primary/secondary

World history	History	Deductive	Secondary
Big history	Multidisciplinary	Deductive	Secondary
World-system approach	Political economy, sociology	Deductive	Secondary
Historical sociology	Sociology	Deductive	Secondary
Civilizational analysis	Sociology, history	Deductive	Secondary

time adopted by a category, the more deductively oriented and secondary source-based it becomes.

Mapping the 12 branches in their singularities, overlaps, and clusters

The first chapter provided us with a definition of each trans-boundary branch of history and applied them to a particular case study. The second chapter revealed that these branches represent categories and networks in the history profession. Now, this chapter has shown that each branch defines space, time, sources, and methods in its own particular way. Many overlaps and singularities coexist in these definitions, as summarized in Table 2.7.

Table 2.7 clearly and simply presents what makes each category singular in regard to time scale, space, method, sources, and discipline. At the same time, the table facilitates a generalized visualization of the many overlaps between branches. Based on these overlaps, the 12 branches can be arranged into clusters in different ways.

For example, based on their similarities along these five parameters and the combination of them, there is a large cluster of branches geared toward analysis of large scales of time and space, the use of the deductive method, and a reliance upon secondary sources. Conversely, another large cluster stands out for branches that are more compatible with studies that analyze smaller scales of space and time, use the inductive method, and utilize primary sources. There are several qualifications to this very broad and generalizing scheme; however, this summary provides a good point of departure for grasping the 12 historiographic projects in their singularities, overlaps, and clusters.

The clustering presented by Table 2.9 is a rather close representation of the main arguments and strategies advanced by this book, namely, clustering by the leading four methods for thinking history globally. As advanced in the introduction, four clusters emerge behind the four big Cs of global thinking: comparing, connecting, conceptualizing, and contextualizing. All of the branches use more than one of these strategies to different degrees; however, each branch can be portrayed as separating itself by the prominence of

Table 2.7 Twelve branches in their singularities and overlaps

Branch	Unit of analysis	Time scope	Inductive/ deductive	Main sources	Discipline
Comparative history	Political entities	Ancient to contemporary, up to 5000 years	Inductive	Primary/ secondary	History
Relational histories	Political entities	Modern and contemporary	Inductive	Primary	History
International history	Nation states	Contemporary	Inductive	Primary	History, international relations
Transnational history	Transnational entities	Contemporary	Inductive	Primary	History, international relations
Oceanic histories	Ocean basin	Mostly modern and contemporary	Inductive	Primary	History
Historical sociology	Political entities	Mostly modern and contemporary, up to 5000 years	Deductive	Secondary	Sociology, history
Civilizational analysis	Civilizations	Up to 5000 years	Deductive	Secondary	Sociology
World-system approach	World (model)	Mostly modern and contemporary, up to 5000 years	Deductive	Secondary	Political economy, sociology
Global history	World (articulated)	Modern and contemporary	Deductive/ inductive	Primary/ secondary	History
History of globalization	World (towards articulation)	Modern and contemporary	Deductive/ inductive	Primary/ secondary	History
World history	World (geographic)	Up to 2.5 million years	Deductive	Secondary	Sociology
Big history	Universe	Up to 14 billion years	Deductive	Secondary	Multi-disciplinary

some of the four strategies. Table 2.9 summarizes the degree, schematically defined as "much," "some," or "none," in which each branch relies on the four big Cs.

Table 2.9 shows that comparative history, historical sociology, and civilizational analysis lean almost exclusively or mostly on comparisons. The other nine branches use connections as the leading strategy to go beyond boundaries. As these 12 branches represent the "global trend" or "spatial turn" of going beyond borders, the ways in which these borders are crossed—by

Table 2.8 Clustering the 12 branches by five parameters

Branches	Scale of unit of analysis	Time scale	Approach and sources	Discipline
Comparative history	Small	Ancient to contemporary	Inductive/ primary	History
Relational histories	Small/ medium	Mostly contemporary	Inductive/ primary	History
International history	Small	Contemporary	Inductive/ primary	History
Transnational history	Small	Contemporary	Inductive/ primary	History
Historical sociology	Small	Ancient to contemporary	Deductive/ secondary	Sociology
Civilizational analysis	Medium	Up to 5000 years	Deductive/ secondary	Sociology/ history
Oceanic history	Medium	Mostly modern	Inductive/ primary	History
World-system approach	Large	Mostly modern and contemporary/ up to 5000 years	Deductive/ secondary	Political economy/ Sociology
Global history	Large	Modern onwards	Deductive/ secondary	History
History of globalization	Large	Modern onwards	Deductive/ secondary	History/ multi-disciplinary
World history	Large	Pre-history onwards	Deductive/ secondary	History
Big history	Huge	Cosmic	Deductive/ secondary	Multi-disciplinary/ history

comparisons, connections, or both—represents a pivotal distinction. This distinction is fully addressed in chapters 3 and 4, while Chapter 5 is devoted to three branches, new international, transnational, and oceanic histories, that embody connections as a method for transcending boundaries.

Table 2.9 also shows that all branches involve some degree of conceptualization. However, those branches rooted in the social sciences—historical sociology, civilizational analysis, and the world-system approach—are the ones that deliberately aim to conceptualize the past by explicitly articulated concepts and models. Chapter 6 is dedicated to them. All branches also contextualize their case studies within the different scales of space and time specified above.

Table 2.9 Clustering the 12 branches by the four big Cs

Branches	Comparing	Connecting	Conceptualizing	Contextualizing
Comparative history	Much	None	Some	Much
Relational histories	None	Much	Some	Much
International history	None	Much	Some	Much
Transnational history	Some	Much	Some	Much
Oceanic history	Some	Much	Some	Much
Historical sociology	Much	None	Much	Much
Civilizational analysis	Much	Some	Much	Much
World-system approach	Some	Much	Much	Much
Global history	Some	Much	Some	Much
History of globalization	Some	Much	Some	Much
World history	Some	Much	Some	Much
Big history	Some	Much	Some	Much

The extents of these contexts are small, medium, large, and huge. Chapters 7 and 8 address those branches that provide the largest frameworks of space and time for contextualization: the history of globalization and global, world, and big histories.

The four big Cs and the 12 branches have been fully displayed in theory and practice, in their singularities, overlaps, and clusters, and performing in the scene and behind the scenes. Now, it is time for a closer and more detailed acquaintance with each of them before fully engaging them again in a second thought experiment in Chapter 9, the last stage in this training for thinking history globally.

3
Thinking History Globally: Comparing or Connecting

The transcendence of political boundaries, moving beyond one's self-enclosed unit, is the necessary condition for thinking history globally. How to move beyond boundaries is, therefore, of crucial importance. As such, this movement deserves its own chapter, which seeks to explain and exemplify at length the two methods of transcending enclosed boundaries. The 12 branches can be clustered once again by their inclinations toward these methods: comparisons and connections.

Comparisons and connections are two very different means of crossing boundaries. Comparisons aim to transcend the single, self-enclosed unit of analysis in order to contrast between two or more units to highlight differences and/or similarities, to test causal attributions, or to formulate a pattern or generalization. This comparative way of moving beyond borders corresponds with the branches of comparative history, historical sociology, and civilizational analysis.

The other major way of transcending boundaries is by connecting units that are usually approached separately and underscoring the ties at play between them. In this case, boundaries are crossed substantially, instead of analytically, as the crossing is indispensable for defining either a unit of analysis larger than usual or the very subject matter of the research. That is, adopting a world-system, an ocean basin, or the globe as a unit of analysis requires the crossing of many political boundaries. Similarly, subjects such as invasions, conquests, cultural diffusions, migrations, economic relations, ecological conditions, and many more inherently involve the crossing of borders, both material and political. The categories that rely upon connecting include the world-system approach, entangled history, international history, transnational history, oceanic history, the history of globalization, global history, world history, and big history.

Let's make these conceptual distinctions concrete by thinking globally about American history. In opposition to national histories, by taking American

Table 3.1 Ways of crossing borders

Categories	Ways of crossing borders
Comparative history	Comparison
Historical sociology	Comparison
Civilizational analysis	Comparison/connection
International history	Connection
Entangled history	Connection
Transnational history	Connection
Oceanic history	Connection
World-system approach	Connection
World history	Connection
Global history	Connection
History of globalization	Connection
Big history	Connection

history beyond the boundaries of the political unit that turned into the United States, its contrasts with and connections to the world will be front and center. This move beyond boundaries can be done comparatively by contrasting America with other self-enclosed units or by connecting America's history to that of other units.

For example, C. Vann Woodward, in his edited collection *The Comparative Approach to American History*, aims to shed new light on the understanding of American history by way of contrasting it with the history of Europe.[1] According to Woodward, the "newness" of the country, its geographical isolation, and a sense of cultural inferiority traditionally detached American history from any wider context. Conversely, following the breakdown of physical isolation, the waves of mass immigration, and the emergence of the United States as a world power, Woodward finds that one could understand American history in a wider context by contrasting the history of British North America (BNA) and the United States as an enclosed unit with that of Europe as a second enclosed unit.

From these contrasting exercises, he draws distinctions, for example, between the rigidity of class structure, the hierarchical social order, and the institutional weight of the Crown, church, and aristocracy in early modern Europe and the openness produced by the frontier and expanding economy, rapid upward mobility, and absence of feudalism in BNA and the United States. The contrast between American and European variants of the Enlightenment's underscoring of "pragmatic rationalism" is another case in point, as is the political preeminence of Marxist-oriented socialist movements in modern Europe and their absence within the American labor movement. These types of contrastive conclusions reflect the basic method that Woodward and the authors of the different chapters within the edited volume employ, namely, matching up American history at a particular chronological point, from "the colonial phase" up to "the Cold War," with comparable units chosen from European history. Thus, British colonies are compared to Spanish ones, and the situation of the United States during the Cold War is compared with the history of ancient Rome, nineteenth-century Britain, and the post-Second World War Soviet Union.

An entirely different attempt to understand American history beyond its physical and political borders is offered by David Russo's *American History from a Global Perspective*. Russo seeks to integrate American history with that of other world regions by focusing on connections, such as economic relations and scientific and popular cultural transfers. In this way, the unfolding of American history is conditioned by its ties with the world. For example, the development of the American economy is contextualized amid developments of the global economy, changes in American society are related to forces coming from outside, and American culture, scientific and popular, is intertwined with cultural developments in Europe.[2]

Ian Tyrell, in his *Transnational Nation*, also claims that forces beyond America have made it what it is today. Moreover, Tyrrell not only describes how the flows of trade, investment, technology transfers, and migrants reshaped the United States in the nineteenth century but also how the local reactions to these transnational forces are important in understanding domestic developments. Most prominently, he emphasizes the rejection of free trade, exemplified by the tariff policies that succeeded in creating a diversified national economy and domestic market. In the twentieth century the involvement of the United States in world politics is evident throughout the major conflicts of the century: the First and Second World Wars and the Cold War.

Altogether, the history of the United States from this transnational perspective is portrayed as a game of musical chairs between state and society vis-à-vis the attitudes to the outer world. In the nineteenth century the outer world made deep inroads into American society, while the American state remained aloof in the international arena. By contrast, the twentieth century witnessed the arrival of the American state on a global stage, while American society retreated inward as represented, for example, by exclusionary immigration policies. It is only in the current period of globalization, starting in the late twentieth century, that this divorce of state and society was brought to an end with both being on board with global integration.[3]

This global integration is reflected in the willingness to revise self-contained American history and connect it globally before the nineteenth century. Looking for connections beyond borders, the early modern period in North America appears as one of "massive environmental change wrought by the exchange of pathogens and biota[,]...forced and free migrations[,]...connections forged by silver trade[,]...European rivalries[, and]...the global institution of slavery."[4]

Now, moving back in time and among many places, the following examples aim to make the distinction between comparing and connecting as strategies for moving beyond borders apparent and understandable in depth.

Exemplifying the comparative–connective distinction

In order to clarify the distinctions between the possibilities opened by the comparative and connective methods in a concrete way, this section depicts three consecutive and related historical topics from both comparative and connective perspectives. These three exemplifying topics are the "dawn of civilization," "imperial history," and "the American Divergence." The "dawn of civilization" refers to the emergence of cities with tens of thousands of inhabitants, which spread their rule over adjacent villages. This development unfolded first in Mesopotamia, contemporary Iraq, during the fifth and fourth millennia BCE and in Egypt, which by 3100 BCE became united as a single kingdom in command of thousands of square kilometers and hundreds of thousands of people.

"Imperial history" deals with the most prominent political structure of world history: empires.[5] Empires pushed forward the centralization of authority, initiated in Mesopotamian city-states and the Kingdom of Egypt, spreading out over larger and larger territories and with more and more diverse ethnic groups living within them. Around 2250 BCE the Akkadian Empire of Sargon, established in Mesopotamia, started the long-lasting career of this type of political formation. In fact, empires were overwhelmingly displaced only recently by nation-states, as the process of decolonization began in 1947, after the Second World War.

By the sixteenth century, however, there was a major turning point in imperial history: the emergence of modernity and with it the appearance of modern empires. Entwined with the emerging capitalist economy and the unfolding Scientific Revolution, these new empires were global in scope (as opposed to regional) and maritime in reach (as opposed to territorial in reach, being limited to contiguous lands). Imperial history at this point becomes closely associated with the third exemplifying topic, "the American Divergence," which refers to the divided fortunes of New World societies created by modern empires from around 1500 BCE onward. In other words, the American Divergence speaks to how North America, north of the mouth of the Río Grande, thrived to the point of giving birth to world hegemonic power, while Latin America was left behind in the Third World or as a developing region.

Let's go back in time and far afield, then, to the very "dawn of civilization" to begin our investigation of the comparative–connective rift. From a comparative perspective, our attention is captured by the stark contrast between Sumerian and Egyptian civilizations. While political centralization was an outstanding feature of the Old Kingdom, Sumerian civilization could not maintain political cohesion. This contrastive comparison could be enhanced into an inductive comparison by attributing the difference to an independent variable such as geographical constraints. The navigability of the Nile River is indeed advanced as the crucial difference conditioning the contrasting political patterns at the dawn of civilization. Controlling access to the Nile River meant rule over Egypt. Hence, a ruler with a modest state apparatus could command the entire country.

From a connective perspective, however, this contrast or even crucial difference is not the focus of attention. Instead, the spotlight is on the interactions between Sumer and Old Kingdom Egypt. In fact, one of the puzzling questions of archaeology and ancient history is why Mesopotamia—where far-reaching communities of merchants established links with Anatolia, the Iranian Plateau, and the Indus River valley—and Egypt did not engage in trade. In pursuing this question, rather than the similarities and differences between the two civilizations, archaeologists were able to come out with evidence of a limited amount of trade sent from Mesopotamia through the Mediterranean coast back in around 4000–3200 BCE. It is only in the Late Bronze Age (the second millennium BCE), when material records show that contact resumed. The mask of Tutankhamen (1323 BCE), ornamented with lapis lazuli that was mined from what today is Afghanistan, and the Uluburun shipwreck (ca. 1305 BCE), found in 1982 near the shores of Anatolia, are two of the most prominent examples of the interactions between Mesopotamian and Egyptian societies.[6]

From this example clearly emerges the difference between histories limited by enclosed boundaries and histories going beyond boundaries as well as the radical difference within the later. Histories limited within political boundaries are written on ancient Egypt or ancient Mesopotamia, but not on both. By contrast, histories going beyond boundaries engage both cases at once but approach this matching differently. Comparative histories deal with ancient Egypt and ancient Mesopotamia by keeping them as self-enclosed units with the aim of contrasting them, stressing their similarities and differences for the sake of detecting patterns of recurrence or causal inference. Connective histories also adopt both ancient Egypt and Mesopotamia but focus on the connections between the two.

The above examples show how the establishment of differences and/or commonalities, on the one hand, or searching for relationship between units, on the other hand, is the radical difference between comparative and connective methods. Moreover, this difference of purpose has repercussions in two other fundamental dimensions: the definition of time and the formulation of causal relations. Frank's quotation above addresses the definition of time dimension: "the same thing through different times," that is, a diachronic perspective on time, versus "to relate different things and places at the same time," that is, a synchronic perspective on time. The procedure of contrasting enclosed units implies that these units brought together can be selected by the historian from the entire time span. That is, it is possible not only to compare ancient Egypt and ancient Mesopotamia but also ancient Egypt, Hellenistic Egypt, and Muslim Egypt or the Maya classical period (ca. 200–1000 CE). Contrary to that, when the aim of bringing together two units or more is to underscore their relationship and ties, the synchronic dimension of time prevails, as simultaneity is a requirement for such a relationship. There was never a relation in real time between ancient Egypt and Muslim Egypt or between ancient Egypt and the Mayas in their classical period. Ancient Egypt instead was truly connected in real time with ancient Mesopotamia. This means that works in comparative history, civilization analysis, and historical sociology can select for comparison whatever units from the entire time span as it suits the aims of the project. This freedom of choice is very prominent in the study of imperial history.

For example, the study of imperial history conducted from a comparative perspective can contrast imperial histories taken from different periods. In this way, for example, Ronald Syme compared the Roman, Spanish, and British empires in order to elucidate the causes of imperial disintegration. He found that the crucial difference that explained the long-lasting endurance of the Roman Empire, as opposed to the shorter duration of the Spanish and British empires, had to do with local elites. Presumably, the absorption of local elites into imperial institutions, as in the case of Rome, warranted stability. On the other hand, the Creole aristocracy of the Spanish Empire, which was never employed in high-level administration, led to the empire's disruption and downfall. A similar outcome occurred in BNA, as the integration of the local elite into the imperial machinery was only partial.

A similar comparison, although with a different conclusion, was advanced by Peter A. Brunt. In his study of the Roman and British empires, the reasons for the faster collapse of the British Empire are found within the modern conditions of its existence. Arguments about the reasons for long-lasting or short-lived empires aside, these examples taken from comparative history clearly show that dealing with enclosed units of analysis allows us to bring together several of them, even if they existed in different historical periods. This possibility of engaging units taken from different times leads us to describe comparative histories as diachronic—that is, they can analyze disparate historical events across and over time.

For connective histories, for which the interactions between units are their subject of study or interpretative context, these units must coexist, must be simultaneous or synchronous. The flows, transferences, networks, diffusions, interdependencies, and entanglements occur in real time. This distinction between the diachronic possibility of comparisons versus the synchronic necessity of connections becomes very clear if we revisit imperial histories from a connective perspective.

For connective histories, what matters about empires has to do with their synchronicity. It does not make sense to bring the Roman and British empires together from a connective perspective. If we are to bind the history of the Roman Empire to that of another empire, then we should look for contemporaneous empires. That is the way world historians handled things from the classical work by Teggart, correlating turmoil in Rome and China and relating it to nomadic societies' migrations and conquests from the Tarim Basin east and westward. William McNeill, another example, stressed the fact that the Roman, Parthian, Kushan, and Han empires ruled simultaneously across Eurasia at the beginning of the Common Era. This imperial simultaneity represented political stabilization on a continental scale and enabled economic integration, the "first closure of Ecumene."

Transportation, communication, trade, and migration were enabled and enhanced by this imperial stabilization. Ultimately, the tightening of contacts across the Eurasian landscape of stabilizing empires resulted in the diffusion of epidemics that contributed to the collapse of all of these empires almost simultaneously. Occurring at the same time was the impact of Central Asian nomadic societies upon the sedentary societies under imperial rule, sealing the fate of those empires and bringing the first closure of Ecumene to its end.[7]

At this point, another feature of the comparative–connective distinction becomes apparent: the tendency to rely upon endogenous versus exogenous causal relations in comparative and connective methods, respectively. An endogenous causation is one in which the responsible factors for a particular outcome reside within the unit under scrutiny. Conversely, an exogenous causation points toward factors beyond the limits of the unit under study as responsible for a particular outcome within that unit. The exemplification of this dichotomy was already implicit in the contrast between diachronic and synchronic macro-historical perspectives on empires.

The comparisons between the Roman, Spanish, and British empires resulted in envisioning either the fate of local political elites or the presence of modern conditions as internal factors determining the durability of these empires. These were endogenous causations. The entanglements between Eurasian empires in antiquity, instead, resulted from exogenous causations, as the collapse of every empire was determined by forces external to them such as a pandemic outbreak or nomadic invasion.

The relation between enclosed units, diachronic time, and endogenous or internal causation as opposed to that of interrelated units, synchronicity, and exogenous or external causation becomes apparent. As far as each unit remains self-enclosed, it proceeds along its own historical timeline. Therefore, the causes for whatever outcome should lie at some previous stage of this same timeline.

By contrast, when attention is directed to some processes permeating the units under scrutiny, a synchronic view of these entangled units prevails. In this framework, it is only natural that the reasons for whatever outcome have to do with these interactions.

The relation between enclosed units under comparison and endogenous causation normally prevails even if the compared units belong in the very same chronological period. The study of "the American Divergence" offers a wide window into synchronic comparisons, as there is a vast amount of comparative history literature contrasting the Spanish and British empires and the underlying crucial differences for the divergent paths of Spanish and British America.

For James Lang, for example, it is the declining power of the Cortes (representative institutions, that is, parliaments) in Spain as opposed to the rising power of the Parliament in England, together with the territorial character of the Spanish colonial enterprise in place of the English maritime commercial emphasis, among several other differences, that are behind the diverging fates of North and Latin America. Anthony Pagden, instead, suggests that the sources of this divergence between modern empires reside with the land of destination, not the land of departure. That is, areas as densely populated, wealthy, urbanized, and politically articulated as the Aztec and Inca empires generated the ambition and provided the resources for tight colonial control. By contrast, areas sparsely populated and without valuable resources, as was the case in North America, kept motivation and profits low in order to evolve a centralized colonization, paving the way instead for local and autonomous initiatives. Out of these constraints in the loci of arrival, two different types of empires, and later on of nation-states, were to emerge regardless of the cultural and historical luggage brought from the Old World.[8]

These alternative explanations of the American Divergence exemplify the link between enclosed units and endogenous explanations, even when the units being comparison are contemporaneous. Unsurprisingly, this tendency to privilege endogenous causation remains in place precisely because the units are enclosed and, therefore, the causes are to be found within the boundaries of each of the units. Either by finding causes in the society of departure (England versus Spain) or the lands of arrival (Aztec and Inca empires versus North America East Coast) in all cases, these causes for North American success and Latin American failure are endogenous.

This endogenous perspective is epitomized by modernization theory. Modernization theory proposes that a process of differentiation transformed traditional societies by creating new specialized institutions in the economic, political, cultural, and social sectors of society. In order for this transition to occur, a series of preconditions, involving societal values, institutions, and motivations, had to be fulfilled. After meeting this set of preconditions and undergoing the process of differentiation, every society could move from the traditional stage toward modernization. Failure to make the move toward modernization was a testament to a society's not being able to meet the preconditions on its own, in which case outside influence from already modern (that is, Western) societies could "right the ship," so to speak. In this way, modernization theory considers each society in an enclosed fashion, consisting of internal structural features that are essential for its modernization and with the possibility of corrective input from the outside fostering development.[9]

Contrary to that view, dependency theory provides a connected history of the North Atlantic and Latin America that accounts for the development of the former and the underdevelopment of the later. The entanglement between the two worked through "unequal exchange": the capacity of stronger states to obtain surplus value from weaker states in their trade because of the relatively monopolized products of the first as opposed to the relatively low-added value products exported by the latter. This entanglement offers an exogenous causation for both the development of the North and the underdevelopment of the South.[10] The 13 colonies gained their independence by detaching themselves from the emerging global empire by relying upon the support of the declining powers of France and Spain. The Latin American road to decolonization inverted this equation by expelling a declining empire by inviting a powerful emerging one to its shores. Subsequently, the collision between the industrializing North and the agro-exporting South ended with the North prevailing in the American Civil War (1861–1865). The result was the exact opposite in the War of Paraguay (1864–1870), in which agro-exporting Argentina, Brazil, and Uruguay devastated industrializing Paraguay.

In short, by achieving independence, the United States managed to disentangle itself from unequal exchanges with European powers and, later, by embracing industrialization, succeeded in imposing unequal exchanges on Latin America for its own benefit. Latin America, instead, deepened its unfavorable unequal exchange, as its independence resulted in the displacement of the Spanish and Portuguese empires by the advent of the much more powerful British informal empire. Finally, by the time that the power of the British Empire waned, the United States was in full strength and capable of following in its footsteps and inheriting the unequal exchanges with Latin America.

This contrast between a comparative perspective such as modernization theory and a connective one as *dependency theory* not only insists on the divergent paths of contrasting versus connecting but also on diachronic versus synchronic dimensions of time and endogenous versus exogenous causal relations. Modernization and dependency theories are also revealing in that by thinking globally about history we can aim to achieve broad generalizations. In the case of comparative histories, this is just one option among a range of possibilities offered by the comparative method.

Table 3.2 Thinking history globally: The comparative–connective divide

Thinking globally / Defining features	Comparative	Connective
Way of transcending national boundaries	Comparatively	Connectively
Space dimension	Several enclosed units	Several entangled units or transboundary inclusive unit
Time dimension	Diachronic	Synchronic
Causality attribution	Endogenous	Exogenous

The comparative method

Reflections on the comparative method lead comparative historians and historical sociologists to devise several typologies of comparisons. These typologies recognize two, three, or four categories of comparison. According to the most parsimonious typology, there are two major categories of comparisons: comparisons aiming to study individual units by contrasting them, and comparisons for the sake of generalization by discerning consistent patterns running through several units.

For example, Otto Hintze dealt with comparisons designed to expose an underlying generality and comparisons intended to bring out the individuality of a specific unit. A. A. van den Braembussche labeled these two modes the "contrasting type" versus the "universalizing type." In George Fredrickson's view, these types are related to two different traditions: the illumination of the particular in the humanities and the development of theories in the social sciences that foster "grand manner" comparisons. An additional dual typology along similar lines was advanced by Victoria Bonnell. However, the "generalizing, universalizing, grand manner" type of comparison is subdivided into two variants: comparative or illustrative. The comparative variant explains common or contrasting patterns by identifying independent variables underlying equivalent units. The illustrative variant assesses theories by comparing equivalent units to a particular theory. By making this distinction, Bonnell is in fact pointing toward a tripartite typology.

A clearly stated tripartite typology for comparisons was proposed by Theda Skocpol and Margaret Somers. Their tripartite typology of comparisons includes contrast-oriented comparative history, macro-analytical comparative history, and parallel comparative history. These types of comparisons coincide to a great extent with the types of comparisons appearing in the above bipolar typologies: the "individualizing, contrasting, particularizing" type; (b) the comparative variant of the "generalizing, universalizing, grand manner" type; and (c) the illustrative variant of the "generalizing, universalizing, grand manner" type.[11]

Practically speaking, these three categories represent concrete procedures of comparative analysis. A contrast-oriented comparison is one in which two units of analysis, or the same unit itself at different time intervals, are presented side by side. The aim of this comparison is to stress the contrast between the units or time intervals, emphasizing the singularities between the two. For example, in *The Changing Land: Between Jordan and the Sea* B. Z. Kedar gathered, selected, and matched aerial photographs of rural and urban landscapes in Palestine and Israel dating from the First World War, the 1940s, the late 1960s, and the 1990s. The aim of this "do-it-yourself" comparative exercise is "to allow the reader to confront, through the visual texts proffered by aerial photography, some of the physical changes that took place during this stormy century in a number of localities throughout the country." A similar method was applied by John Elliott in *Richelieu and Olivares*. The author refers to his book as "a historiographical Wimbledon," as it shifts from one character to the other from chapter to chapter as the biographies of both statesmen unfold.[12]

The category of macro-analytic comparison represents a substitute for the experiment in the natural and social sciences. Its aim is to determine causation by discovering the independent variable responsible for a determined outcome. For instance, what variable or set of variables leads toward social revolution, economic development, or technological innovation? With this type of clearly defined goal in mind, one possible research design is to choose several units in which the phenomenon in question—for example, revolution in France, Russia, and China—took place in order to isolate a shared variable or set of variables present in all of them. It is the presence of this shared variable or set of variables—for example, combination of domestic conflict in an agrarian society and international threat—that the final outcome was actually attributed to by Theda Skocpol.[13]

This procedure is what John Stuart Mill had called the method of crucial agreement. That is, no matter how different France, Russia, and China are, as long as there is a crucial agreement in these three, for example, the combination of domestic conflict in an agrarian society and an international threat, all of them underwent the same outcome: revolution. An alternative method envisioned by Mill is that of the crucial difference. That is, no matter how closely similar two societies are, one significant difference between them might prove to be crucial, as entirely different outcomes are observed in each of them.[14]

For example, for all the similarities within the Spanish Empire in the Americas, a drastic distinction emerged around the question of emancipation among colonial elites. Colonial elites waged wars of independence in the Viceroyalties of Nueva Granada and Río de la Plata, while loyalty to the Spanish Crown was adopted by colonial elites in the Viceroyalties of Mexico and Perú. The social structure and composition of the workforce was accounted for as the crucial difference responsible for such bifurcation in the history of the Spanish Empire. In the Viceroyalties of Mexico and Perú, heavily dependent on forced labor, the elites feared ending up as a republic of slaves, following Haiti's example. Conversely, in the Viceroyalties of Nueva Granada and Río de la Plata, which were less dependent on forced labor, the elite looked at its prospects as more likely to resemble the path of the confederation in North America: getting rid of a monarch abroad while keeping the forced laborers at bay.[15]

The methods of crucial agreement and crucial difference make up the basic toolkit of the experimental-like thinking represented by macro-analytic comparisons. However, there are several additional possible designs for this type of comparison. While crucial agreement and crucial difference seem to work under an all-or-nothing principle, Emile Durkheim's method of concomitant variations contemplates different degrees for the presence of an independent variable and its outcome rather than its existence or lack of.[16]

Based on these variables precisely, Arnold Toynbee concluded that challenging but affordable environments, in contrast to comfortable and barren settings, encourage cultural flourishing the most. The cultural effervescence of the Río de la Plata region (Buenos Aires), as opposed to Brazil and Patagonia, exemplifies this gradualist scheme, as much as the vitality of Icelandic culture compared to that of Norway and Greenland.[17]

The singularity of the third category of the tripartite classification for comparisons, the parallel comparative history, resides in its deductive dimension. That is, whenever the point of departure is a general conclusion or deductive statement, its validation is discerned by comparing it with case after case in a parallel way. A multiplicity of cases showing consistent agreement with the deductive statement should end up making the case. For example, in *The Founding of a New Society*, Louis Hartz coined the term "fragment" to designate a migrant group that freezes its original motherland culture and reproduces it along generations of newborns in the land of destination. Fragments, then, perpetuate in a deeply conservative vein their motherland culture in their new destination, while in their motherland that same culture keeps changing beyond recognition. This argument is contrasted with different European colonial experiences. The Spanish immigrants arriving in the Americas at the dawn of the Middle Ages imprinted a feudal character to Latin America. The rising bourgeoisie and the gentrification process in Britain at the moment of departure to North

America, instead, originated liberal societies. Finally, the wave of foundational migration to Australia amid the Industrial Revolution created a radical society there. For all of their differences, all of these colonial experiences, according to Hartz, incarnate the pattern captured by the concept of fragment and therefore validate it, making it a useful tool in understanding the founding of new societies.[18]

Finally, some scholars have classified the comparative method into four categories. Jonathan Smith distinguishes cultural, historical, combined, and hermeneutic comparisons. The cultural comparison establishes a "we/they" contrast, for example, "the West and the rest," whose later variants as presented by Niall Ferguson, according to whom there are six features in the West lacking in the rest that explain the success of the former, namely: a more fragmented political setting that worked to encourage competition and innovation both between and within states; a predilection for open inquiry and a scientific attitude toward nature; property rights and the representation of property owners in elected assemblies; modern medicine; an Industrial Revolution based on both a supply of sustained innovations and a demand for mass consumer goods; and, finally, a work ethic that included more productive labor with higher savings and capital accumulation.[19]

The historical comparison contrasts the past and the present. That is the typical "before and after" experiment. For example, how does a society look before and after a thorough application of a set of neoliberal policies? In a nutshell, national economies supportive of local production, aiming to supply the local market while restraining imports, were replaced by exporting oriented toward the world market. The retreat of the state led to social polarization, as redistributive policies declined and identity fragmentation follow the divestment of "melting pot" state-sponsored policies.[20]

The combination of these two types of comparison, "we/they" and "before and after," results in the third type, which aims to establish the historical reasons for any kind of "we/they" contrast. For example, in the above "West versus the rest" cultural comparison, a plethora of crucial differences is advanced as crucial moments of divergence: the regeneration of empires in Eurasia following the collapse of classical age empires, except in the West where political fragmentation became the rule; the emergence of capitalism, Protestantism, or the exploitation of a subsoil reach in coal, among many other possible turning points that resulted in "before and after" moments.

Comparison as a hermeneutic device constitutes Jonathan Smith's fourth type and consists of approaching the unknown unit by means of the unit already known. Its goal is to take advantage of our acquaintance with one unit in order to underscore similar features or processes in the lesser known unit. For example, acquaintance with a process of industrialization in one society can guide the study of this same process in another society. Moreover, and in a more subtle way, a phenomenon apparently unique to one society—for example, the binding of women's feet in China—can guide the search of seemingly sexual aesthetic preferences in other societies, such as the long, extended necks of women among the Kayan people in Burma and the South Ndebele people in the southern part of Africa (contemporary Zimbabwe and South Africa). In this example, although these are two entirely different practices, bound feet and lengthened necks, the hermeneutic comparison might reveal that beyond the uniqueness of sexual aesthetic preferences both cases function similarly as control measures over women. Bound feet cannot walk far from the husband's control; a woman's weakened neck is at the mercy of a husband, the coil holds the head in place and the respiratory system functioning safely.

This application of the hermeneutic comparison is closely related to the notion of "homologies," coined by Fritz Redlich. By homologies, Redlich meant functional analogies. That is, two different features that for all their difference actually have the very same function in their respective societies. For example, sermons and preaching during the European Middle Ages might be approached as homologous to modern mass media in their function as public opinion generators.[21]

Jürgen Kocka's fourfold classification, consisting of the heuristic, paradigmatic, descriptive, and comparative categories, can be juxtaposed with Jonathan Smith's cultural, historical, combined, and hermeneutic comparisons. Smith's hermeneutic comparison overlaps with Kocka's heuristic and paradigmatic comparisons. According to Kocka, a heuristically oriented comparison serves to identify issues in one unit facilitated by the acquaintance of another unit but without necessarily contributing to its interpretation. Conversely, the paradigmatic function opens new venues of inquiry for the better known unit based on the novelties provided by the least known unit. The fresh insight provided by this unit opens up the better known unit to alternative possible interpretations and to the elimination of unexamined assumptions.[22]

For example, by studying the principle of the divine right to rule, the process of constructing an imagined order can be scrutinized, making sense of political regimes alien to our political experience. The relatively easy deconstruction of the divine right to rule as just an imagined order rather than a self-evident truth can help the deconstruction of an imagined order based on self-determination, popular sovereignty, equality before the law, and human rights despite the fact that all these principles look to us as self-evident truths. In other words, Kocka's heuristically and paradigmatically methodological functions are two faces of the same revealing process. Exposure to a unit of comparison inspires new issues for the least known unit and at the same time undermines implicit assumptions regarding the better known unit.

Kocka's remaining two methodological categories are the descriptive, depicting individual cases more clearly by contrasting between units, and the comparative, functioning as a substitute for experiment to enable the testing of hypotheses. Besides this fourfold classification of comparison, Jürgen Kocka also coined the idea of "asymmetrical comparisons." This label refers to the addition of a second case to the case study of expertise. Whereas a scholar is able to research the case of her or his expertise based on primary sources, the original language, and full command of the historiography, the second case is included to shed a comparative light, even if the scholar's command of this case is based only on a partial knowledge of the secondary literature. For example, a Sovietologist researching the collapse of the Soviet Union can gain a broader perspective by taking a comparative look at China, even if all of the research on China is based on secondary sources in languages that she or he is able to read.

Charles Tilly's four categories derive from two parameters: the number of units in which the phenomenon is present (only one case to all cases) and the quantity of forms of the phenomenon (from single to multiple). From the combinations of these parameters, his four categories of comparison emerge: individualizing (aiming at the peculiarities of each unit), universalizing (seeking to explain a general pattern), identifying difference (trying to establish the concomitant variation of a particular phenomenon along several units), and globalizing (following the changing relationships between the components and the system in which they are immersed).[23]

Ultimately, all these typologies can be reconciled if they are arranged in a scale ranging from the most general to the most specific, as in Table 3.3.[24]

Table 3.3 Comparison typologies reconciled

Bipolar Typologies

Otto Hinze	Individualizing	Generalizing	
A. A. Van den Braembussche	Contrasting	Universalizing	
George M. Fredrickson	Particularizing	"Grand manner"	
Victoria E. Bonnell		Comparative	Illuminating

Triple Typologies

Theda Skocpol and Margaret Somers	Contrasting	Macro-comparative	Parallel

Quadruple Typologies

Jonathan Z. Smith	Hermeneutic		Cultural	Historic	Combined	
Jürgen Kocka	Heuristic	Paradigmatic	Descriptive		Comparative	
Charles Tilly	Individualizing		Difference		Universalizing	Global

Connections as method

The comparative method garnered almost a century and a half of scholarly attention, producing multiple treatises specifying its practice, varieties, and classifications. A considerable part of that literature is presented above. When it comes to connections as method, however, there is not such a body of methodological literature for these much newer sets of methodological options. Nevertheless, several methodological resources to establish connections can be recognized and classified along three broad categories: enlargement of geographic units of analysis, attention to historical linkages between units of analysis, and adoption of units of analysis or themes that are intrinsically cross-boundary in nature.

The simplest way to establish connections is by erasing boundaries as larger units of analysis are defined. That is, by moving up in the scale of space and redefining space units, connections are instantly established. For example, the moment that a unit named East Asian, African, or Latin American civilization is addressed as the unit of analysis, many boundaries—most prominently political and linguistic ones—disappear. Otherwise enclosed units, such as China, Vietnam, Korea, and Japan for East Asia, Zimbabwe, Mali, and Ethiopia for Africa, or Mexico, Brazil, and Chile for Latin America, are brought into contact.

Similarly, whenever an ocean basin is adopted as the unit of analysis and as a liquid road for communication and transportation, boundaries are also erased between space units even farther apart than those connected by the concept of civilization. A Pacific Ocean unit brings together not only the four East Asian nation-states mentioned above but also Mexico and Chile, among many others. An Atlantic Basin connects the shores of west Europe and Africa with those of the eastern Americas. The ultimate way to erase all boundaries on the planet is by adopting the world as the unit of analysis. Such a connection could be conceptual—that is, adopting the world as a geographic unit to be looked upon as a whole—or historical, which means that connections worldwide were actually established.

These two alternatives, conceptual as opposed to historical connections, underline a general distinction for connections as a method. Enclosed units can be brought together by merely enlarging the geographical scope as exemplified above by the adoption of civilizations, ocean basins, and the world as units of analysis. But an enclosed unit could also be connected by concentrating on the linkages established between them regardless of their belonging to a mutually encompassing unit. That is, China and Japan can be connected by adopting East Asia as the unit of analysis and, regardless of this possibility, China and Japan can be connected by scrutinizing their linkages. Japan and Chile can be connected by adopting the Pacific Rim as a unit of analysis, but they can also be connected by tracking their linkages. The two hemispheres can be brought together within the encompassing unit of the world while the search for the actual connections between them is the alternative modus operandi of connections as method.

As long as connections are fostered by enlarging space units, the possibilities most frequently offered are the following: civilizations, ocean basins, hemispheres, and the world. The connection method as space enlargement, then, can almost be depicted as a matryoshka or nested doll. Almost because the fit is not perfect: civilizations fit in hemispheres and those in the world. But ocean basins and hemispheres do not fit neatly, the Atlantic and Pacific oceans spill over both hemispheres. Neither do civilizations and ocean basins fit well; back to back Chile and Argentina belong together in the Latin American civilization, but Argentina belongs in the Atlantic, Chile in the Pacific.

On the other hand, whenever connections are pursued through linkages, it is not size but intensity that matters. That is, the strength and regularity of the mutual impacts imprinted by the connected units on each other. The departing point with the lowest degree of intensity between two or more units is that of contacts, that is, initial and sporadic communications carrying occasional one-directional or mutual impacts. Sustainability of contacts, though, leads toward interactions: an ongoing process of communication with some measure of regularity yielding to cumulative and mutual impacts on the parties involved. Lasting and deepening interactions become interdependent relations, that is, a mutual and permanent conditioning linkage between units.

Finally, long-lasting interdependent relations becoming structural features may be argued to constitute a system, that is, the units tightly connected through such interdependent relations actually become a complex whole. In other words, the individual units interdependently entwined end up being absorbed into a larger unit of analysis: the system. In this way, the system as a method of connection combines both categories presented so far, connection as space enlargement and connection by actual linkages between units.

This combination of the previous two strategies actually represents a third category for connection as a method out of which the system is only one possibility. As with space enlargement, this third methodological category consists of adopting a new type of unit of analysis. The contours of this new type of unit, however, do not derive from size enlargement. Instead, and in consonance with the attention to actual existing linkages, the realm of the new type of unit emerges by encompassing all agencies immersed in some form of intense linkage, such as interaction or interdependency. This is the case for the adoption of social networks as an analytical framework for approaching connections as a method.

Social networks are webs of interconnected groups or individuals across space. These interconnections often times go beyond boundaries. Tracing the geographical scope of a network might reveal that it is simultaneously immensely larger *and* smaller than many of the space units discussed so far. A network of breast cancer researchers can span from Japan to China, Russia, the European Union, Canada, and the United States making this space unit much more widespread than any civilization, ocean, or hemisphere and yet immensely smaller than any of them.

The institutionalization of a transnational network, or perhaps the other way around coming from the top-down, the waiving of transnational networks by an institution result in a formalized version of social networks: the transnational organization. The adoption of a transnational (or trans-boundary for pre-national times) organization as a study case represents an additional avenue of connection as method. The study of FedEx, Human Rights Watch, or Catholic Relief Services exemplifies this avenue.

Finally, a twist to this is to approach a transnational or trans-boundary theme or subject rather than an organization. An environmental theme such as draught, flooding, climate change, or soil degradation, among many others, can be studied while circumscribed to the borders of a particular space unit (generally a nation-state). However, as the environment knows no political frontier, the adoption of such a theme encourages border crossing and the establishment of connections between the units affected by the phenomenon in question. What is true for the environmental variable also applies to other themes that intrinsically embodied border crossing: the study of trade relations in economic history, migration in demographic history, disease in epidemiological history, and conquest in political and military history constitute some prominent examples of trans-boundary themes that bring the study of connections to the forefront of their methodological agendas.

For all of the clear-cut distinctions summarized in this table, it is important to stress that these different ways of establishing connections are not mutually exclusive. They were analytically charted here for the sake of clarity, aiming

Table 3.4 How to connect? A typology of connections as method

Expand the units of analysis into different geographical scopes	Focus on links of different intensity between units of analysis	Let the links define new types of units of analysis or subjects
Civilizations	Contacts	Social networks
Ocean basins	Interactions	Transnational, trans-boundary organizations
Hemispheres	Interdependency	Transnational, trans-boundary themes
World	System	

to offer a succinct methodological menu. However, in practice, these different ways for the establishment of connections share fundamental features, enhance one another, and even easily combine.

Starting with the shared fundamental features, these include a preference for the synchronic time dimension, an inclination toward the formulation of external explanations or causal relations, partially a prominence in the use of secondary sources, and a predilection for topics involving movement. On the time dimension, connections encourage a shift from a diachronic to a synchronic perspective. This means that instead of giving priority to the successive stages of progression within a given enclosed unit of analysis—say China, Vietnam, Korea, and Japan—by enlarging the geographic scale, priority is given to developments occurring simultaneously across the encompassing unit, in this case the civilization of East Asia. The same applies to the contrast between the diachronic disposition of time within a civilization as opposed to a synchronic disposition of time on a hemispheric scale encompassing multiple civilizations.

For example, the time dimension circumscribed to the European civilization is framed by the successive progressive stages of antiquity, the Middle Ages, early modernism, and modern history. By contrast, the encompassing of the eastern hemisphere shifts the attention toward simultaneous developments across this larger space, including, for instance, the emergence of medieval Europe, the rise of Islam, and the reunification of China under the Sui and Tang dynasties. This simultaneity is also what matters while approaching connections by focusing on the links between these units, which requires doing so in real time. From this perspective, and following the previous example, what was crucial for Europe around 700 BCE was the presence of Islam in the Mediterranean Sea, rather than classical antiquity. The important time dimension is the real time in which the units interact with one another rather than the previous or successive stages in which each of them is embedded separately.

Finally, synchronicity is also necessary for studying networks, trans-boundary entities, and themes. Studying a network of traders in that period such as the Radhanites, a trans-boundary entity such as the Cistercian monastic order, or a trans-boundary theme such as the prominence of Aristotelian philosophy tends to privilege a synchronic dimension of time. Synchronicity is necessary in order to show how the Radhanites, Jewish medieval merchants, coordinated their trade operations from locations in China and India throughout Central Asia and the Middle East and up to Western Europe. Synchronicity is necessary to research the extent to which decisions made by the General Chapter, or general assembly, of the Cistercian order in Cîteaux were adopted and adapted throughout Europe in the approximately 500 monasteries belonging to this monastic order. Synchronicity is necessary while interpreting why and how Ibn Rušd

(1126–1198) and Maimonides (1135–1204) became influential around the same time in Islam and Judaism, respectively, with Thomas Aquinas (1225–1274) bringing Aristotelian thinking into Christian theology soon after.

By giving priority to a synchronic perspective of time, connections as a method are prone to formulate exogenous causal relations. As long as the geographical scope is enclosed and time dimension contemplated vertically as a progression of stages or periods, causal relations are found within the enclosed unit of analysis and a step back in the line of time progression. Once the geographical constraints are eliminated—either by enlarging the units of analysis, highlighting the links between them, or defining new types of integrated units—and a synchronic view of time prevails, it is possible to think upon the reasons for simultaneous processes in many areas.

In this way new perspectives on causal inference arise. The above example on the successive stages of European civilization invites us to revisit the opening story of the fall of the Roman Empire. The transition from antiquity to the Middle Ages is identified with this development. The collapse of the Roman Empire is attributed to the internal structural weaknesses of this empire, ranging from its economic structure to the metal content of its water pipes. In the farthest internal attributions, the neighboring Germanic peoples play a role in the empire's demise. By contrast, contemplating Afro-Eurasia synchronically allows the visualization of the simultaneity between the end of the Pax Romana with the collapses of the Parthian, Kushan, and Han empires. This perspective leads us to attempt exogenous explanations such as climatic changes, epidemiological bursts, and nomadic prevalence upon settled societies.

Last but not least, the enlargement of spatial scale and/or chasing after links, mobile entities or subjects may require a different approach to sources. Depending on their genre and scope, work fostered by connections as a method may rely preferentially or extensively on secondary literature and/or translated primary sources. This last feature represents a major divergence from the fundamental disciplinary duty of pursuing sources in their primary form. Nevertheless, conditions had changed in the balance between the bulk of primary and secondary sources since this disciplinary rule was established. After more than a century of professional historiography, there is huge body of secondary literature in need of connection and synthesis. By pursuing this goal, the application of connections as a method converges with the historical discipline in its unique way.

On the other hand, the application of connections as a method can be fostered while sticking to the most rigorous disciplinary demands regarding the use of primary sources in their most primary form. The study of a transnational or trans-boundary institution usually relies on the original records created by that institution. The same is true for the study of social networks. The study of trans-boundary themes is more challenging in this regard, as tracking such a subject across space means changing language zones and, therefore, confronting primary sources potentially in more languages than a researcher can master. However, a multilingual historian can tackle this challenge too.

Even when it comes to connections by the enlargement of space, research can be conducted on primary sources. In our contemporary globalized world, the eight most commonly spoken languages are used by more than 40 per cent of the world's population.[25] This current situation is the long-lasting result of centuries of expansions, colonization, and acculturations. Methodologically speaking that means that the histories of huge areas and populations of the world can be studied from primary sources even while mastering very few languages.

Moreover, the enlargement of space does not necessarily mean that all of it would be covered. Rather, all of it will be considered as the encompassing relevant context while only some locations within it would be studied in depth through primary sources. In this regard, thinking globally about history is analogous to nationally based or boundary-enclosed histories. A great deal of that historiographic production does not address the entire nation-state, or any alternative enclosed unit, but rather smaller units—a city, a county, a province, and so on—within it. Such smaller units are taken as partial, representative, conditioned, or subordinated to the whole. The same principle applies for smaller units immersed in spatially enlarged contexts.

The adoption of a larger geographical unit also encourages the study of entities or subjects spread out throughout it or in motion within it. These entities and subjects include peoples, ideas, commodities, artifacts, seeds, plants, germs, and so on. This also works the other way around: the study of entities and subjects that imply linkages and mobility demands the enlargement of spatial frameworks. In short, the prominence of these mobile entities and subjects exemplifies how the different ways of connecting as method enhance one another: space enlargement encourages the tracking of mobility; following the footprints of linkages, networks, trans-boundary entities, or themes enlarges the space chartered.

Finally, besides their sharing of the time dimension, external explanations, subject preferences, and singular reliance on sources as well as their mutual enhancement, the different ways of establishing connections as a method can be perfectly combined. A network within a civilization, a system in an ocean basin, and a trans-boundary theme in a hemisphere can be suggested as examples: Al-Qaeda in the Muslim world, the modern world-system in the Atlantic Basin, and the effects of the depletion of the ozone layer on the southern hemisphere represent each of these, respectively.

From comparing to connecting

The first branches that diverged from space-enclosed historiography were those that embraced the comparative method. After some attempts during the first half of the twentieth century, it was finally during the 1950s and 1960s that comparative history, historical sociology, and civilizational analysis emerged as well defined and established academic fields. However, it was the world-system approach that developed crucial features such as connectedness, synchronicity, and exogenous causation. The world-system approach emerged during the 1970s out of the entangled histories of development and underdevelopment of the North and the South, respectively, as outlined by dependency theory. In this third wave of history writing beyond borders amid current globalization, these features are now the backbone of global thinking.

The transition from comparative toward connective methods is clearly visualized in the emergence of world history as represented by the writing of one of the leading founders of the field, William McNeill. His foundational, all-encompassing synthesis on world history, *The Rise of the West*, is organized by a principle of balance between civilizations (focusing on the Chinese, Indian, Middle Eastern, and Western civilizations) and, therefore, based on a comparative perspective.[26] According to this principle, the rupture of balance between civilizations results in a challenge that stimulates transformations. Following this principle, chronology is broken into three major periods: 3000–500 BCE in which Middle Eastern civilization destabilized the balance through the agricultural revolution and birth of cities; 500 BCE–1500 AD characterized by the relative stability between civilizations, although shaken by the diffusion of Hellenism, Indian culture, and the rise of Islam; and 1500–1990 in which Europe first and then the West broke the balance between civilizations through the impact of the Ancient Regime and the twin revolutions (industrial and democratic).

Each of these major periods is broken down following a second organizing principle: the basic social patterns involved. The agricultural revolution led to the emergence of agricultural and pastoralist nomadic societies. Relationships between these two basic patterns, through commerce and diplomacy or war, made a major imprint in the history of Eurasia up to the contention of the pastoralist nomadic societies by Russia (beginning in the fifteenth century). Following this second principle, then, the first major period (3000–500 BCE) is divided by three turning points provided by nomadic invasions: Charioteers invasions (ca. 1800–1500), invasions by iron weaponry holders (ca. 1000), and cavalry invasions (ca. 700). Similarly, the second major period (500 BCE—1500 AD) is internally divided by the successive Turk, Arab, and Mongol invasions. The third major period (1500–1990), in which the nomadic societies were progressively marginalized, is split into two: before and after the unfolding of the twin revolutions.

The contrast between these organizing principles and those of McNeill's new book, *The Human Web: A Bird's Eye View on World History*, illustrates the novelty of the current wave of global thinking in history by transitioning from a comparative toward a connective perspective.[27] Instead of enclosed civilizations, the basic building blocks are cross-boundary networks. The interactions and exchanges along these networks, and not the disruption of balance between civilizations, constitute the fundamental process.

Concomitantly, chronology also changed. Language revolution enabled the creation of networks that, nevertheless, were volatile until around 12,000 BP. By then, more thick networks evolved, up to the consolidation of the "metropolitan webs" around 6000 BP, with the emergence of cities. Some 2000 years before the present, and following the intermittent increase of flows and contacts, the "Old World Web" emerged all across Eurasia and North Africa. The mastering of navigation along the Pacific Ocean waved the "cosmopolitan web." Finally, for the last century and a half, starting with the telegraph, this network begins its electrification that resulted in the current "single global web."

The transition from comparing to connecting was a rather drastic shift. These two ways for moving beyond boundaries had appeared back in the 1990s as two mutually exclusive options. Later on, fortunately, a more balanced, nuanced, and inclusive trend in historical writing started offering several bridges of collaboration between these two big Cs. This transition from exclusiveness to inclusiveness is unpacked, explained, and exemplified in the next chapter.

4
Thinking History Globally: Comparing and Connecting

As Chapter 4 begins, a plethora of comparative historical studies have already been presented and analyzed while discussing the comparative–connective rift as well as in the exposition of the comparative method. As a quick reminder, and in chronological order, the following works on comparative history were addressed: the stark contrast between Sumerian and Egyptian civilizations; Ronald Syme's study on colonial elites in the Roman, Spanish, and British empires, and Peter Brunt's comparison of the Roman and British empires in order to reach an understanding of imperial endurance;[1] the vast comparative history literature contrasting the Spanish and British empires, and the underlying crucial differences that led to the divergent paths taken by Spanish and British America; John Elliott's *Richelieu and Olivares* that contrasts the biographies of both statesmen; Woodward's edited collection, *The Comparative Approach to American History*, that sought to shed new light on the understanding of American history by way of contrasting it with the history of Europe; the comparative study of colonial emancipation across the Spanish Empire in the Americas; and B. Z. Kedar's *The Changing Land: Between Jordan and the Sea*, in which matched aerial photographs of rural and urban landscapes in Palestine and Israel, dating from the First World War, the 1940s, the late 1960s, and the 1990s, are offered for comparative analysis.[2]

Many more works on comparative history can be presented, analyzed, and classified; however, a more promising course is to investigate the growing criticism of comparative history during this third generation of cross-boundary writing as well as the alternatives offered by some historians of this last generation. Additionally, this chapter will assess the contributions of comparative history to the history profession at large, regardless of the growing criticism surrounding it, and the ways in which criticism can be channeled toward constructive ends that enhance the asset that is the comparative method for global thinking and the history profession as a whole.

Criticism of comparative history and its alternatives: Relational histories

Comparative history has been on the defensive since its institutionalization. The editorial introductions of both comparative history journals adopted an apologetic tone vis-à-vis the traditional procedures of monographic history. In the preface to its first issue, the *Recueils de la Société Jean Bodin pour l'histoire comparative des institutions* observed that confusions and misunderstandings still prevail regarding comparative history, seeing it as an enterprise of mechanical and unfruitful juxtapositions of idiosyncratic histories. With the aim of clarifying the journal's intention to foster a relationship between nationally framed and comparative history, the former is recognized as the primary path for historical research. Nevertheless, comparative history is posited as an indispensable complement for gaining a comprehensive view of civilizations. In the editor's words: "L'analyse et la synthèse, l'èrudition et la comparaison doivent se compléter [analysis and synthesis, erudition and comparison should complement each other]."[3]

In a similar vein, the first issue of *Comparative Studies in Society and History* opened by describing dismissive reactions toward comparative history. To reverse this situation, the editor advocated information exchange in matters of wide concern rather than jeopardizing sound scholarship (nationally framed research) by spreading research into probable superficiality (comparative history).[4]

However, increasingly, the more critical appraisals of comparative history and the use of comparisons at large come from the world-system approach first and practitioners of connective methods next. These latter practitioners offer alternative procedures of entanglement instead of contrast. Their task of associating discrete units at the same point in time, and assessing the interplay and mutual influences between them, confronts head on the basic procedure of seeking similarities and differences between two or more enclosed units, which characterizes comparative history. This is the core of the criticism brought about by practitioners of connective histories vis-à-vis comparative history.

For example, in discussing Victor Lieberman's comparative work on the history of East Asia, Sanjay Subrahmanyan argues that the author "downplay[s] the global and connected character of the early modern period, in order to reify certain chosen national entities."[5] In his view, these national entities or geographical units are self-imposed straitjackets used as building blocks for comparisons. Lieberman's work, for its part, unfolds along the standard procedures of a comparative study: the selection of cases to be compared, the selection of variables or parameters for comparison, the detection of similarities and differences. Lieberman's units are Burma, Siam, Vietnam, France, Russia, and Japan. The variables contemplated for comparing between these six enclosed units include climate, population growth, disease patterns, international exchanges, and military competition. Finally, a series of crucial agreements are advanced based on this comparison: during the early modern period a transition from political fragmentation toward centralization evolved in these units, accompanied by the growth of coercive state apparatuses, standardization of culture and ethnicity, commercialization, and a "military revolution."

For Subrahmanyan this comparative exercise is biased because only the most congenial examples were chosen in order to sustain the argument. Moreover, this comparative process can only determine if each compared case belongs or not within the general trend. Finally, there is no engagement whatsoever with the interactions between these units and between units and broader trends. This is the standard connective criticism of comparative history: units of analysis are plugged into networks and immersed in processes of circulation not enclosed behind insurmountable boundaries.

Out of this criticism, Subrahmanyan offers his alternative of connected histories that are attentive to local, regional, supra-regional, and global interfaces. From this perspective, when it comes to the study of state building in early modern South East Asia, connections are to be found as the foundations for such growth. The Ayutthaya Kingdom (1351–1767) in Siam or the Arakan Kingdom (1429–1666) in Myanmar, for example, emerged in tandem with Persian influences transmitted throughout the networks of commercial exchange operating in the Bay of Bengal and connecting the Coromandel Coast with Burma, Mergui, and the Malay coast. To these regional connections, Subrahmanyan also adds trans-regional and global connections established by the circulation of bullion (staples can also be added), firearms, and the military revolution that contributed to the transition from political fragmentation to centralization. Most crucially, though, he emphasizes the traveling of ideas. Subrahmanyan tracks the synchronic interest throughout Afro-Eurasia in millennialism, Messianism, and the impending end of the world, as well as the legend of Alexander the Great as the ultimate world conqueror, while tracking their circuits of circulation. In his explanation the simultaneous interest in these ideas and the traveling of these "ideological constructs" are related to state formation throughout early modern Afro-Eurasia.

At core, then, connective criticism of comparative history sustains that the latter misses the interactions between and beyond units that are so decisive a factor in understanding history while at the same time it reifies the enclosed units under comparison. However, as if this criticism would not be enough, there is yet a more radical critical argument that questions the neutrality of the comparative method. This criticism claims that research conclusions are biased by the mere framing of a comparison because the ways in which comparisons are designed actually define what is at stake in the research subject. Moreover, as comparative historians position themselves as translators bridging gaps between two languages, two cultural systems, and two places in a time period other than their own, they are actually agents of transnational exchange rather than mere scholars.

Micole Seigel had articulated this type of criticism and exemplified it by addressing the comparative historiography on race in the United States and Brazil, the pair most chosen for comparisons based on "racial relations" in the twentieth century.[6] In her view, this literature had helped construct race as well as notions of national character, while the authors of this literature have facilitated the circulation of people, ideas, cultural forms, and had created transnational networks. In a nutshell, the comparisons between the United States and Brazil resulted in the depiction of the first as a place of a dual racial system and overt racism, while the second emerged as based on subtle multiplicity.

Rather than a depiction grounded in colonial and postcolonial social history, Seigel sees this conclusion as stemming from eighteenth- and nineteenth-century intellectual history. In her argument, this ongoing contrast between the United States and Brazil was what abolitionists and later civil rights activists wanted to see (that is, the viability of harmonious racial relations) as well as what allowed racist eugenicists in both countries to point toward the risks of miscegenation. Similarly, the comparison also provided nationalist historians with material to construct a profile of their nations' character: modern, industrial, practical, and fast paced, progressing even if at the cost of racial conflict for the United States; cordial, sensual, and plural even if progressing at a slower pace for Brazil, a "racial democracy." Seigel's antidote for this stereotypical contrast in the simultaneous service of both supremacist and antiracist as well as nationalistic agendas is "to call a moratorium on comparative study" and move instead toward related and global perspectives. Comparison should be embraced as a subject of study rather than as a method.

As a result of these kinds of criticisms, several approaches are in the making, although their degree of formulation and acceptance is by far less than all other presented branches. Many of these approaches are the ideas of one or a small group of scholars, and their institutionalization is virtually nonexistent. As a whole, these initiatives can be defined as a family of relational approaches. What brings them under this shared familial umbrella is their goal of relating their units or subjects of study to one another while focusing on the crucial role played by the connections between the units or subjects under scrutiny.

These relational approaches present the "historian as electrician," pursuing of connections, crossings, intersections, and entanglements. That is, the historian's task is to reconnect all the cords, cables, and plugs between units or subjects.[7] This task would shed light on the past because many links and connections between units get lost during more than a century of enclosed historiographies that sealed the boundaries between units. Cross-national comparisons discourage attention to interactions between units as much as nationally based studies because they keep units enclosed for the sake of contrast. The underlying assumption of relational histories is that interactions between units are crucial for their historical trajectories, as they reciprocally modify one another. The family of relational approaches includes entangled history (*histoire croissé*), connected histories, shared histories, and the history of transfers.

Pairing two states, such as Germany and Russia, particularly Nazi Germany and Soviet Russia, provides an additional illustration of the relational approach and its difference with comparative history. Since Leon Trotsky described Fascism and Stalinism as "symmetrical phenomena" in his *Revolution Betrayed*,[8] a fair amount of comparative literature on Nazi Germany and the Soviet Union has been written. Deductive comparisons stressed the concept of totalitarianism: an all-embracing organization in full command of force and ideology or the combined subjugation of state and society under a utopian, non-political claim to exercise rule.[9]

Analytical comparisons confronted the component parts of these regimes: a totalistic ideology, a single party committed to this ideology led by a dictator, a fully developed secret police, and monopolistic control of mass communications, operational weapons, and all the organizations involved in a centrally planned economy.[10] Contrasting comparisons stressed the ideological divide between these regimes, the degree of consistency between ideology and practice, and the fundamentally different goals of their policies.[11] Similarities and differences, the heart of comparative historiography, are not generally found at the core of relational histories. Connections, transfers, influences, and mutual influences instead are front and center.

Therefore, the parallel fashion of tracking the unfolding histories of these two states from a comparative perspective is replaced by attending to the transversal forces that interpenetrate the so far enclosed boundaries. Relational histories can depart from a parallel process unfolding in late Wilhelmine Germany and Romanov Russia. The emergence of an antimodern, antiliberal, and anti-Semitic extreme right on the one hand and left-wing revolutionary parties on the other hand at the margins of the political landscape is a case in point. Then, these parallel processes become entangled as cross-border interpenetrations unfolded in multiple directions as time passed by.

The German occupation of the Ukraine and the Baltic area during the First World War allowed for the transfer of ideas (for example, *The Protocols of the Elders of Zion*) and people (for example, Ukrainian nationalists and German Balts) from the Russian Empire to Germany. Conversely, 1.5 million Russian prisoners of war in German camps provided ample opportunities for interactions that formed and strengthened German stereotypes about Russians.

Such stereotypes even contributed to alienating comrades. German Communists continued to perceive Russia as a backward society despite the Bolsheviks' attempts to present it as the revolutionary vanguard. Conversely, Russian Communists perceived their German counterparts as too bourgeoisie. These perceptions and the different socializations that brought them about contributed to blocking the construction of an effective transnational revolutionary movement. And yet Lenin's aim to export the Communist revolution to Germany was matched there by the Spartacus League, a revolutionary movement willing to establish a second dictatorship of the proletariat in the most industrialized European economy. The suppression of this movement by the Free Corps enhanced the power of the later, which became instrumental in the rise of Nazism. Besides, former Communist converts to the extreme right influenced both Nazism and German images of Russia.

Additional influential forces in this direction came from the White émigrés. The defeat of the Whites—the loose alliance of anti-Communist forces—in the Russian Civil War (1917–1922) resulted in many of them being exiled to Germany, where they plotted with the extreme right. The political, financial, military, and ideological contributions of these White émigrés are claimed to be fundamental in the making of National-Socialism.

Moreover, German–Russian collaboration in confronting the Treaty of Versailles (1919), the German–Russian Treaty of Rapallo (1922), Goebbels's borrowings from and responses to the Soviet propaganda, the Molotov–Ribbentrop Pact (1939), and the Great Patriotic War on the Eastern Front (1941–1945) are some additional examples of instances calling for the study of entanglements, connections, and transfers. Their pursuit opens new venues left aside, unexplored, or under explored by the comparative literature bringing Germany and Russia side by side. However, enthusiasm for these more innovative projects should not be detrimental to recognizing the strengths of comparative history.[12]

And yet the singular contribution of comparative history[13]

If comparative history once was on the defensive, making room for itself beside canonical national histories, lately growing criticism coming from connective histories brought it back to that position. Paradoxically, however, the singular contribution of comparative history is precisely being able to facilitate the communication and transition from close boundaries into border-crossing historiography. Three factors make comparative history the pivot of historiography, making it able to bridge between these two historiographical blocks: its dealings with the unit of analysis, its grasp of the comparative method in its manifold varieties and uses, and the actual inclusion of comparative publications amid both close boundaries and border crossing publications.

Attention to the unit of analysis served as our point of departure for distinguishing "methodological nationalism" from the 12 border-crossing branches of history. Comparative history's dealings with the unit of analysis represent a middle ground between close boundaries and border-crossing historiographies. As in close boundaries historiography, the unit of analysis for comparative history is usually the nation-state or its political predecessor. But a solitary unit can never in itself provide the framework for a comparative study; there has to be at least two units. In this sense, the difference between nationally framed and comparative history is quantitative more than conceptual. Conversely, it is precisely this quantitative dimension that holds out a bridge toward global thinking.

By considering more than one nation-state, comparative history moves closer to historical sociology. It is true that a qualitative difference separates both comparative history and historical sociology from other connective histories, which have adopted larger units of analysis (civilizations, continents, ocean basins, and the entire world). Nevertheless, by abandoning the single enclosed unit, transitioning into at least two of them, comparative history succeeds in transforming the historiographical dichotomy "border closed–border crossed" into a continuum. The first deals with the nation-state unit, a smaller unit within it, or a predecessor political entity. Comparative history deals with two or more such units. Historical sociology usually deals with more than three nation-state units. Civilizational analysis brings many nation-state units into a larger unit of analysis: a civilization. Oceanic histories and the world-system approach incorporate units beyond the boundaries identified by civilizational analysts. Finally, global, world, and big histories present the largest units of analysis. Historiography as a whole, then, covers the entire spectrum of units of analysis, with comparative history facilitating the transition from the enclosed unit into the crossing of its borders. Chapter 1 clearly illustrates this point, as the enclosed boundaries of Perón's Argentina were wide open to the global context, starting with a comparison to Nasser's Egypt.

The second reason that comparative history is in a pivotal role derives from its very nature, namely, transforming a method of inquiry into a historiographical approach. The defining character of comparative history is the transcendence of enclosed nation-state boundaries in order to study the commonalities and differences affecting a particular phenomenon, process, or institution present in two or more units of analysis. It is the deliberate and systematic application of the comparative method that turns comparative history into an independent subfield of historical knowledge and writing. Comparison as a basic mode of thought, however, is common to all forms of historical study. All historical knowledge is comparative knowledge.

Even if the method is not deliberately, systematically, or even consciously applied, all historical knowledge and subsequent writings derive from the insights gained from the use of comparative thinking. To the extent that history studies continuity and change in all domains of social life, these situations can only be discerned by comparison: demographic growth, social polarization, economic slowdown, political democratization, gender inequality, all historical developments in their continuities and changes are discernible by comparison and by comparison alone. In the case of border-closed history, the comparisons are usually between different stages of development of the nation-state for the purpose of analyzing its degree of political stability, economic growth, innovative ideas, and so on.

Also histories moving beyond borders rely on the comparative method, as is evident both in historical sociology and in studies of civilizations (also known as the comparative study of civilizations). But connective histories are likewise based on numerous unstated applications of the comparative method. For example, the periodization of world history as well as the identification and characterization of its successive stages, the identification of influences and processes of circulation and diffusion, are all the result of hidden comparisons. Similarly, the regional division of the world, the logistic and Kondratiev waves, and the hegemonic cycles on which the world-system approach is based (see Chapter 6) result from comparative insights.

Being that comparison is a ground common to all historiography, it is appropriate for the historiographical branch that transforms this method into a specific approach to become a source of methodological refinement for the other branches. Since comparative history is the historical subfield that reflects on and conceptualizes the comparative method shared by all historiography, it is qualified to be the bridge uniting the full dichotomic historiographical field. Alongside the significant list of methodological differences between comparative history vis-à-vis border closed and border crossed, there is a wide and radical denominator common to all three: the comparative method. The discipline of history as a whole, from border closed and nationally based to connective histories, may profit from the theoretical formulations that inform comparative history.

Indeed, as exposed in Chapter 3, comparative historians reflected very closely on the multiple ways to deploy the comparative method. To name only a few such formulations: Mill's analysis of agreement and difference, Durkheim's method of concomitant variations, Bloch's hypothesis-testing design, Redlich's homologies (functional analogies), Thrupp's comparing of notes (taking into account information arranged thematically and not only by nations), Hammel's adhesions (confronting sets of similar cultural traits), and Elliot's refutation of stereotypes; all of these could inform the implicit comparisons undertaken in nationally based and cross-boundary historical writing.[14] Acquaintance with the comparative methodological tool kit as well as with the literature that stems from its use represents a valuable source for the enrichment of historians and students of history from all walks of historiography.

The third reason that renders comparative history as a bridge between closed border and border crossed historiography is not conceptual (as are the previous two)—its unit of analysis as a middle ground and comparison as the basic device common to all forms of historical knowledge—but practical. As discussed in Chapter 2, history journals clearly reflect professional categories and networks. The most prominent type of those is defined by space units (that is, national history and area studies), while others are defined by time period, dimension, subject, and perspectives. Among these perspectives, all 12 branches of cross-boundary history are also represented with the exceptions of relational histories and big history. Although there are specific journals for the publication of comparative history, in practice comparative articles are published throughout all categories of journals.

For example, *French Historical Studies*, the *Journal of Contemporary History*, and the *Economic History Review*—just to illustrate space, time, and thematically oriented journals—include comparative articles. These examples are less arbitrary once viewed against the bigger picture provided by the largest databases. Since 1958, the *annus mirabilis* of comparative history,[15] up to now, the *Historical Abstracts* include no less than 5457 articles clearly defined by their authors as comparative by displaying the words "comparative," "compared," "comparison," or "comparing" in their titles. Proportionally speaking this huge volume of publications in comparative history is rather marginal in the context of history articles as a whole (less than 1 percent). However, articles on comparative history appear everywhere. No other historiographical category shares this prerogative, demonstrating that in practice, as much as conceptually, comparative history is positioned as the bridge between closed-boundary and border-crossing historiographies. This is its outstanding singularity from which it derives its unique contribution and positions comparative history in an important place despite all criticisms. Moreover, the insights provided by these valuable criticisms can be harnessed to enhance the comparative method, comparative history, global thinking, and historiography as a whole.

Zero sum game or win–win situation? Inclusiveness: Vision and practice

Comparisons and connections are presented, so far, as two alternative sets of methods (Chapter 3). Concomitantly, all 12 cross-boundary projects are divided into comparative and connective branches. Moreover, radical and uncompromising criticisms on the use of the comparative method are articulated from connective perspectives. In short, everything seems to indicate that comparative and connective branches represent mutually exclusive options for moving beyond enclosed boundaries. And yet there are several methodological strategies aiming to overcome this situation by combining both entangling and contrasting procedures to achieve a fruitful synthesis. Indeed, such a combination represents a methodological upgrading that capitalizes on the singular insights derived from comparing and connecting.

Back in the days when world history was just in the making, Marshall Hodgson had already noticed the problematic relationship between comparing and connecting. In an article dedicated to the conditions of historical comparison, he stressed the importance of taking into account the relationship in which each compared unit is involved vis-à-vis its region. For example, both Vikings and Polynesians engaged in maritime exploration and colonization. Their enterprises were, strikingly, simultaneous; however, while tracing this comparison Hodgson stressed that Vikings' and Polynesians' connections to their respective contexts were very substantially different. The Vikings' explorations were part of a wider configuration, namely, Afro-Eurasia or Hodgson's Oikoumene. The Polynesians, instead, were isolated explorers.[16] This preliminary observation represents a harbinger in addressing both comparisons and connections. In recent years several attempts to adjust comparative and connective methods were made by practitioners of different cross-boundary branches.

The Great Divergence by Kenneth Pomeranz combines comparative and global history along the lines of Hodgson's reasoning. Contending that comparison and connections are inseparable, Pomeranz's methodology is based on comparisons between selected parts of his units—Europe, China, Japan, and India—which are similarly positioned within their worlds. That is, the units under scrutiny are simultaneously connected to their socio-economic wider context and compared with each other. Through these connections and comparisons, Pomeranz moves progressively toward larger units, from the local to the regional and beyond, such as the Atlantic Basin, until he finally adopts the whole world as the unit of analysis. From this connective perspective he is able to make comparisons that highlight the crucial differences that resulted in the "great divergence." Namely, Europe moved ahead due to a large series of intertwined factors that includes the legacies of the feudal past and the richness of subsoil in coal, as well as the combination of maritime trade with naval power and the collaboration between entrepreneurs and states, and, last but not least, the exploitation of African slaves and American resources.[17]

This strategy for combining comparisons and connections was formalized by Philip McMichael, who also coined the expression "incorporated comparison" to define it. This type of historical comparison, instead of juxtaposing several enclosed units, adopts connected and mutually conditioning units or processes as its subject of comparison. Compared–connected units are also approached as part of the same whole or system.[18] Indeed, even from within the world-system approach, the first connective branch that has challenged the disconnected, diachronic, and endogenous inclinations of comparative branches, not only has the "incorporated comparison" emerged but also the "comparative world-system approach" has developed.

In his "Cross-World-System Comparisons," Christopher Chase-Dunn points out that world-systems range from small to global in terms of the populations linked and the spatial extent of their interactions. Moreover, world-systems are articulated by different forms of accumulation of wealth: kin-based, tributary, and capitalist modes. Given these new parameters for what once was a one and only modern capitalist world-system, Chase-Dunn defines ten types of world-systems: nomadic foragers, sedentary foragers, big man, simple chiefdoms, complex chiefdoms, primary states, primary empires, secondary empires, commercializing systems, and modern world-systems.

Counting on such a variety of world-systems, Chase-Dunn analyzes them comparatively, stressing their crucial similarities and differences. His explicit comparative design takes into account variations in information flow, politico-military competition, trade in prestige goods, and the bulk goods trade along the ten types. Based on his findings, he offers a parsimonious scheme of four categories of world-system: kin-based, tribute-based, market-based, and socialist.[19] Methodologically speaking, enclosed units are connected first into a comprehensive system and next these systems are brought into comparison. Substantially speaking, the incorporation of the comparative method for the connective world-system approach is helpful in addressing the chronological divide within this approach (see Chapter 6). Whereas previous authors engaged in discussing whether the world-system originated 500, 800, or 5000 years ago, the "comparative world-system approach" states that different world-systems are not mutually exclusive but comparable.

This type of combination between connections and comparisons by sequencing them in the same research is a strategy very prominent in the study of the history of globalization (see Chapter 7). In this case a process of connection, namely globalization, is compared at two chronological stages: the last part of the twentieth century and the second half of the nineteenth century.[20] The recurrent comparison between "today's globalization" and the "first great globalization" of 1850–1914 results either in agreement or in crucially different conclusions. Conspicuous among the first are economic openness, export and GDP ratios, lowering of tariff rates, rate of capital flow, and the "hegemonic stability" provided by a single state that has sufficient power to influence or coerce other states, as in the case of the British Empire and the United States, respectively. On the other hand, conclusions oriented toward differences note the qualitative distinctions between the two waves of globalization by stressing, inter alia, the drop in cost of the transfer of ideas, acceleration of information flow, and decentralization of production.[21]

Sequenced connections and comparisons, incorporated comparison, and the comparative world-system approach confront head on the criticism of comparative history that emphasized the lack of interactions between and beyond units. These strategies actually provide venues for stressing those interactions without relinquishing the analytical advantages of comparisons.

Back then to square one, to the earliest historical case approached through the compare–connect dichotomy, Mesopotamia and Egypt. Now we see that it is not only possible both to compare and to connect the two but also to combine comparisons and connections by asking why the connections between Egypt and Mesopotamia were so loose and interrupted while Mesopotamia held a sustained and vast trading sphere from Anatolia to the Indus River valley?

Such optimistic prospects, however, need to address yet another stream of criticism, a more radical one. This more radical criticism revolves around the neutrality of the comparative method. The comparative method is indicted of constructing the subjects that it is supposed to research and of facilitating notions of national character. In the above example, these claims were illustrated by the construction of race and the articulation of the American and Brazilian national characters, respectively. Arguably, the notion of race was constructed far more often outside of comparative studies than by them. Similarly, national characters were articulated so much more by non-comparative nationally framed studies relying on implicit comparisons than by comparative studies. Remember, the institutionalization of comparative history came in the wake of the First World War to confront nationalism. And yet it is worth addressing these serious charges against comparative studies through an additional example.

A simplified standard history of the writing systems departs from pictographic scripts (one picture equals one object), continues through ideographic script (one picture one idea), logographic script (one picture represents a word or meaningful components of a word), and ends up with alphabetic script (one picture one sound). This sequence may imply a process of abstraction with manifold consequences such as simplification, effectiveness, and democratization both of knowledge and society at large. A comparison between a logographic and an alphabetic script would show that it takes a relatively short time to learn the 26 characters of, say, the Latin alphabet and become a reader and writer soon after. However, it would take several years, instead, to learn the 3000 basic Chinese characters before becoming a proficient reader and writer at beginner level. Concomitantly, the relative accessibility facilitated by the 26 letters of the alphabet is conducive to easier achievement of higher rates of literacy than that allowed by the barrier posed by the incorporation of 3000 and more Chinese characters. Conversely, literacy rates can be correlated to the democratization of knowledge and social life at large.

In short, a comparison between the Latin alphabet and Chinese characters would indicate that the first is simpler, more effective, more accessible, and more democratic and, therefore, represents a more advanced writing system.

Such a comparison replicates in a more extreme fashion the flaws observed by Seigel. This comparison on writing system constructed the subject—writing systems—as a history of progression in cognitive abstraction and social complexity while at the same time articulating the characters of the Western and Chinese civilizations.

Seigel attributes this flaw to the very nature of the comparative method, as "comparison is the process of relational self-definition." That means that the definition of whatever unit—self (I am different from you) or nation (we are different from them)—emerges from a more or less explicit comparison. Interestingly enough, this radical criticism on the comparative method concedes that all historical knowledge is comparative, as sustained by the above claim of comparative history as the pivot of history. More to the point, coming to the criticized one-sidedness observed in the above examples of race and writing systems, it is worth remarking that this bias is not intrinsic to the comparative method as such but only to some of its forms. *Cultural* comparisons, as defined by Jonathan Smith's contrasting "we/they" and exemplified by Neil Ferguson's "the West and the rest," are clear examples of that problem. However, the antidote for that bias comes not only by displacing comparisons by connections but also from within the comparative method in the form of "mutual comparisons."

A mutual comparison is one in which we not only compare the unit best known to us with a lesser known unit but also the other way around. In other words, the contrast between units A and B is not only made when A is considered "we" (in the above examples, the United States, the West) and B is considered "they" (in the above examples, Brazil, China) but also when A is considered "they" and B is considered "we." By applying a "mutual comparison" to the study of writing systems, a whole lot of different conclusions might be reached.

The idea of alphabetic writing as simpler, more effective, more accessible, and more democratic compared to the logographic one is transformed by reconducting the comparison from East to West. For all of the advantages of alphabetic writing, the Latin alphabet would allow a reader acquainted with it to read, among other languages, English, Portuguese, Spanish, French, Italian, Dutch, German, Polish, Hungarian, Romanian, and Turkish, understanding virtually nothing in most of these languages except from her or his own language. Hence, in many cases, alphabetic writing provides accessible literacy for a relatively short geographical radius. Moving beyond that radius would demand the study of an entirely new language to make sense of the Latin alphabetic script.

Here comes a trade-off, the intelligibility of the Latin script demands the mastering of the languages that it expresses. This demand posed by an alphabetic writing system does not apply to a logographic writing system, which allows intelligibility of the characters regardless of the spoken language. In this way, speakers of Gan, Guan, Hui, Jin, Kejia (Hakka), Min, Wu, Xiang, Yue, Ping, and Ba-Shu, to name some of the languages using Chinese characters, can read and understand them to some extent. It turns out that the long investment of Chinese character memorization pays off, as it opened up literacy to a radius of thousands of kilometers as opposed to radiuses of hundreds of kilometers frequently allowed by the Latin alphabet.

In short, a "mutual comparison" on writing systems shows that when it comes to alphabetic and logographic systems, there is an ongoing trade-off between the two. The logographic system requires a huge learning investment up front but grants huge geographic literacy coverage. The alphabet represents a learning-time and effort-saving system providing, however, a much-limited geographic coverage. Once we contextualize this realization historically, it makes perfect sense that the political fragmented history of Europe, with its relatively small political units, is better suited for an alphabetic system while the long-lasting imperial Chinese past, with its huge extension, was better served by a logographic system. This "mutual comparison," then, deconstructed the history of writing as progression, a provincialized Europe, and challenged ethnocentrism at large, one of the driving forces and commitments of comparative history as envisioned by its founder practitioners.

Summing up, the rise of connections as method was correlated with a growing criticism of the comparative method. However, several attempts have been made in recent years to move from the zero sum game, offered at first by the relational approaches, into a more inclusive approach that transforms the game into a win–win situation via the combination of connective and comparative designs. This combination has been made possible either by concentrating on the functional relationship of the units compared to their contexts and/or wholes or by comparing a world process at different historical stages. Awareness of the potential biases built into the comparative method and overcoming them represents an additional venue of mutual enhancement between connections and comparisons.

Moreover, for all of the above prescriptive pleas for a better integration of comparisons and connections, it is important to stress that, descriptively speaking, comparisons and connections are intermingling in many ways. For example, since 1999 the *American Historical Review* has perceived both realms as close enough to be combined into a single historiographical category. Moreover, the very specialized journals on connective histories accommodate comparative articles in their issues. For instance, the inclusiveness of comparative history within connective histories is observable in the leading journals on world history and global history.

The *Journal of World History* aims to transcend national frontiers and study such phenomena as population movements, economic fluctuations, climatic changes, transfers of technology, and so on;[22] it clearly entails a connective agenda. Nevertheless, the *Journal of World History* includes comparative articles on such worldwide phenomena as government, nationalism, and imperialism. Even further, this journal contains even strictly comparative articles that contrast discrete units with regard to a particular topic such as, for instance, hunting in Kenya and India, military affairs in Europe and Japan, and borderlands in Eurasia, Africa, and America.

Even the most uncompromising entangling branch, the world-system approach, includes in its journals—*Journal of World-System Research* and *Review*—articles on comparative history. Similarly, articles cross the comparative history bridge in the opposite direction. The journal *Comparative Studies in Society and History* provides comparative perspectives on such connective phenomena as the transfer of technology or cultural diffusion.

World history textbooks are another instance of entwinement between connective and comparative histories. Very many of them construct their narratives by relying on connections and comparisons. The underlying dichotomies behind titles such as *Traditions and Encounters*, *Worlds Together, Worlds Apart*, and *World Civilizations: The Global Experience* are actually comparisons (traditions, worlds apart, and world civilizations) and connections (encounters, worlds together, and global experience). Finally, comparative and connective historical branches as a whole are combined into synergic projects, producing comparative–connective histories such as the historical sociology of international history, comparative world history, and transnational comparative history.[23]

Even in a more concrete way, the above discussion between compared versus connected visions of totalitarianism in Nazi Germany and Stalinist Russia had been productively combined recently. Precisely because of evolving new ways of studying these regimes, Michael Geyer and Sheila Fitzpatrick edited a volume that both compares and relates the two. Interestingly, in terms of content, the comparative chapters stress the crucial differences between these regimes in direct opposition to the previous comparativist generation in totalitarian studies. However, the most important innovation at the methodological level is the combination of comparisons and connections, which represents the win–win situation described above. Nazi Germany and Stalinist Russia are compared in their methods of governance, uses of violence, and processes of socialization. And yet there is still room for presenting their interpenetrations in the forms of mutual image making, transfer of culture and ideas, and warfare.[24]

To conclude, solid conceptualization and clear-cut typologies are invaluable analytical tools when it comes to organizing reality, in this case historiographic and methodological reality. However, their aim could not be the crystallization of typologies and the entrenchment of categories and networks. To the contrary, as conceptualizations and typologies charter the map of historiography clearly, they should facilitate bringing the different branches into synergetic collaborations. Comparisons and connections already appear regularly combined in practice, and the sky is the limit when it comes to the creativity that their synergy can bring.

5
Thinking History Globally: Varieties of Connections

Criticism of comparative histories led historians such as Bénédicte Zimmerman and Michael Werner, Sanjay Subrahmanyam and Serge Gruzinski, and Huri İslamoğlu-İnan and Peter C. Perdue to formulate the alternatives to *histoire croisée* (entangled history), connected history, and shared histories, respectively. None of these relational approaches became widely established and institutionalized in the ways that the other cross-boundary branches are with their professional associations, periodic conferences, and journals.

However, the types of approaches and subjects fostered by relational histories overlap to a considerable extent with two very well established cross-boundary branches: international history and transnational history. In fact, the new international history can be portrayed as a particular type of entanglement or connection between two societies entwined via interstate relations. State-mediated entanglements between societies and cultures determine the approach and subject matter of the new international history. Hence, all entanglements are subordinated to foreign relations. In transnational history, by contrast, nothing is subordinated to foreign relations. Transnational history focuses on phenomena or entities, such as processes of cultural transfer and transnational organizations, that by definition go beyond nation-states. Attention to these subjects is what makes transnational history unique.

In a sense, these overlaps allow us to envision an enlarged family of relational approaches in which international and transnational histories are included. On the other hand, as mentioned, these last two are fully established branches as opposed to the former. Most crucially, the endeavors of international and transnational history imply the existence of nation-states, constraining these two branches temporally to approximately the last 200 years and the twentieth century in particular. This temporal focus sharply contrasts with the dedication of connected histories primarily devoted to the early modern period. And timing is not all, as the centrality of the state as the unit of analysis and agent as well as the preponderance of the political sphere, particularly omnipresent in international history, is rather alien to the relational approaches.

It is in these regards that the relational approaches are more akin to another well-established branch: oceanic histories. Also oceanic histories are about connections, entanglements, sharing, and transfers, in their case specifically facilitated by bodies of water. Moreover, oceanic histories work within an open chronology in which the early modern period is prominent and the political dimension is mostly secondary. Oceanic histories, however, are border crossers first and foremost by defining enlarged geographic units of analysis. The pursuit of connections is circumscribed by units such as the Mediterranean Sea, the Indian Ocean, the Atlantic Basin, or the Pacific Rim. Relational histories, instead, follow the tracks of linkages unbounded by a particular region of the world. Wherever the tracks would go, related histories would be ready to follow suit.

This same distinction applies to the contrast between oceanic and the new international and transnational histories. Each of these three represents in this order the three categories of connections as method: enlargement of geographic units of analysis (that is, ocean basins), attention to historical linkages between units of analysis (that is, nation-states), and adoption of units of analysis or themes that intrinsically cross boundaries (that is, transnational entities or processes). Oceanic histories are thematically broader than new international histories and chronologically more comprehensive than both new international and transnational histories.

Finally, both oceanic and new international and transnational histories share very important methodological aspects with relational histories. All of these branches are inductive, that is, based on bottom-up reasoning and a meticulous collection and analysis of information gathered by a careful scrutiny of primary sources anchored in archival research. In short, as summarized in Table 5.1, there are substantial reasons to think about relational, international, transnational, and oceanic histories as an enlarged family. And yet there are no less valid reasons to identify the singularity of each.

Time now, then, to address and exemplify the singularities of the well-established members of this enlarged relational family: international, transnational, and oceanic histories.

The new international history

As the emergence of history as an academic discipline is closely related to the consolidation of the modern nation-state, foreign policy, diplomacy, and war were among the leading subjects of study from the very beginning. Therefore, international history is as old as the discipline of history itself. Similarly, international history and the discipline of history at large in its earliest stages shared themes, goals, sources, and method: statecraft, nation building, official records, and archival research, respectively. The subsequent development

Table 5.1 Unity and variety in the enlarged relational family

	Unifying methodology	Diverging variety of connection	Chronological range	Organizing variable	Degree of branch institutionalization
Relational histories	Inductive, primary sources	Linkages Cross-boundary themes and units	Mostly early modern onward	None	Low
International Histories	Inductive, primary sources	Linkages	Mostly 20th century	Politics	High
Transnational Histories	Inductive, primary sources	Cross-boundary themes and units	Mostly 20th century	None	High
Oceanic histories	Inductive, primary sources	Enlarged geographical units	Mostly early modern onward	None	High

of the profession in so many directions—social, economic, cultural to name but a few—with the concomitant innovations in themes, goals, sources, and methods, profoundly transformed the historiographical landscape.

International history, however, remained closely attached to its original endeavors, having a reputation as a conservative field. By the 1990s, however, international historians decided to close the widening gap opened within the profession by entwining their original concerns on foreign policy, diplomacy, and war with those of the profession at large, namely, society, economy, culture, gender, race, and ethnicity. This thematic renovation, referred to as the "culturalist turn," also resulted in the expansion of relevant sources and ways to interpret them. Emphasizing multinational archival research instead of relying on sources from only one country's archives exemplifies the first type of expansion. The adoption of insights from critical theory, cultural studies, and postmodernism exemplifies the second one.[1]

These renovations resulted in the *new* international history, in which foreign relations, diplomacy, and warfare are entangled with the societies, cultures, and multiplicity of groups under the rule of the states in question. These constituencies and constructions appear as agents as much as subjects in forging and conditioning foreign relations. In this way, social and cultural developments within states are addressed as the sources of foreign relations as much as the trajectories of foreign relations are scrutinized for their impact upon social and cultural developments within states.

The following brief series of short examples shows how culture, ideology, race, class, and gender are entwined with international relations, starting with the most prominent one: culture. Entangling the cultural dimension within international history means to attend the ways in which nations and peoples deal with each other through assumptions, perceptions, prejudice, the arts, popular entertainment, and fashions in addition to political calculations, strategic considerations, and economic interests.

In short, the incorporation of culture into international history added the "imagined" dimension of given "realities." A particular cultural subject privileged by international history is that of cultural encounters and transfers. The process of Americanization is on center stage in this regard, being examined in manifold instances: popular culture, consumerism, domesticity, and journalism among others. Nevertheless, the process of Americanization is not depicted as a unidirectional process. Synchronically, far from being one-sided, the process of Americanization is presented as a cultural dialogue resulting in creative mutual creolizations. Diachronically, international historians confront the evolution of America's cultural relations from the era when American culture represented the derivative assemblages of an insecure peripheral society up to the reversal of the direction of cultural influence.

For example, Kristin Hoganson in her *Consumers' Imperium: The Global Production of American Domesticity, 1865* shows how foreignness in the late nineteenth and early twentieth centuries was central to the production of American domesticity at home through imported household objects, fashion, and cooking, among others. It was precisely the economic ascendency of the United States that allowed these imports from abroad, enhancing outside cultural influence and changing the physical makeup of the American household.[2]

Another instance of cultural influence in the same direction is portrayed by Jessica C. E. Gienow-Hecht in her *Sound Diplomacy: Music and Emotions in Transatlantic Relations, 1850–1920*.[3] In this case music is on center stage with nineteenth-century Americans looking increasingly to Germany as the source of the art's transcendent power. A two-way relationship is portrayed between German-speaking instrumentalists, conductors, writers, scholars, religious leaders, and educators, on the one hand, and Americans eager to disseminate a canon of musical compositions among a broad public on the other, as well as American music students educated in Germany bringing serious musical *Kultur* back to Americans. In this relationship the musicians were motivated by a surprisingly explicit missionary desire to roll back the tide of American ignorance and share the benefits of German culture with the world. The American audiences, for their part, sought to acquire the imprint of European cultural sophistication.

This initial exchange paved the way for a reversal of cultural influence following the Second World War, when, provided with a strongly German-based repertoire, American orchestras visited Europe during the Cold War as a way to create solidarity by highlighting transatlantic cultural unity. On this stage of reversing the direction of cultural influence, Jessica C. E. Gienow-Hecht's *Transmission Impossible: American Journalism as Cultural Diplomacy in Postwar Germany, 1945–1955* analyzes the history *of Die Neue Zeitung,* an American-sponsored German-language daily through which attempts were made to introduce American values and perspectives in the Western zones of post-Second World War Germany.[4]

Indeed, studies dedicated to the flow of American culture to the world are more abundant.[5] The year 1898 is offered as a turning point that opened up the reversal of cultural influence from America toward the world by Emily S. Rosenberg.[6] Following campaigns in Cuba, Puerto Rico, and the Philippines, Theodore Roosevelt, who had no qualms himself about outright imperialism but believed that the American electorate would not accept long-term rule over other nations, proposed that progress could come about alternatively by American experts helping other nations to stabilize their markets and monetary exchange policies through the scientific application of economic laws. Since the administrations of Theodore Roosevelt, William Howard Taft, and Woodrow Wilson, financial management has been regarded as an alternative to imperialism.

Such financial management meant the allocation of American loans in exchange for the right to manage other nations' customs, taxation, investment, and foreign trade policies according to the dictates of "scientific" gold standard economics. Under the auspices of this arrangement, American policymakers, investment bankers, and professional economists reached the Dominican Republic, Haiti, Nicaragua, Mexico, China, and Liberia to spread the gospel of standardized monetary and financial arrangement to less developed nations and teach the "natives" good economics. This study of the cultural dimension through the analysis of transferring ideological and conceptual frameworks responsible for the management of national economies complements the otherwise widely researched Dollar Diplomacy.[7]

This complimentary feature is characteristic of the culture-centered new international history that provides new perspectives on diplomatic history, pointing toward more historical agents active in international relations as well as toward the complexities in the relations between states and their respective societies. The incorporation of popular culture in diplomatic history contributed, for example, to the discernment of a dual image of the United States in the view of Europeans, who on strictly political grounds condemned American foreign policy, mainly since the Vietnam War, but continued to embrace American popular culture, such as rock music. A kind of duality was also observed in the line drawn by Anglo-American music benefactors in the United States between Germany's political and cultural identities as the First World War erupted.

Moreover, the incorporation of culture not only enlarged the range of historical agents active in international relations and nuanced the nature of relations between states but also, at times, resulted in alternative explanations, as, for example, in Hoganson's *Consumers' Imperium*. In contrast to William Appleman Williams's influential "open door" thesis, according to which the export of capital and goods provided the central dynamic in American foreign policy and national life, it was the import flow that created American domestic life. These kinds of fresh insights contribute to focusing attention on the soft power of culture as an increasingly central theme in international relations at large.

Besides culture in general and ideology in particular, the relations between domestic and foreign dimensions are also explored by international history through subjects such as ethnicity, class, and gender. In *The African American Encounter with Japan and China: Black Internationalism in Asia, 1895–1945*, Marc Gallicchio presents the role that Japan and China play in the evolution of African American views and in removing the illusion of "white supremacy." According to the author, Japan and China assume a symbolic importance in African American discourse about "white supremacy" and their challenge to the American order that has sought to relegate them to the margins. Japan and China both invalidated the idea of "colored inferiority" through their respective challenges to American preeminence in the twentieth century. Moreover, Asia revealed the limits of American power also in the Korean and Vietnam wars.

Gallicchio argues that since Japan's rise to power following the Russo–Japanese War (1904–1905), black internationalists hoped that Japan's challenge to white supremacy would eventually convince the American government of the inevitability of improving their status. Moreover, African American respect and admiration for Japan bloomed after the First World War, when the Japanese representatives at the Versailles Peace Conference fought to include a resolution denouncing racism in the League of Nations charter. Despite the defeat of this Japanese motion at Versailles, more and more African Americans came to see Japan as a "champion" for people of color around the world. Subsequently, with the Japanese discredited because of their imperialist policy during the Second World War, African Americans gradually turned their attention to China. However, the Chinese never reciprocated the African American interest and signs of friendship. Chiang Kai-shek, intent on winning the war against the Japanese and keeping his Communist enemies in China at bay, never pressed the United States on racial matters either during or after the war. Gallicchio concludes that the African American belief that foreign "champions" such as the Japanese or Chinese would involve themselves with America's civil rights problem was sadly misplaced. Nevertheless, the entanglement of civil rights with international relations resulted in more significant results after 1945.[8]

In *The Cold War and the Color Line: American Race Relations in the Global Arena*, Thomas Borstelmann describes the dramatic changes in post-Second World War race relations. The narrative follows the parallel struggles for civil rights within the United States and against colonialism and white supremacist regimes abroad. The central thesis of the book is that these processes influenced each other. Changing American race relations affected the way the United States fought the Cold War and responded to the end of European colonial rule, while the Cold War influenced the domestic civil rights movement in various ways. Notably, that was the case because racial discrimination and violence at home was a continuing source of embarrassment to the United States abroad. That occurred in a context in which the United States tried to recruit nonwhite allies when many new African and Asian states became independent during the Cold War. This kind of global contextualization shows the benefits of revisiting domestic history from fresh perspectives of international history.[9]

This last example shows how the once considered conservative field of international history can actually be innovative in addressing social, racial, ethnic, and gender questions from a fresh perspective. Conversely, the previous examples have shown how the incorporation of culture and society into international history transformed the field and brought about the new international history as an updated branch thematically, methodologically, and conceptually. However, for all of this updating, current globalization brought to the forefront of world affairs concerns such as global warming, species extinction, and pandemics as well as the implosion of transnational agents such as multinational corporations and nongovernmental organizations. All of these concerns and agents that go far beyond the reach of states stimulated the emergence of an additional branch that goes beyond international history.

Transnational history

Transnational history represents yet a further step in de-centering politics as the privileged dimension and particularly the state not only as the main agent but also even as the basic unit of analysis. Transnational history replaces the state as both a unit of analysis and as the main agent by focusing on processes that are transnational by definition—for example, cultural transfer, global warming—or transnational agents such as intergovernmental, nongovernmental organizations, or other non-state actors. Intergovernmental actors (IGAs) are organizations comprised of states in search of accorded policies and regulations (for example, the UN or WTO). Nongovernmental organizations (NGOs) are institutionalized groups organized around a particular concern (for example, human rights, the environment, jihad) and often active in multiple societies.

Other non-state actors (NSAs) galvanize around a particular concern or identity even if their organization is less formal and institutionalized. People created these organizations for coping with problems that transcend the borders of states in response to their "sense of transnational interconnectedness." Multinational or transnational business corporations represent an additional form of transnational organization made distinctive by their major goal, namely, profit.

International cooperation was already in place during the last decades of the nineteenth century in matters such as lighthouses, telegraphs, and the standardization of silver coinage throughout Europe. Moreover, the increased range and speed of communication and information flow allowed also for the creation of transnational NGOs and NSAs such as the International Council of Women (1888), the International Peace Bureau (1892), and the International Olympic Committee (1896). The number of these types of organizations reached about 330 by the outbreak of the First World War. Then, the war became a great catalyst for their further expansion addressing six types of issues: humanitarian relief, cultural exchange, peace and disarmament, development assistance, human rights, and environmentalism. Later, during the Cold War era, grassroots movements emerged striving for the abolition of nuclear weapons, humanitarian relief, human rights, and the protection of the environment. The end of the Cold War allowed for the expansion of these types of organizations further. Today the number of NGOs deployed transnationally is around 40,000.

The growing proliferation of these organizations in tandem with the emergence of a global consciousness has resulted in what Akira Iriye has defined as a transnational society or global community.[10] This community represents a wider world over and above separate nation-states in which individuals and groups, no matter where they are, share certain interests and concerns. Transnational history addresses the history of this emerging global community by studying natural and cultural forces that do not recognize state boundaries (for example, climate, disease, cultural transfers) and organizations that articulate political, economic, and social forces across the globe.

An example of this global society, in the form of a "transnational disarmament movement," was traced by Matthew Evangelista in his book *Unarmed Forces*. The book tells the story of a network of American, European, and Soviet scientists that opposed the nuclear arms race. Starting with failing attempts during the last years of Stalin's rule (1950–1953), the network became truly successful after the Cuban Missile Crisis (1962). Indeed, the partial Test-Ban Treaty (1963), the Strategic Arms Limitation Treaty (SALT, 1972), and the comprehensive Nuclear Disarmament Program (1986) were all facilitated by the efforts behind the scenes of this transnational network. Evangelista highlights that the mutual on-site inspections stipulated by the 1986 program were carried out by "a transnational coalition of American and Soviet scientists, rather than official interstate organizations." From failed attempts through impact on policy making and up to its implementation, this transnational network of scientists has shown the potential power of states, even superpowers, by a global society and even in such sensitive areas as security.[11]

Attention to transnational processes, rather than transnational agents, is the other major focus of transnational history, as exemplified by "the making of the middle class."[12] Such a making of a social class, sharing a material experience, a political project, and a cultural practice, according to López and Weinstein, did not occur confined within states or regions. Certainly it was not the prerogative of North Atlantic societies only subsequently imitated by the rest of the world with different degrees of failure or success. Rather, "the meanings, subjectivities, and practices of being middle class were mutually—and coevally—constituted across the globe."[13] At the same time, the transitionally created middle class shaped the contours of modern societies throughout the world. These are the two entwined transnational processes addressed: the transnational formation of the middle class and the transnational formation of modernity that the middle class had contributed to shape.

A transnational middle class is just one of the multiple transnational social categories and networks that constitute the global community. It is this global community or society with its transnational processes, organizations, and grassroots movements that transnational history has defined to be its subject of study. These particular subjects of study help in defining the singularity of transnational history vis-à-vis international history. However, beyond this distinction, methodologically both branches share the same procedures of archival research. This type of research grounded upon solid scrutiny and analysis of primary sources is also shared with another branch within the wide relational family: oceanic histories. Although much more circumscribed by its units of analysis, oceanic histories are also longer, even much longer, in their chronological ranges.

Oceanic histories

Oceanic histories transcend enclosed political and regional boundaries by privileging bodies of water rather than the terrestrial domains ever at the core of all historiographical approaches. This move into lakes, rivers, seas, and ultimately oceans allows historians to look at human societies in and by bodies of water and, most crucially, at rather surprising connections between human societies. In order to visualize these kinds of surprising connections, think, for instance, about the place of Chile in the globe. Drawn by our implicitly assumed terrestrial perspective, Chile would be considered part of the Southern Cone together with Argentina, Uruguay, and Brazil. From a deliberately oceanic perspective, instead Chile would be connected with New Zealand, Australia, the Philippines, and China through the Pacific Ocean. The same exercise can be applied for most countries and regions in the world. From a terrestrial perspective, Nigeria can be contemplated beside Tanzania, Uganda, and Ethiopia. But from an oceanic perspective, Nigeria can also be considered amid the Arab, Persian, and Indian worlds by way of the Indian Ocean. Finally, New Orleans belongs within the southern states of the United States—for example, Mississippi, Alabama, and Georgia—as much as with the islands of the Caribbean Sea and the western shores of Africa and Europe.

Oceanic histories then, including Pacific, Indian, and Atlantic Ocean histories, complement regional studies (for example, Latin American, African, and East Asian studies) defined by landmasses in a Gestaltic way. While the latter looks at landmasses often times encapsulated within the perimeters of shores, oceanic histories connect between pairs of shores or multiple shores through the seas.

Far from being mutually exclusive, terrestrial and aquatic oriented historiographies are fully complementary. From New York you can look at Los Angeles and a lot could be seen in that trajectory. At the same time making a 180 degree rotation at the same point of observation will lead to many discoveries between New York and Amsterdam, while there will be much to spot too by taking a similar rotation in Los Angeles toward Shanghai. Land- and water-based historiographies are complementary, as they point toward different spaces.

Land- and water-based historiographies are also complementary as alternative kinds of research projects. Whereas the terrestrial viewpoint was extensively applied, the fresher oceanic take brings its own newer outlooks,

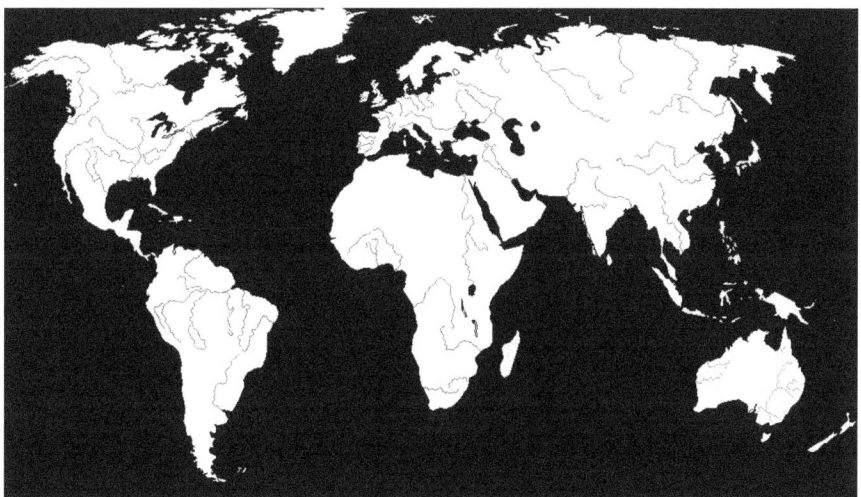

Figure 5.1 "Gestaltic" terrestrial and oceanic world maps

Figure 5.2 "Gestaltic" terrestrial and oceanic world maps

perspectives, and themes that open up additional venues of research, interpretation, and contextualization.

Finally, this complementary character of terrestrial and aquatic historiographies is not only geographical, perspectival, and thematic but also historically grounded. That is, both solid and liquid roads connected societies simultaneously, in tandem, and while their relative weight oscillated from time to time. An example of terrestrial and aquatic synchronicity can be seen in that both the Silk Road along Inner Asia and the Spice Road across the Indian Ocean brought Han China and imperial Rome into contact.

During other periods, predominant cross-boundary interactions through landmasses were surpassed by integration between societies primarily by water masses and vice versa. For instance, the integration of Euro-Afro-America peaked during the first decade of the nineteenth century across the Atlantic Ocean, following three centuries of building connections. Later, the shrinking of colonial empires in the wake of the wars of independence in the Americas (1776–1820) and the subsequent disruption of commerce combined with the abolition of the slave trade (1807), the laying of railroad systems (1830 onward), and the articulation of national economies tipped the balance in favor of land-based railroad integration for the rest of that century.

Yet again the political stabilization of the new republics throughout the Americas around the 1880s allowed for the resumption of economic relations with European powers, a new cycle of European imperialist expansion in Africa and Asia, reaching its zenith by the 1880s, and the widespread use of steamships and subsequent technological advances in maritime transportation that reinvigorated oceanic connections until the last decades of the nineteenth

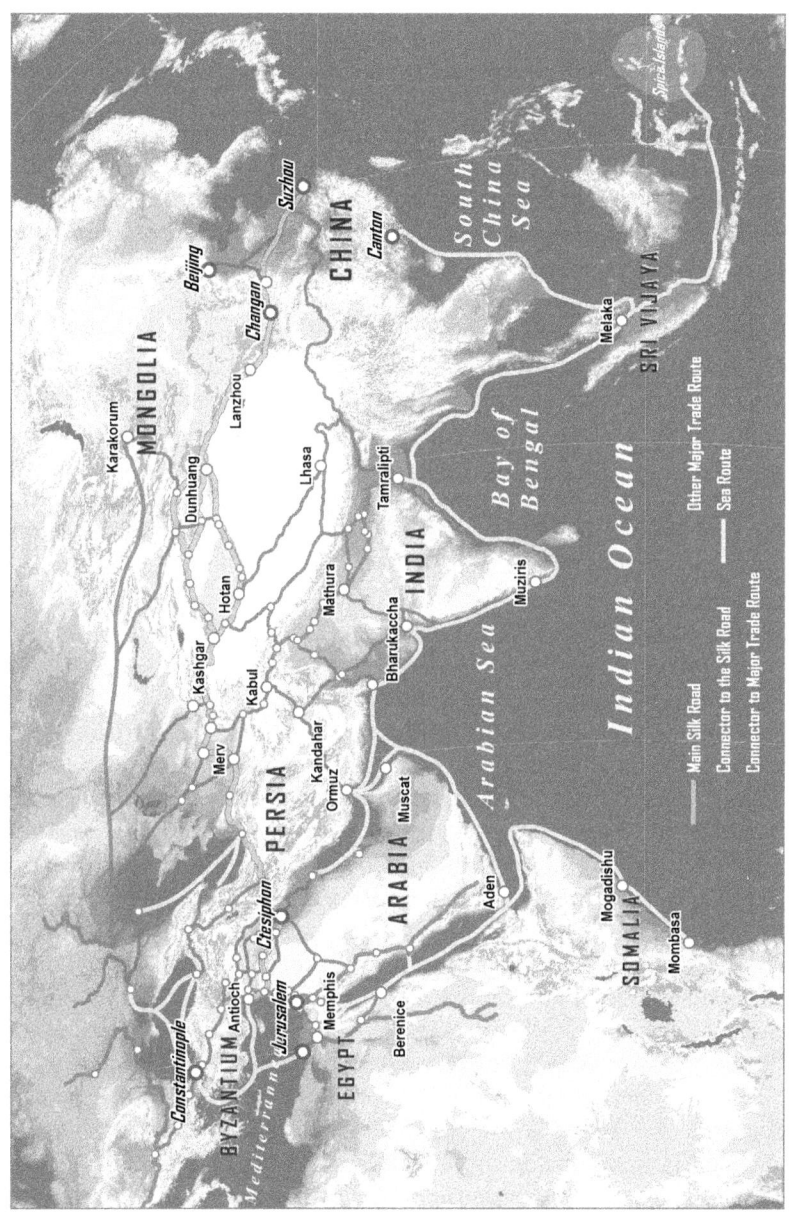

Figure 5.3 Silk and Spice roads[14]

century. Moreover, the carving of the Suez (1866) and Panamá (1917) canals connected the Atlantic Ocean with the Indian and the Pacific Oceans, respectively. Those relatively minor cosmetic surgeries on the face of the planet connected the three oceans unmolested since by any landmass obstacle. Virtually one continuous body of water surrounds all continents—a global sea has emerged.

Space, perspectives, themes, and historicity are instrumental not only in showing the complementary character of land- and aquatic-based historiographies but also in defining the core features of oceanic histories themselves. In terms of space, the Indian Ocean, the Pacific Rim, and the Atlantic Basin are the biggest possible spaces for oceanic histories. However, works aiming to encompass an entire ocean basin are the exception rather than the rule. Dealing with the history of an entire ocean, an approach referred to as "circum-oceanic," is the largest scale for oceanic histories and is unusual. "Cis-oceanic" and "trans-oceanic," the other two approaches, as extensions of those defined by David Armitage for the Atlantic Ocean, are much more common. Cis-oceanic refers to the study of particular places in their interactions with the wider oceanic rim. Trans-oceanic histories establish comparisons within the same oceanic rim. Exemplifying these three approaches, with each example coming from a different ocean, provides an additional glimpse into this form of global thinking.[15]

As its title indicates, *Trade and Civilization in the Indian Ocean: An Economic History from the Rise of Islam to 1750* by K. N. Chaudhuri embodies the circum-oceanic approach as applied to the Indian Ocean. This book, spanning for a whole millennium and encompassing the entire Indian Ocean, engages a broad array of oceanic themes related to navigation and trade. Among the first, Chaudhuri studied the wind system, the techniques and lines of navigation, the technologies of shipbuilding, and the social attitude toward the sea. Trade themes include the study of markets and commodities, the merchant classes at sea, land, and their interface, trading diasporas, urbanization, and cultural transfers.[16]

Steven R. Fischer applied the cis-oceanic approach to the Pacific Islands amid their larger context and in interaction with the entire ocean. *A History of the Pacific Islands* opens by portraying the Pacific Ocean as the reservoir and means for peopling the islands that allowed for the formation of local societies, economies, and belief systems. All of these local traditions entered a phase of deepening transformations as the ocean subsequently brought whalers, sealers, traders, missionaries, colonists, a world war, nuclear testing, and tourism. Besides these impacts from the outside inward, the book also examines the reverse situation by looking at the Pacific Islander Diaspora. Finally, it combines outer and local interactions by showing the ways in which the thorough transformations arrived from the ocean but were co-directed by the islanders.[17]

Trans-oceanic history, as a comparative enterprise, is represented by John H. Elliott's *Empires of the Atlantic World: Britain and Spain in America, 1492–1830*. The book explores how "occupation," "consolidation," and "emancipation" evolved in English and Spanish America, two great Atlantic enterprises, along similar lines. At the same time the comparison stresses the differences between the two empires institutionally, demographically, and culturally—differences with roots mostly found in contingency, serendipity, and chance: striking on precious metals and large populations in Mexico and Peru as opposed to the lack of both factors in BNA. This trans-oceanic comparison shows that besides comparing New England to England additional insights are to be gained by comparing New England to New Spain.[18]

At the same time that these three books show three different approaches to oceanic history, they also hint at three different histories of oceans. The Indian Ocean is presumably the one with the longest history, dating back to the interconnections between the three earliest foci of civilization in Mesopotamia, the Indus River valley, and the Nile River valley ca. 3000 BCE. It is hypothesized that around that same time Polynesian people began spreading throughout the islands of the Pacific Ocean. Its circumnavigation, though, and the establishment of lasting connections throughout this one-third of the planet's surface, waited until the nineteenth century. Atlantic history is temporally the shortest, comprising the connection of four continents over five centuries.

Each of these histories brings its singular themes. The multiple transitions of political configurations for oceanic navigation, trade, and contacts since ancient times, throughout the age of classical empires, the rise of Islam, and the penetration of European colonialism are unique to the study of the Indian Ocean. With more than 20,000 islands, the Pacific Ocean stands out as the insular ocean. Hence, its history comprises very much the multiplicity of social and cultural experiences of these localities in their interactions with the oceanic and global frameworks. However, the history of the Pacific also entails the four continents that frame it. Therefore, transpacific connections between Asia, Australia, and the Americas provide an additional dimension of singularity. Although transatlantic relations are also about connections between four continents—Europe, Africa, and the Americas—singularity derives from the uniqueness of its relations: the slave trade and plantation complex and colonial empires and societies.

Besides these singularities, all oceanic histories focus on bodies of water that facilitate the transit of people, biota, germs, goods, and ideas; they share a wide range of common themes: action, interaction, and motion; travel, discovery, navigation, cartography, trade, traders, and maritime workers; pilgrimage, proselytization, and religious orders; warfare, sailors, soldiers, and pirates; migration, exile, and diasporas; colonization, the spread of ideas, and struggles for independence. At the end, all of the above singular subjects combined

112 *Thinking History Globally*

Table 5.2 Oceanic histories

	Indian Ocean	**Pacific Ocean**	**Atlantic Ocean**
Circum-oceanic	Encompassing the whole Indian Ocean	Encompassing the whole Pacific Ocean	Encompassing the whole Atlantic Ocean
Cis-oceanic	Connecting locations in the Indian Ocean and/or with the Indian Ocean at large	Connecting locations in the Pacific Ocean and/or with the Pacific Ocean at large	Connecting locations in the Atlantic Ocean and/or with the Atlantic Ocean at large
Trans-oceanic	Comparing locations in the Indian Ocean	Comparing locations in the Pacific Ocean	Comparing locations in the Atlantic Ocean
Smaller body of water	e.g. the Arabian Sea	e.g. the Sea of Japan	e.g. Caribbean Sea
Smaller still	e.g. Caspian Sea, Amazon River, Lake Victoria		

with these shared themes embody the openness of boundaries and the replacement of borders by connectedness, permeability, and porousness encouraged by oceanic histories.

And yet despite this generic name, oceanic histories do not only demand dealing necessarily with an ocean but also with smaller bodies of water, such as the Mediterranean, Caribbean, Black, or Chinese seas, and smaller still, such as the Great Lakes in North America or Central Africa. Oceanic histories are not so much fixed to a particular space as they are a style of inquiry (Table 5.2).

Oceanic histories move beyond the boundaries of any single empire or future nation-states, emphasizing interregional contacts, flows, and networks reminiscent of transnational history. Nevertheless, transnational history reaches throughout the globe in the age of nation-states, while oceanic histories cover much longer time periods within ocean basins. Both branches, however, are approaching the stage of global history: transnational history due to its global reach; oceanic histories tackling big slices of the globe. The innovations provided by these two as well as the renewal of international history following the "culturalist turn" and more generally the flourishing of the extended relational family at large—presented in the last two chapters—all stem from the processes of globalization. The history of globalization and its pivotal place in defining world and global histories as the providers of the largest frames for contextualization, together with big history, waits ahead. Now it is time to turn to the singular contribution coming from the social sciences: the third big C that stands for conceptualization.

6
Thinking History Globally: Conceptualizing through Social Sciences

Historical sociology and civilizational studies are among the very first attempts to think globally about history. Sociology emerged as a field of history trying to make sense of the transformation beyond recognition brought about by the "twin revolutions": the French Revolution and the Industrial Revolution. The comparative method was at the core of this effort, with Marx comparing modes of production, Émile Durkheim comparing traditional and modern societies, and Max Weber comparing religions, their economies, and societies. This last project, in fact, arranges the world as a set of civilizations derived from the major religions: Confucianism and Taoism in China, Hinduism and Buddhism in India, Judaism and Islam in the Middle East, Catholicism and Protestantism in Europe. This overlap between historical sociology and civilizational analysis exemplifies their cognate nature. Both stem mostly from sociology, rely heavily on the comparative method, and are pathfinders of global thinking.

The origins of civilizational analysis can be tracked to times previous to the carving of the world into nation-states in the writings of Vico, Montesquieu, and Herder among others. However, a defining moment for the emergence of the field was the aftermath of the First World War with the publication of the influential *The Decline of the West* (1923) by Oswald Spengler and *The Study of History* (1934–1961) by Arnold Toynbee. Both historical sociology and civilizational analysis grew into pioneering and inspirational fields for the present wave of the writing of history beyond borders, not so much because of these early origins but because of key publications by remarkable authors in both fields starting in the second half of the twentieth century: Seymour Martin Lipset, Neil Smelser, Reinhard Bendix, Theda Scokpol, Barrington More, Charles Tilly, and Perry Anderson among others in historical sociology, Fernand Braudel, Shmuel Noah Eisenstadt, Samuel Huntington, Johann Arnason, Benjamin Nelson, and Björn Wittrock among others in civilizational analysis.

Historical sociology

Historical sociology concentrates on the study of social and political structures—such as modes of production, empires, and states—and their transformations either by long-lasting processes—such as the rise of capitalism or democratization—or by drastic changes brought by revolutions and social movements. Historical sociology is a theory-oriented field and therefore its research and writing is rooted in and geared toward clear conceptualization and modeling of historical structures and transformations. Conceptualization and modeling, in their turn, are conducive to comprehensive explanations of historical structures, patterns of change, and generalizations of these two. Conversely, the study of historical cases allow for testing existing theoretical explanations and the formulation of new theories. This dialogue between the conceptual and the historical reflects the merging of the two disciplines of sociology and history in terms of their interests and methods of study.

The singularity of historical sociology among the 12 cross-boundary branches can be appreciated by presenting its unique approach to the very same topics advanced as examples in the previous chapter: the rise of civilization in the ancient Near East, imperial history, and the American Divergence. The rise of civilization in Mesopotamia is the point of departure for Michael Mann's analysis of the history of social power. His analysis is based on the distinction between four main forms of power: political, economic, military, and ideological. Far from mastering all four forms of power, the Sumerian civilization was a multi-power-actor in which different cities and hinterlands, institutions and groups shared power in its different forms. Nevertheless, as this multi-state cultural and diplomatic geopolitical power organization grew consolidated by militarism, it represented the first effort moving in the direction of power concentration.

This attempt is compared to five additional and rather synchronic instances in which civilization emerged independently, including ancient Egypt, the Indus Valley, the Yellow River, Mesoamerica, and Peru. Subsequently, the fourfold framework for conceptualizing power is applied diachronically into later polities. Starting with the age of classical empires, the mastering of power in its four dimensions was coming to fruition. The Roman Empire, in command of the political and military spheres, relying on its institutions and army as well as gaining ideological and economic power through Latinization and trade networks, exemplifies this development. The four volumes of *The Sources of Social Power* continue this dialogue between the fourfold conceptualization of power and the unfolding of history up to the current age of globalization.[1]

Shmuel Eisenstadt's book *The Political System of Empires* is another take on empires from a historical sociological perspective, and it aims to reveal the common political characteristics of bureaucratic empires. After analyzing dozens of cases, Eisenstadt concludes that the common underlying characteristics include territorial centralization, the differentiation of social, political, and economic hierarchies, and the constitution of the political sphere as a distinct organizational framework equipped with autonomous goals. These characteristics result in the definition of the necessary and sufficient conditions for the emergence of such empires. On the one hand, the presence of a ruler striving to implement innovative goals and able to mobilize resources for their achievement (an equipped and autonomous political sphere) is necessary. On the other hand, a sufficiently complex and productive society to provide these resources is also mandatory (differentiation of social, political, and economic hierarchies). Finally, a delicate balance between these two, rulers and elites, with the first accomplishing centralization while the second enjoys autonomy. The sustained presence of these three requirements conditioned the emergence and longevity of empires.[2]

By looking at empires, their durability, and beyond, James Mahoney addresses the American Divergence by looking into the impact of colonialism on post-independence economic development in the western hemisphere. Spanish Latin American countries are compared with one another first and with British and Portuguese colonies second. The territories of the Spanish Empire are divided between colonial centers—such as Peru, Guatemala, and Bolivia—and peripheries—such as Chile, Argentina, Uruguay, and Costa Rica. Colonial centers concentrated large populations and massive wealth and these colonies were ruled by the mercantilist policies of the Habsburgs. The peripheries, instead, enjoyed more liberal policies, as applied after 1700 by the Bourbon dynasty. The path dependent result of this conditioning was that postcolonial states emerging out of the periphery of the Spanish Empire were better off than those evolving out of its center. Along this same line of argumentation, settlement colonies of British North America, as well as Australia and New Zealand, thrived in post-independence due to the application of liberal policies during the colonial era. Brazil represents a mixed scenario in which its northeast region with a mercantilist past fell behind the country's south that enjoyed more liberal policies during the colonial era and faster economic development since independence. In this way, this wide historical comparison led to the sociological identification of a recurring pattern in the transition from colony to state.[3]

These three examples provided by Mann's, Eisenstadt's, and Mahoney's works illustrate that historical sociology deals with social and political structures (in these examples, power and empires) and transformations (from states to empires and from colonies to states). The examples also show the centrality of conceptualization and modeling (fourfold dimensions of power; three conditions for empire; colonial path dependent conditioning on contemporary economic performance). These examples are also representative of historical sociology in that comparison is the methodological backbone of the field.

Moving beyond methodology and into substance, relying on comparison means that the multiple units selected in the above examples remained self-enclosed (for example, Mesopotamia, Byzantium, and Uruguay), the privileged dimension of time was the diachronic one (for example, power from 3000 BCE to 2011; Habsburg colonialism, Bourbon colonialism, independence), and endogenous causal explanations prevailed (the capability of an empire to claim the four types of power or to achieve a balance between autonomous rulers and elites determined the crystallization and perpetuation of empires; the colonial past of Peru is the cause of its contemporary economic performance). Finally, these three examples on the very same issues discussed in Chapter 3—the dawn of civilization, empires, and postcolonialism—highlight the singularity of historical sociology. This singularity stems out of the combination of these features listed above as well as from its use of the "grand manner" or "universalizing type" of comparison, also reflected in the above examples.

Civilizational analysis

Civilizational analysis is an historically oriented branch of sociology, the subject of which is civilization in the singular and/or civilizations in the plural. As a subject of study, civilization refers to the evolution of the social life of humankind as a whole in all of its dimensions. As a unit of analysis, civilizations refer to geographical areas in which a distinctive trajectory in the evolution of social life is recognizable. As several societies and polities are identified as offspring of each distinctive trajectory, civilizations as a unit of analysis incorporate several societies with shared cultural, economic, and/or geographical features under its umbrella. In this way, polities and societies under their rule such as city-states, kingdoms, empires, or nation-states typically adopted as units of research are assembled by civilizational analysts according to their cultural affinities and embedded within these larger units defined as civilizations.

Occasionally, a full overlap can occur between a political unit and a civilization. The Chinese civilization and Chinese Empire are a case in point. However, by and large civilizations are units larger than a single polity and include many polities, as with the cases of Western civilization, African civilization, Muslim civilization, and so on. With these larger units in place as a point of departure, studies in civilizational analysis either compare or relate between the particular trajectories in the evolution of social life experienced by them.

Once again by approaching the same subjects discussed so far—the dawn of civilization, empires, and the American Divergence—the specificity of civilizational analysis is made apparent. So far, the dawn of civilization was presented from a comparative perspective that highlighted the similarities and differences between ancient Mesopotamia and Egypt or a connective viewpoint that stressed the links between the two. From a historical sociological perspective, these two cases, along with many others, were instrumental in conceptualizing the origins of social power. Now, from the standpoint of civilizational analysis, the dawn of civilization is the departing point of the evolution of the social life of humankind as a whole in all of its dimensions. In this context, ancient Mesopotamia and Egypt can be combined as a first stage of evolution linearly leading up to the global civilization in which we live today.

That is how David Wilkinson presents the history of the evolution of the social life of humankind as a whole. In his view, ancient Mesopotamia and Egypt collided and fused by 1500 BCE resulting in the "Central Civilization." This Central Civilization expanded, incorporating the Mediterranean and Indian societies first. Northern European and African societies were also absorbed next. The civilizations of the Americas and the Far East were added in the wake of colonialism and imperialism. By the end of the nineteenth century eventually most of the globe had become part of the Central Civilization. In this linear way, all original independent civilizations end up submerged under a single global civilization that began in ancient Mesopotamia and Egypt. Although Wilkinson's work departs from the use of civilizations in the plural as the original trajectories of social life that emerge in specific areas of the world, his emphasis is on civilization in the singular as one particular trajectory—that of ancient Mesopotamia and Egypt—prevailing by progressively absorbing all the rest.[4]

An example that privileges the plurality of trajectories, instead, is provided by Eisenstadt's work on the "Axial Age." The Axial Age is a period from the eighth to the fifth centuries BCE and defined as the foundational moment of many major intellectual traditions. In China, many philosophical schools had emerged during this period, out of which legalism, Daoism, and predominantly Confucianism stand out. In India, Buddhism and Jainism had emerged, fostering the reformulation of Hinduism. In the Middle East, Zoroastrianism appeared in Iran as a dualist religion, while Judaism as a monotheist religion entered its prophetic phase. In time, this tradition was continued by Christianity and Islam. Last but not least, Greece witnessed the emergence of rationalistic philosophy.

All of these diverse intellectual traditions flourished rather simultaneously and resulted in the transformation or emergence of major civilizations such as Imperial China, the Hindu and Buddhist civilizations, Zoroastrian Iran, ancient Israel, and ancient Greece. Moreover, by presenting the Axial Age as a series of conceptual revolutions along time rather than a sole episode, Eisenstadt also included the emergence of Christianity and Islam as Axial Age civilizations. The unity of the Axial Age amid the diversity of its civilizations is given by a series of underlying shared features. According to Eisenstadt, all Axial Age traditions institutionalized the division between the mundane and transcendental orders. This institutionalization is represented by the emergence of a new social type of elite, a spiritual leadership that challenges and restrains the already established political elite. Based on moral considerations, this new spiritual elite restrained the old political one and demanded accountability from it. The reordering of the world of knowledge, ideas, ideals, and morality also led to the reordering of the political and social spheres.[5]

Eisenstadt's move from historical sociology in his *The Political Systems of Empires* to civilizational analysis resulted in the displacement of empires by civilizations as the basic unit of analysis and hence in a dramatic reduction of the amount of units analyzed. This shortening from 32 political systems to eight civilizations reflects the comprehensive character of civilizations as units of analysis. The use of this larger unit of analysis and the study of a unifying trajectory undergone by all societies within it are two of the features that make civilizational analysis a singular branch.

Viewed from a civilizational perspective, the American Divergence can be portrayed as the result of two different trajectories in the evolution of social life. That is how the case is presented by Samuel Huntington. In his book *The Clash of Civilizations and the Remaking of World Order*, Huntington argues that in the post-Cold War era and the waning of ideological contention the new generation of global conflicts will revolve around cultural tensions and confront different civilizations. There are eight different civilizations that Huntington recognizes: the Western, the Latin American, the Islamic, the Chinese, the Hindu, the Orthodox, the Japanese, and the African (a Buddhist civilization is also identified but underrepresented in international affairs). In terms of the American Divergence, what matters here is that North America, north of the mouth of the Río Grande, is brought together with Europe, Australia, and New Zealand, while Latin America is considered to belong on a different trajectory of social life.[6]

This distinction was made explicit in full by Huntington in *Who Are We? The Challenges to America's Identity*. In a nutshell, the English institutional heritage and the dissenting Protestant culture resulted in a social life based upon a democratic, limited government accountable to its constituencies and matched by commitment to individualism, equality, freedom, and work ethic. The trajectory stemming out of these principles cannot be attained by the Hispanic Catholic tradition depicted as lacking in initiative, self-reliance, ambition, and prioritization of education. In Huntington's view, this civilizational gap is responsible for the American Divergence in the sense that North America parted ways with Quebec, Mexico, and Brazil because the latter were settled by French, Spanish, or Portuguese Catholics, while the former was settled instead by British Protestants. Moreover, this same gap accounts for the challenge posed by Mexican migration and the potential bifurcation of the United

States resulting from the Hispanization of those areas adjacent to and acquired from Mexico.[7]

The above examples show some of the possibilities and dichotomies embedded in civilizational analysis. Civilization can be adopted in the singular as a unifying process concerning humanity as a whole. Civilizations, instead, are defined in the plural as manifold trajectories undertaken by different large groups of people. Then, to the extent that civilizations are adopted in their plurality, a comparative or connective perspective could be applied. A comparative perspective on civilizations stresses the singularity of each as well as their underlying commonalities. In the Axial Age example, each civilization is unique and yet they are all based on the institutionalization of the division between the mundane and transcendental orders.

A connective perspective on civilizations, instead, emphasizes interactions between them, a dimension entirely missing in the Axial Age argument. Yet when interactions are the main focus for civilization analysis, they can be creative and constructive or conflicting and destructive. Wilkinson's argument of the Central Civilization is leaning closer to the first alternative. Huntington is a clear example of the second option. In short, civilizational analysis is a branch fostered by diverse and even competing approaches. In this regard, it is similar to historical sociology, as in that branch too, different approaches (for example, functionalist, state-centered, Marxist) offer alternative explanations. That is not the case, however, with the next branch, which fully overlaps with a singular approach.

The world-system approach: The first connective macrohistory

The world-system approach is the first connective branch. It is connective because it deals primarily with cross-border phenomena, such as capital accumulation, world division of labor, and the struggle for political hegemony, which transcends political boundaries connectively resulting in long-lasting interdependent relations. The enclosed units tightly connected through such interdependent relations actually became a complex whole, a system. This system is the unit of analysis and is referred to as the world-system, even if the entire globe was not yet incorporated into it from its beginnings back in the sixteenth century.

This *world* of the world-system approach is a unit of analysis deductively, preconfigured by a hierarchy determined by the organizing concepts of world division of labor, accumulation of capital, unequal exchanges, and interstate relations. Societies whose economy is based on quasi-monopoly products are located higher in the hierarchy of division of labor and are named core societies. This type of economy is created and fostered by a high accumulation of capital and high technological development. Conversely, societies located at the bottom of the hierarchy, named peripheral societies, are characterized by economies based on raw materials and/or on competitive products. The concentration of such products, whose production is possible anywhere else, allows for a narrower surplus than that of quasi-monopoly products. This is the self-perpetuating result of low capital accumulation and low technology production. The resulting trade between core and peripheral societies, therefore, has been called "unequal exchange." Between these two extremes is an in-between category of societies partially orientated toward both core-like and peripheral-like production called the semi-periphery.

The social result of this categorical tripartite division of labor is that at the core flourish societies based on broad populations enjoying high wages, high consumption, low exploitation, and low coercion. In contrast, at the periphery most of the members of the societies are low-skilled workers suffering low income, low consumption, high exploitation, and high coercion. This social profile is shared by semi-peripheral societies side by side with moderately skilled urban workers. As for the political results, states in the core have a wide fiscal basis on which the efficiency of its bureaucracy and the power of its armies depend, while the limited resources of peripheral countries allow for a weak and usually corrupt state, whose army's main function is to police social unrest. The strength of semi-peripheral states varies along the spectrum created by the former two patterns.[8] The characteristics of these components are permanent but their agents are not. Upward and downward mobility exist in the system.[9]

The economic, logistic, and Kondratiev cycles and the quest for hegemony represent major criteria for periodization. Logistic cycles are long economic trends of about three centuries divided in a phase of overall expansion, such as the "long sixteenth century" (1450–1640), and a phase of general stagnation and decline (1600–1750). Kondratiev cycles describe periods of 40–60 years launched by a technological innovation. Such innovation promotes economic growth until the market is overflowing, resulting in stagnation and recession. A new technological breakthrough would open the growth phase of a new cycle.

The quest for hegemony brings the most powerful states in the core to contend for achieving supremacy over the system as a whole. These conflicts resulted in the rise and fall of the hegemonic powers and their challengers throughout the history of the system: Portugal and Spain, the Dutch Republic, Britain, and the United States among the former; France and Germany among the later.

This modeled world that the world-system approach created started to emerge since the last part of the fifteenth century by encompassing mainly the Atlantic Basin. Only later was the rest of the world progressively integrated into the system. That was how Immanuel Wallerstein in his *The Origins of the Capitalist World-System* (1974) and Andre Gunder Frank in his *World*

Table 6.1 The world that the *world-system approach* has created

	Core	Semi-periphery	Periphery
Economy	Quasi-monopoly products, high accumulation of capital, high technological development, dominate the world-economy	Both core-like and peripheral-like production	Based either on raw materials and/or on competitive products. Narrower surplus than that of quasi-monopoly products. Low capital accumulation, low technological production
Society	High wages, high consumption, low exploitation, and low coercion. Formulate the discourse that interprets the world	This social profile is shared by semi-peripheral societies	Most of the members of the societies are low skill workers suffering low income, low consumption, high exploitation, and high coercion
Politics	Wide fiscal basis, efficient bureaucracy, powerful armies, and strong states in the core aim to perpetuate and foster the well-being of their societies establishing the rules of the interstate system	States vary along the spectrum created by the former two patterns	Weak and usually corrupt peripheral states' main aim is to repress their pauperized societies

Accumulation, 1492–1789 (1978) defined the starting point of the world-system. Later works by Immanuel Wallerstein and others as well as the studies published in *Review*, the journal dedicated to the study of the world-system, further developed this perspective and widened its geographical scope by the progressive incorporation of world regions into that system beyond the original focus on the Atlantic Basin. Moreover, its time span was also expanded from 500 to 5000 years. Premodern world-systems were identified besides the modern one with the most ancient of them starting from as early as 30,000 BCE.[10]

The singularity of the world-system approach is self-evident, as it represents not only a particular branch with its unit of analysis and method but also a particular approach with its concepts, models, and premises outlined above. However, for the sake of illustration, the same exemplifying topics applied

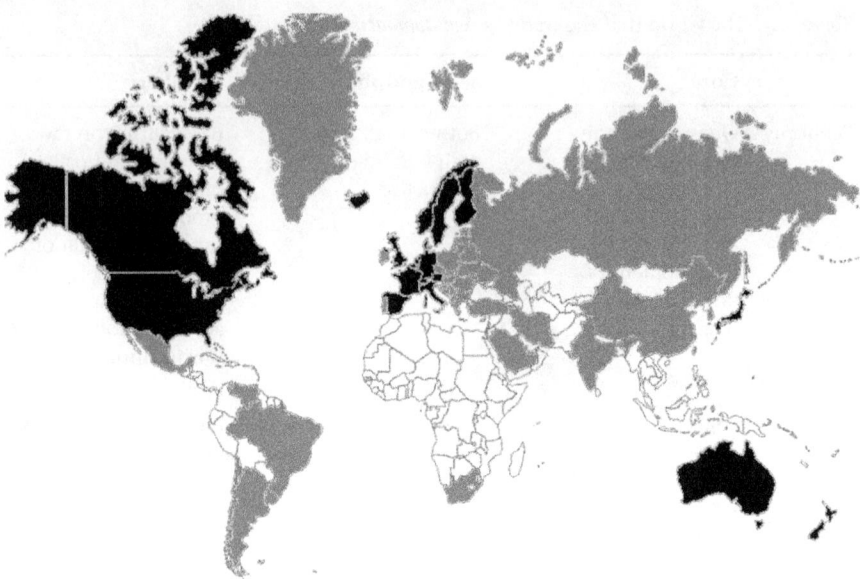

Figure 6.1 Core, semi-peripheral, and peripheral states

so far—the dawn of civilization, empires, and the American Divergence—are displayed once more.

Viewed from the world-system perspective, the complex and hierarchical societies that emerged in Mesopotamia about 5000 years ago were integrated by using networks through which important, two-way, ordinary interaction linked peoples and created a world-system. That is, the space was arranged along a scheme of strong core polities and weaker and dependent peripheral societies, with semi-peripheral societies in between. Cyclical patterns of urban and empire growth and decline and expansion and contraction of trade networks influenced by climate change unfolded in recurrent cycles. The first two cycles consisted of the expansion of Uruk and the consolidation of the Akkadian Empire. Uruk expansion was accomplished by founding colonies and colonial enclaves within existing towns across a vast region in order to gain access to desired goods and to control trade routes. The Akkadian Empire is considered the first instance of a core-wide empire resulting from the conquest of a number of older core states.

The application of the world-system approach to ancient times despite its original formulation for the modern world was in fact generalized by Andre Günter Frank, one of the founding figures of the approach, who took the big leap backward in the dating of the emergence of the world-system. In *The World-System: Five Hundred Years or Five Thousand?* (1993), he claims that the main dynamics of the world-system oriented the course of history since its very beginnings. The process of capital accumulation, the establishment of core-periphery relationships, the operation of cycles of expansion and contraction, and the existence of hegemony and rivalry relationships, all apply equally well to premodern as to modern times. These dynamics were taking place from the interactions between Mesopotamian and Egyptian societies in about 3000 BCE and have expanded in size and scale ever since. This overreaching statement is accompanied by the tracing of eight long cycles that are presented as the economic and political history of the eastern hemisphere between 1700 BCE and 1700 CE.[11]

Coming to "imperial history" from the perspective of the world-system approach, empires represent large geographical and political entities in which vast economies and economic trade developed. However, a world-system encompasses larger economies than a single empire because it incorporates trade networks going beyond the political boundaries of any empire. Moreover, regardless of the difference in size and its consequences (for example, varieties of soils, climates, natural resources, and demography that shape economy and trade) a crucial distinction between the two is that an empire is in command of the whole economy within its boundaries, whereas no single political authority is in command of the world-system. In this sense, the adoption of a world-system as a unit of analysis is rather an alternative to "imperial history," regardless of how important empires may be to the understanding of a world-system.

Janet Abu-Lughod's book *Before European Hegemony: The World-System A.D. 1250–1350* illustrates how the Mongol Empire was crucially instrumental in facilitating the coalescence of a world-system that reached far beyond the Mongol Empire both geographically and economically. This world-system was articulated in Eurasia and North Africa by eight commercial "circuits": northwest/Mediterranean Europe, the eastern Mediterranean and Black Sea basins, the Middle East, the Steppe of central Asia, west and east India's coastlines, Southeast Asia and China. Although these circuits had been weaving commercial links previously, between 1250 and 1350 the *Pax Mongolica* provided the political stability and infrastructures that allowed these links to thrive.

According to Abu-Lughod, in contrast to the European modern world-system, this world-system was based on cooperative and mutually interdependent relations, without a single participant dominating it all. Instead, most of the participants benefited from coexistence and mutual tolerance, since it was not based on "short term plunder [but on] long-term exchange." However, the system bore in itself the seeds of its own destruction: the spread of the bubonic plague from China throughout Asia toward Europe. It is precisely the disruption of this system that paved the way for the subsequent European capitalist hegemony, as the collapse of this Afro-Eurasian world-system is portrayed as a precondition for the Atlantic Basin and European-controlled world-system to emerge.[12]

In this modern world-system, empires once again held a central place as cyclical hegemons on top of the system: the Portuguese, the Spanish, the Dutch, and the British empires. But the modern world-system remained more than the sum of its component empires. Finally, as for the American Divergence, the world-system argument is essentially the same as that of dependency theory, which represents one of its major sources of inspiration. In fact, the world-system approach was formulated at first to account for the divergences that evolved in the modern world.

In conclusion, the world-system approach offers a singular global perspective from the social sciences geared toward conceptualization. The world that the world-system approach has created is a powerful tool to analyze global processes. But besides conceptualization, the world-system approach has also fostered many crucial features of historical global thinking, such as interdependent relations, synchronicity, and exogenous causation. These features are now the backbone of all connective branches of history. The world-system approach also defined a broad context against which all phenomena are discussed. This is a key procedure replicated by all branches thinking history globally, namely, the fourth big C of contextualization.

The pending four branches—the history of globalization, global history, world history, and big history—are those providing the broadest frameworks for contextualization. These branches are informed to varying extents by the world-system approach. For example, the internal division within the world-system approach, generated by chronological considerations regarding how old the world-system is and if just one or many world-systems, had emerged was later reenacted and expanded by the history of globalization. Furthermore, this chronological debate about the origins of globalization is tightly connected to the differentiation between world history and global history. These are the concerns to be addressed in the next two chapters.

7
Thinking History Globally, Thinking Globalization Historically

The understanding of two of the major history branches, world history and global history, with which the current wave of history writing beyond borders is identified, is punctuated by three interrelated conceptual problems. First, there is not a widely accepted distinction between the two concepts. The aims of world history, as stated by Jerry Bentley in the *Journal of World History* editorial, are "to transcend national frontiers, and study forces such as population movements, economic fluctuations, climatic changes, transfer of technologies," and so on from the very beginnings of human history.[1] This definition was consolidated during the first two decades of world history's use, as reflected in Patrick Manning's definition of it as "the study of connections between communities and between communities and their environments" in the first encompassing book on the historiography of world history.[2] The editorial of the *Journal of Global History* mentions a *"subtle difference* between the closely related endeavors of global and world history" without any further specification.[3] In their survey on historiography in the last 18 years, Georg Iggers, Q. Edward Wang, and Supriya Mukherjee also point to the fact that it is not clear how the concepts of world history and global history differ: "The term 'global history' overlapped with 'world history' and was often identical with it, but tended to deal more frequently with the period after the explorations of the fifteenth century and often referred to the process of globalization since the last third of the twentieth century."[4]

The second conceptual problem is that despite the tight and intricate relationship between the current processes of globalization and the writing of world and global history, there is not a clear analysis of the relationship between world and global history vis-à-vis the history of globalization. This second problem is closely related to the third one: the lack of a clear chronological and conceptual framework for the history of globalization. Although the usual fate of central concepts in history such as slavery, feudalism, capitalism, imperialism, or modernity is the existence of a wide range of definitions, chronologies, and different research paths, the situation with the concept of globalization goes well beyond that, as the disagreement on its coverage ranges from the past 30 to the last 200,000 years. This chapter presents the history of globalization and many of its chronological, conceptual, and methodological debates. Besides its own merits, the understanding of the debates on the history of globalization is key in the search for the subtle distinction between world and global history.

The history of globalization

The depiction of current globalization processes as the integration of an interdependent economy relying on information and communication networks that simultaneously contribute to enhancing a global culture may suite many historical accounts.[5] The common feature of all of these works is the attempt to establish a point of departure for the phenomenon of globalization. The idiosyncratic feature of most of them is that any work provides its own starting point. The first part of this chapter arranges the approaches to the history of globalization into three main categories following the dating of globalization: the extremist, moderate, and conciliatory approaches. Nevertheless, the multiplicity of periodizations implies that several conceptual problems are at stake. The second part of this chapter, dedicated to the conceptual issues, examines the implicit debates underlying the search after *l'idole de l'origine* between and within these three categories. Profiting from the insights obtained from conceptual debates, the third part of this chapter offers some conclusions on the definition and chronology of globalization.

Periodizing globalization: Extremists, moderates, and conciliators

Several historians have defined different starting points for the process of globalization. Among the most prominent plausible origins of this process are current globalization, industrialization, mercantilism, discoveries in the Atlantic Basin, Eurasian commercial "circuits," Islamic world civilization, and world empires of antiquity and the ways in which they interacted. Other scholars view the first civilizations and their interrelationships as the initial stage of globalization, and some even view various prehistorical periods as the initial stage, thus pushing back even further the origins of globalization. From this wide range of historiographical possibilities emerges a simple comparative conclusion: there are extremist, moderate, and conciliatory approaches to the phenomenon of globalization. The extremist approaches envisage globalization as a present condition, either as contemporary or as a continuous present. The moderate approaches relate the contemporary developments to previous times but, at the same time, establish clear-cut distinctions between a precise definition of globalization and several types of other interregional or global flows. Finally, a conciliatory approach attempts to combine several definitions at once.

From a contemporary extremist perspective, the age of globalization, dated to the second half of the twentieth century, represents "an entirely new epoch." The reasons for this sharp break from the past are a new spatial dimension, the "spaceship earth," that is, the thrust into space and the resulting possibility of envisaging the globe as a unity, and the effects of new factors in human existence. Conspicuous among these factors are nuclear power, satellite communications, the rise of multinational corporations, environmental problems, and the emergence of "global consciousness." Another prominent characteristic is the withdrawal of previous institutions: the territorial state is now for the most part unable to protect its citizens.[6]

From a past continuous extremist perspective, the integration of the world is a long-lasting process and result, offering in this way a wide range of premodern options for the origins of globalization. For example, Roland Robertson and David Inglis recognize in Roman cosmopolitanism the starting point of globality in the sense of interconnectedness and the emergence of global consciousness.[7] David Wilkinson pushed the origins of globalization backward to the twenty-third century BCE by understanding globalization as a scaling up process, moving toward ever-larger spatial units covering ultimately the entire world. A more extremist proposal by Fernandez Armesto claims that the Ice Age was a kind of globalization in that economy, technology, and key elements of culture were homogeneous all over the inhabited world, whereas divergence was the ruling process. Finally, for Robert Clark the spread of humankind from Africa, starting about 150,000 years ago, constitutes the first global process in which the world was truly encompassed by *Homo sapiens*.[8] Encompassed yes, but not connected.

From a moderate perspective, the beginning of globalization could occur only once the globe was not only fully encircled but also connected. That happened "[w]hen the Old World became directly connected with the Americas in 1571 via Manila." Since then, interactions among trade, ecology, demography, and back to trade again represented a "path dependent process" that created a global system functioning as an organic whole. The crucial developments for each of these variables were the silver trade, the "Columbian" and "Magellan" exchanges, the dramatic growth of the Chinese population, and a second wave of silver trade, respectively.[9] David Armitage added to this chronological framework the dimension of consciousness. By tracing expressions of awareness to globality among cartographers, cosmographers, jurists, and philosophers, he opened many paths toward a multilayer history of globalization.[10]

In contrast with the above multiplicity of departing points of globalization, the moderate approach to globalization offers two main alternative origins for globalization. Besides the sixteenth-century beginning, there is a nineteenth-century date. Two groups of scholars, one gathered by the National Bureau of Economic Research (NBER) and the other associated with the world-system approach, are developing the study of globalization mainly by comparing the economic integration of the last part of the twentieth century with that of the second half of the nineteenth century. This strategy has become the major current trend in the research of economic globalization in history.[11] Prominent among the publications proceeding from the first group is Kevin H. O'Rourke and Jeffrey G. Williamson's *Globalization and History* in which they deal with globalization as the movements in labor, capital flows, and trade in goods and services. They designed the work as a comparison between "today globalization" and the "first great globalization" of 1850 through 1914. Between these two waves of globalization, the world war period represents a loss of previous globalization achievements. They find crucial agreements between the economic openness in the final years of the nineteenth and twentieth centuries. The export and GDP ratios for today's Organisation for Economic Co-operation and Development (OECD) countries are not overwhelmingly higher than those in 1913 (8.2 percent of total GDP in 1913 and 12.8 percent in 1987). The authors contrast land prices and real wages in immigration and emigration countries (fall of land prices and rise of wages in the latter, the reverse in the former). Globalization appears as a contributor to convergence, the process of diffusion of growth from richer to poorer, by narrowing the differences in productivity because of new methods of organization and production available to those economies capable of using them. The forces that fostered the processes of globalization were economic in the first place, particularly a decline in transport costs, and they were political second—the lowering of tariff rates, the end of restrictions on emigration, and the maintaining of minimal barriers against immigration. It was also a period with limited international warfare or other political disturbances. Conversely, the withdrawal from globalization is attributed to increased tariffs imposed in Europe because of pressure from agriculturists and the New World countries' attempts to gain protection for their manufacturing industries. The success of these policies was accelerated by war and depression.[12]

Along the same lines, stressing the relationship between globalization and convergence, Williamson dedicated an article to the recurrent topic of the origins of globalization. Here globalization is defined as the integration of international commodity markets represented by a decline in the wedge: falling transport costs or trade barriers lead to falling import prices, rising export prices, commodity price convergence, and an increase in trade volumes. The only irrefutable evidence for globalization is the commodity price convergence. That is to say, trade-creating forces must change domestic commodity prices, which in turn induce a reshuffling of resources in order to influence the scale of output, the distribution of income, and the quality of life. The application of this perspective on chronology results in the establishment of the origin. Prior to the eighteenth century, long-distance trade was limited to non-competing goods. Since the early nineteenth century, the rise of trade in basic competing goods and the spectacular decline in transport costs fostered a price convergence. The present era has seen trade in both basic and highly differentiated manufactured commodities. Michael Bordo added to these arguments the flow of capital, resulting in a similar U-shaped figure. The first wave of a high rate of capital flow occurred during the period 1870–1914, followed by a withdrawal of foreign investment in the years 1914–1973, and a restored increase in capital flow since 1973.[13]

One comprehensive example of the group associated with the world-system approach is an article by Christopher Chase-Dunn, Yukio Kwano, and Benjamin Brewer that provides another view of globalization for a similar chronological framework. According to their definition, globalization is "the increasing worldwide density of large-scale interaction networks relative to the density of smaller networks." They propose three waves since 1795 in which international trade as a proportion of global production increased significantly. Although the authors have established a clear distinction between economic and political globalization, they stress the importance of "hegemonic stability"—that is, the greater order when a single hegemonic state has sufficient power to influence or coerce other states or other international actors—as a necessary condition for the enhancement of economic globalization.[14] Moreover, the particular features of any wave of globalization are presented as molded by the political leadership. In this way, Giovanni Arrighi distinguishes between British hegemony, characterized by pushing vigorously for international free trade, and American hegemony, which relies more heavily on global firms and global governance. Through this "enlightened global Keynesianism," growth in other geopolitically strategic core regions, such as Japan and Korea, was allowed by preventing American corporations and financial capital from marginalizing those countries. The result was a balanced world of capitalist growth until the decline in competitiveness of the American economy. By then, at the beginning of the 1970s, big companies and finance capitalists had returned to power.[15]

The chronology that derives from the figures indicates that

> from the 1830s there was a rise to a high mound between 1850 and the late 1880s, then a decline until 1905 and then another wave that rose before

World War I, declined a bit during it, and then rose again for the roaring twenties. A big downturn corresponded with the stock market crash of 1929, and with some wiggles it descended to a very low level reached in 1949, and hence began the most recent great wave of trade globalization.

The main factual difference with respect to the previous works belonging to this category is that they indicate three, instead of two, waves of globalization. The third wave is dated from 1905 to 1929. The main interpretive difference is that the reason for the waves of globalization is not the cost of transportation, which did not radically increase when globalization collapsed; instead the authors point to the correspondence between the first and last waves of globalization and the rise and consolidation of the British and American hegemonic powers, respectively. In contrast, protectionist policies appear in their scheme as a reaction to trade contraction and not as the cause of it.[16]

This U-shaped scheme and its comparative framework have been widely adopted in the last decade, up to the point of becoming the leading historical narrative on the history of globalization. In the latest publications, this periodization appears as generally assumed rather than argued.[17] As such, it gained the attention and criticism of social scientists, who insist that it is only the uniqueness of contemporary phenomena that deserves to be named globalization. They dismiss three key indicators—trade, investment, and migration statistics—as relative. In addition, the scale of contemporary telecommunications, air travel, transworld civil society associations, and global awareness are presented as arguments in favor of the uniqueness of current globalization.[18]

Besides this external criticism, the history of globalization confronts the internal problem posed by its chronology. Several attempts were made to bridge the gap between the several extremist and moderate approaches, resulting in a third way, a conciliatory approach. This approach appears as the adequate solution following the assumption that "it is probably best to think in terms of 'globalizations' instead of 'globalization.'"[19] In *Globalization in World History*, A. G. Hopkins and others approach globalization the way "extremists" do, but they respond to different definitions at different historical stages. Instead of detecting globalization's point of departure, the authors assume world history to be organized according to several waves of globalization. Each wave of globalization is different by definition, and they do not follow a linear pattern of succession. Moreover, different waves of globalization can overlap, interact, compete, or symbiotically intermingle. Therefore, this approach implicitly combines two historical strategies. On the one hand, it deliberately adopts arguments about the present in order to guide our understanding of the past. On the other hand, it rejects an inverted teleological view of history. The combination of these moves results in a tense equilibrium between Bloch's proposal of understanding of the past by the present and Loewenthal's recall of the past as a foreign country.

The first type of globalization is called "archaic" and refers to the entire historical time span before industrialization and nation-state formation. Its generative agents are kings and warriors, merchants and pilgrims responsible for the creation of "globalizing networks," both sea borne and land based. The major social formations created by these agents are alternatively pre-modern empires or city networks. These formations preserve the original diversity of the component parts rather than thrusting toward standardization. Their goal is to coordinate rather than to assimilate. The limitations of the impact of these formations are attributed to technical and institutional constrictions, as well as to the market sizes and the extent of the division of labor. Once these limitations were banished, after industrialization and nation-state formation, a global integration of producers of raw materials and manufacturing centers of Europe occurred. In this second type of globalization, called "modern globalization," the political integration was characterized by the formation of an international system of relations, whose strategies of control are assimilation and association. However, a third type of globalization is distinguished in between the two previously mentioned, during the sixteenth and seventeenth centuries. This type of globalization is called "proto-globalization." The main argument is that on the eve of the major transformations of the nineteenth century, preindustrial manufacturing, financing, and services grew considerably. Simultaneously, political entities strengthened the links between territory, taxation, and sovereignty, a process presented as "military fiscalism." Both developments enhanced the circuits of exchange as the salient characteristic of this type of globalization. The fourth and last type of globalization is the contemporary one, in existence since the 1950s. Called "postcolonial globalization," it is presented as a product of one hegemonic superpower, new forms of regional integration, and the creation of supra-territorial organizations. Outstanding among its most prominent impacts are the elimination of isolation, the collapse of the nation-state and a redefinition of frontiers in the frame of a supra-national borderless world, according to circuits of trade, financial flows, patterns of migration, and systems of belief.[20]

Samir Amin provided a more simple subdivision from a world-system perspective. Again, globalization, being assumed to be the existence of significant relations between various regions, encompasses the entire chronological span. The first globalization involved Eurasia and Africa, from 500 BCE until 1500 CE. The outstanding features of this globalization are its coverage of 80 percent of the world population within the center regions, its unpolarizing nature (the wealth gap between regions perhaps did not exceed a ratio of two to one), and its upward mobility (Europe was able to "catch up" between 1000 and 1200, and even "overtake"). The globalization of 1500–1800 constituted a mercantilist transition in which the old feudal mode of production and the new capitalist mode of production fought against each other. In addition, strife arose between the old global system (centered in China, India, and the Middle East) and the new one (which integrated the Atlantic basin with Europe). Finally, the capitalist globalization, from 1800 on, embraces 20 percent of the world population in its centers, while the wealth gap between the centers and the peripheries is today 60 to one.[21]

This strategy of embracing all possible origins of globalization and formulating a periodization of globalization was also adopted by scholars that see in the sixteenth century the origins of globalization, that is, in a moderated way. Jürgen Osterhammel and Niels Petersson provide a fully developed chronology for a "path dependence globalization" framework, which includes a first stage of empire building up to the mid-eighteenth century, the age of imperialism, industrialization, and free trade as a second stage between 1750 and 1880, a third phase of global capitalism and crisis between 1880 and 1945, and globalization split into two during the Cold War.[22] In this case, the research of social scientists coincided with that of historians of globalization. For example, the political scientist David Held and the sociologist Roland Robertson delineated different stages of globalization. Although departing from different stages—Held, starting from the greatest empires, and Robertson, opening with the transformations of the fifteenth century—both studied the successive shifts in the eighteenth and second half of the nineteenth centuries.[23]

Conceptual discussions

Underlying the attempts to establish the chronology or periodization of the history of globalization are important conceptual discussions. The present extremist stance for globalization leaves no room for discussing the place of globalization in history. The deepest chronological divergence, then, creates a rift between present continuous extremists and moderates. This discrepancy revolves round the existence of globalization before or only since the modern period. Differently formulated, the debate is about the existence of globalization in the framework of tributary systems or the capitalist system alone. Two key conceptual issues lie beneath this periodization discrepancy. The first issue relates to the definition of space. All the pre-modern definitions of globalization adopt Eurasia and North Africa, entirely or partly, as the unit of analysis. The modern definitions adopt the entire world once the globe has been encompassed. The second issue concerns the character of the definitions. The pre-modern definitions are absolute in the sense that the mere existence of contacts, connections, circulations, flows, and influences serves as evidence of globalization. By contrast, the modern definitions are relative because the

Table 7.1 Approaches to the history of globalization: Three main analytical categories

Extremist approach (present continuous)	Moderate approach		Extremist approach (contemporary)
	Early modern	Modern	
Abu Lughod, J.: 1250–1350, "commercial circuits"	Wallerstein, I.: 16th Ct., Atlantic basin World System	Hobsbawm, E.: 19th Ct., Industrial Revolution	Global History: 1960s "Spaceship Earth"
Hodgson, M.: 7th Ct., "Oikoumene"	Flynn, D. & Giráldez, A.: 16th Ct., "Path Dependence"	NBER: 1850–1914 "First Great Globalization" 1973 onward "Today Globalization"	
McNeill, W.: 1st Ct., "First closure of Ecumene"		WSA: 1850–1914 "British Hegemony" 1949 onward "American Hegemony"	
Frank, A.: 3000 BCE, "World System"			
Conciliatory approach			
Hopkins, A. (Ed): "Archaic Globalization"	"Proto Globalization"	"Modern Globalization"	"Post-Colonial Globalization"
Amin, S.: "Fist Globalization"	"Mercantilist Transition"	"Capitalist Globalization"	
Norel, P.: "Empires de l'Antiquité"	"Etats mercantilists"	"Première globalisation"	"Mondialisation proprement dite"

presence of globalization depends not only on the mere existence of interregional flows but also on their significance in relation to local ones or to other processes. In this way, they claim that the rise of trade volume—which could be the result of population growth, the colonization of uninhabited lands, capital accumulation, technological change, and other factors—does not necessarily represent globalization. Only when the local commodity prices are relatively adjusted to those of the world market—the prices converge—does the rise of trade volume indicate globalization.[24] Similarly, in the study by Chase-Dunn, Kawano, and Brewer presented above they defined globalization as "changes in the density of international and global interactions relative to local or national networks." In another article Chase-Dunn operationalizes economic globalization as "the proportion of all world production that crosses international boundaries," "all invested capital in the world that is owned by non-nationals," and "the extent to which national economic growth rates are correlated across countries."[25]

This contrast between absolute versus relative definitions of globalization represents the main divide within moderate approaches, namely, between the sixteenth and nineteenth centuries as starting points. In the course of a recent debate, Flynn and Giráldez claim that by 1640 a price convergence had already occurred on the global silver market, aiming to provide the sixteenth century case with a relative dimension. Moreover, they maintain that global trade before the eighteenth century was not restricted to luxury items, since luxuries (sugar, porcelain, tableware, silk, and ceramics) evolved into everyday necessities over time. However, the strongest argument for a relative dimension in the sixteenth-century definition comes in qualitative rather than quantitative form. The time lag impacts of trade on environment and demography is fostered as the ultimate measure of globalization. At this level the "Columbian" and "Magellan" exchanges produced deep transformations worldwide. Therefore, quantitative measures such as the trade to GDP ratio are not assumed as an exclusive tool for assessing globalization in relative terms.[26] O'Rourke and Williamson dismissed these arguments mainly for being incommensurable with their conceptual framework.[27] However, the discrepancy between sixteenth- and nineteenth-century origins embodied a deeper, implicit, and undeveloped discussion around the relationship between globalization and industrialization. Did the action of mercantile capital construct a global economy? Or could this enterprise be accomplished only by industrial capital?

Nevertheless, the most striking differences appear in the nineteenth-century versions, precisely because of their chronological agreement. Those differences appear both in the factual and interpretative realms. The sharpest factual debate confronts Jeffrey Sach's arguments with Paul Bairoch's refutation. The interpretative collision comes from contrasting the arguments of the participants of the NBER conference on globalization in historical perspective with those proceeding from the scholars associated with the world-system approach. The factual debate concerns three crucial claims and counterarguments. First, according to Sachs, from the 1860s onward, low tariff barriers and lower transportation costs fostered international trade. Bairoch presents this claim as inconsistent because of the variations across countries and over time regarding both trade policies and growth. Second, Sachs claims that the aggregation of appropriated legal institutions, the spread of the gold standard, convertible currencies, and Great Britain's financial leadership resulted in large and stable international capital flows. While Bairoch generally agrees—apart from some rectifications—with those features, he focuses on the destinations of capital flows, stressing that a high proportion went to wealthy countries (27 percent to Europe,

24 percent to the United States) or to the wealthiest countries of each region (Argentina and Uruguay absorbed more than 60 percent of capital flows to Latin America). Third, Sachs concludes, the combination of the above-mentioned developments drove the world economy toward growth and convergence, a path promised also for the countries opening up to the globalization wave of the late twentieth century. On the contrary, following his critical comments, Bairoch's conclusion is that the wealthiest countries concentrated the rapid growth of international production and financial activities. Moreover, industrial production—"the real engine of growth"—developed in core countries, causing polarization instead of convergence. Summing up, according to Bairoch's evidence, Sach's construction of nineteenth-century globalization is a "collection of myths and realities."

In contrast, the scholars associated on the one hand with the NBER and on the other hand with world-system analysis concur not only on the dating of globalization but also on its general trends and internal periodization. This fact is outstanding considering the apparent isolation of both groups, as suggested by the sporadic inter-reference. The wide gap between those groups, however, is evident in the interpretation of the data and the overall picture that emerges from it. There are two main reasons for this gap of interpretation, despite the overall agreement regarding the figures: the role of politics in the study of economic globalization and the underlying assumptions regarding the type of relationships between states within the framework of globalization.

The scholars who had participated in the NBER conference on globalization tend to marginalize the role of politics. Despite the affirmation that the major spurt of globalization did not occur until after the Napoleonic wars, no linkage is suggested. The "liberal policies" practiced in most of Asia since the 1860s and 1870s are recognized as being applied "[r]arely by choice" and without relation to expanding imperialism. The period between the two waves of globalization is detached from the phenomenon as unrelated. At most, it is suggested that the backlash of globalization may have been a key cause of the First World War. On the contrary, for the scholars associated with the world-system approach, politics could be detached from the study of economic globalization only for comparative purposes, not as an organic state of affairs. From that assumption follows the centrality of the processes of political hegemony related to the two main waves of globalization.

A crucial concept for the scholars related to the NBER is that of convergence. One of the definitions provided for this concept maintains that convergence is the ability of any country to reach the level of the leading countries in a series of economic parameters. This definition brings us back to the theories of development, with its linear scheme and assumption of the independent situation of every state. By contrast, due to the framework of political hegemony, most of the states are constrained to a situation of deepening dependency.

Those states, being both controlled and unable to control others, are unable to emulate the leading countries. The supposed road toward convergence is in fact a road to divergence. The scholars gathered by the NBER recognized the figures of "enormous divergence" but attributed it to the lack of "openness" and to the "poverty traps and bad governments," "factors other than globalization."

The interesting part of the argument comes with its application to history by J. Bradford Delong and Steve Dowrick. According to these authors, in the interwar period Latin America, the USSR, and Africa had joined the "convergence club." However, during the 1990s, those three blocks had left the club.[28] The twofold movement of these countries matches exactly the arguments of the underdevelopment theories, since the most opened countries in the 1990s were those of Latin America and Russia, which conversely were closed during their alleged "convergence." In fact, the same is true for the "convergence" of the United States and Germany by the end of the nineteenth century allowed by the protectionist policies in favor of their economies.[29] Finally, if openness is the indicator of prosperity, we should expect a highly developed Third World, and the United States and the European Union to be developing countries.[30]

Toward future definitions

Major concepts in history—for example, feudalism, capitalism, and imperialism—have multiple definitions, and consequently multiple origins are proposed for them. That is already the case for the relatively new concept introduced to historiography: globalization. The present chapter provided a comparative classification of the multiple origins and definitions of economic globalization by historians, stressing the conceptual differences between and within each category. Not a single definition should appear to disrupt the typical polyphony of major concepts. However, by way of conclusion, a supplementary chronological classification of approaches to the history of globalization is provided along with some criteria for comprehensive definitions in order to clarify the nature and scope of the history of globalization.

There are three possible broad chronologies to the history of globalization: "reversed teleological globalization," "deus ex machina globalization," and "path dependence globalization." By reverse teleological globalization, I refer to the attempt either to force all or much of world and global history onto an inevitable track that brings us up to current globalization or, conversely, to force the present upon all or much of world and global history by depicting it as a series of different waves of globalization. By deus ex machina globalization, I refer to the globalization that the invisible hand of the market created through relative advantage, cost-effective rational choices, maximization of profits, and price convergence, as if power has no say in human societies or rather as if when power appears, globalization is banished, being two mutually

Table 7.2 Histories of globalization classified chronologically and comparatively

Chronological classification	Comparative classification
"Reversed teleological globalization"	Present continuous extremist approach & conciliatory approach
"Path dependence globalization"	Early modern moderate approach
"*Deus ex machina* globalization"	Modern moderate approach & contemporary extremist approach

exclusive conditions. By introducing coercion and power into this chronological framework, a much more complete picture of globalization appears, although globalization still appears as emerging without preliminary conditions already in place. This is precisely the perspective provided by the third road, which I call path dependence globalization. According to this paradigm, worldwide trade, as well as coercion, power, and exploitation, were articulated by European empires and their offshoot societies when the process of encompassing the globe began in the sixteenth century. It is this early construction of global structural relations that deeply conditioned all of the subsequent history of globalization.

Several criteria may assist in focusing the history of globalization. A primary criterion is that of the space dimension. The concept of globalization denotes that the unit of integration should be the globe. In this way, the issue of the multiple origins of globalization will be confined to the question: For how long has the globe been an integrated unit of analysis?

A second important feature is that the definitions of globalization should focus the relative impact of the economic flows across the globe. As the teleological definitions of globalization maintain, the economic flows represent the realm of continuity in history. The study of globalization, in contrast, enhances the study of change by stressing the major shifts in the relative impacts of the local, regional, and global economic flows. Those two major features of globalization, the encompassing of the globe and the relative significant increase in global economic flows, are embedded in political processes. Political institutions and political arrangements, reflecting and articulating social relations, carried out the project of encompassing the globe and establishing worldwide economic relationships. Therefore, the definition of economic globalization must include the study of the political sphere and the social relations within which it evolved and should include the realm of ideas as well.

These three suggestions—the adoption of the globe as a unit, the consideration of the significance of the relative impact of the economic flows, and attention to the political context within which the economic relationships are sustained—constitute the unifying criteria recommended for efforts to define globalization. Although, even with these suggestions, the need for diversifying criteria is also apparent from the previous discussions. The definitions of globalization should stress at least two types of distinctions inside the period identified as global: cyclical and linear. The cyclical distinction should consider the entire span of time since the established origin of globalization, instead of concentrating only on the waves of high economic flows while leaving behind the downturns. These backlashes should not be considered as unrelated developments. On the contrary, the study of those instances of de-globalization and re-globalization are essential to the comprehension of globalization. The linear distinctions should focus on the qualitative transformation that occurred from one wave of globalization to the next. While until now the emphasis was only on the crucial agreement between those waves, the high rates of economic flows, the crucial differences—political contexts, institutional arrangements, technological changes, cultural trends—should also be considered. In this way, the unified phenomenon of globalization will be differentiated according to its cycles and its internal transformations.

As historians biased by continuity, there is much that is attractive in the reversed teleological perspective: contacts, flows, and networks were always present even if at a different pace and scale. But history is also the domain of change: the transformation of the pace and scale of contacts, flows, and networks amounts to a connective turning point from which a new phenomenon emerged. If there is an inescapable meaning to the concept of globalization, it is due to the inclusion of the word "globe" within it. Therefore, it is only when the globe, and not the hemisphere or a lesser part of it, became the unit in which the contacts, flows, and networks evolved that the singularity of globalization occurred. Moreover, a second reason to confront "reversed teleological globalization" is that contacts, flows, and networks must be contrasted with intra-societal histories in order to contextualize their relative impact. For instance, besides being hemispheric and not global, how important were trade relations between Rome and China in the first century CE in the history of each of these empires?

According to these two final suggestions—the encompassing of the globe as a unit and the significant impact of external contacts, flows, and networks in relation to internal ones as necessary conditions for the definition of globalization—the reversed teleological road to globalization is not an appropriated framework for the study of the history of globalization. Before the sixteenth century, it is possible to refer to some prototype dynamics of the regional division of labor, trade patterns, and arrangements or other flows that could be pointed out as remote precedents of globalization. Similarly, some few and remote developments might be identified as early path dependence developments that conditioned globalization, such as the impact of Mongol conquests as a handicap through Asia that did not disrupt the future masters that created and fostered globalization, the Europeans and much later the

Japanese; or the adoption of silver as the basis for the monetary system in China in the early fourteenth century, which ended in fostering worldwide trade. However, the history of globalization is the process of encompassing the globe and its articulation into a single unit. This process had started on the eve of the sixteenth century by the progressive incorporation of most areas of the world into European empires, up to the point that 125 of 188 present states are former European colonies. It is, therefore, the road of path dependence globalization that will best lead us toward the history of globalization.

8
Thinking History Globally: Contextualizing on a Bigger Scale

World or global: What is in a name?

Framing the history of globalization is also instrumental in specifying the singularities of world history and global history that, in effect, remain almost undistinguished. The relationship between the two can be understood sometimes as one of synonymity, for example, as Michael Adas states in his *Essays on Global and Comparative History*, part of a larger series by the American Historical Association also entitled *Essays on Global and Comparative History*, "a new global or world history" is emerging.[1] Sometimes it appears as an attempt at nominal differentiation. For instance, in the United States it seems that the name global history aims to differentiate itself from world history and its association with the Advanced Placement (AP) curriculum or introductory survey courses. In Germany, particularly in the former DDR, world history nomination is avoided due to its unwanted association with past official Marxist historiography. However, beyond nominal considerations, the singularity of world history and global history is not yet specified.

Disentangling world and global history

A pioneering attempt was made in this direction at the very beginning of the emergence of the current macro-historiographical wave by Bruce Mazlish. He began by clearly defining global history as the study of contemporary history as a singular temporal unit with unique characteristics: "spaceship earth," the withdrawal of previous prominent institutions (for example, the territorial state), and the emergence of global phenomena (for example, multinational corporations, environmental problems, and nuclear threats). In this spirit, the *Global History Reader*, which he edited with Akira Iriye, deals with recent history. Second, he devoted a chapter specifically to clarifying the differences between world history and global history. He argued that in the meaning and uses of the words "world" and "globe" lie the difference between world and global history. While the word "world" is polysemic (for example, other world, academic world) and divisible (for example, Old and New Worlds, First and Third Worlds) the word "globe," which means something spherical and rounded, implies an entire and indivisible whole. In addition, two other features were provided by defining global history as the study of the history of globalization and the study of global processes. Therefore, world history and global history "exist on a continuum," and the beginning of globalization represents the boundary between the two.

With these clarifications, Mazlish paved the road toward the conceptualization of the distinction between world and global history, as well as both of their relationships with the history of globalization. World history encompasses the history of the world before globalization; global history deals with the history of the world since the beginnings of globalization. However, Mazlish's specification of world and global history is based in his "dues ex machine" or "contemporary extremist approach" to the history of globalization. In his writing, globalization is an entire new epoch dating from the 1970s. As suggested in the discussion on the history of globalization, the "path dependence" approach provides a better framework for writing the history of globalization. In fact, Mazlish himself refers to the study of globalization as tracing the "factors of globalization" as far back in the past as is necessary and useful.[2]

The adoption of the beginnings of globalization in the sixteenth century clarifies that what makes the world the largest unit of analysis in world history are global climatic constraints, comparable evolutionary processes, and contacts, flows, processes of diffusion, and networks ranging from regional to hemispheric. Global history also studies these same subjects but under the new and particular conditions derived from the establishment of global relationships. These global relationships represent a singular subject for global history. That is the subtle difference between world and global history. The "world" of world history is the largest unit of analysis; the world in global history is a historical unit that globalization created.

By separating world history from the history of globalization and eradicating the reversed teleological road to globalization, all these subjects of world history are freed from "globalization servitude," becoming important in their own right and interpretable in different contexts other than that of globalization. By contrast, global history cannot afford investigation outside the context of the history of globalization because that is the context in which every single phenomenon it studies unfolds.

Interestingly, this conceptual distinction coincides with the implicit understanding of many macro-historians, as reflected by the contents of the *Journal of World History* and the *Journal of Global History*. While the *Journal of World History* covers all historical periods, the *Journal of Global History* deals almost exclusively with modern and contemporary history. Almost a third (38 out of 128) of the articles and a third of the books reviewed (137 out of 402) in the *Journal of World History* since 1996 are dedicated to the pre-modern period. By contrast, the share of the pre-modern period in the *Journal of Global History* is marginal (five out of 35 articles and four out of 30 reviewed books).

Similarly, by contrasting books titled "X in World History" or "World History of X" with books titled "X: A Global History" or "Global History of X" the chronological divide becomes evident once again. The time span covered by world history books is significantly larger than that of global history books, which normally are confined to some portion of the modern period alone. The history of empires that exemplified the singularities of comparative and connective histories in the third chapter can illustrate with the same clarity this chronological divide between world history and global history. In *Empires in World History: Power and the Politics of Difference*, Jane Burbank and Frederick Cooper deal with imperial trajectories during the last two millennia, starting with the Roman and Han Empires and moving all the way toward modern empires via Islamic and Mongol Empires. By contrast, *After Tamerlane: The Rise and Fall of Global Empires, 1400–2000* by John Darwin is about, as indicated in the book's subtitle, global empires and the modern period.[3]

By looking at empires from a world historical perspective, fundamental patterns can be elucidated. That is the case, for example, of "The Imperial Wheel" formulated by Yuval Harari. This "Imperial Wheel" consists of six recurrent faces in the rise and fall of empires throughout world history: the establishment of an empire as a political entity, the consolidation of an imperial culture, the incorporation of that imperial culture by its subjects, the demand for equal status in accordance with that imperial culture by imperial subjects, the loss of command by the founders of the empire, but the flourishing of imperial culture despite and because of that.[4]

A global history account of empires chronologically focuses only on the last column of Table 7.1 and, therefore, whatever the pattern visualized, it would encompass modern empires only. For example, in his *The Dynamics of Global Dominance: European Overseas Empires, 1415–1980*, David Abernethy uncovered the synergy behind European imperial might: the triptych of "power-profit-proselytization." That is, the combination of military superiority, capitalist economy, and religious and moral justification allowed Europeans to conquer or subjugate the entire globe but for a few exceptions (Afghanistan, Thailand, and temporarily Ethiopia).[5] This synergy of "power-profit-proselytization" unfolded in successive pulses of expansion and contraction.

In short, the prescriptive chronological distinction offered here between world and global history is also valid to some extent, although not entirely, as a descriptive distinction.

Table 8.1 Harari's "Imperial Wheel" throughout world history

Stage	Rome	Islam	European imperialism
A small group establishes a big empire	The Romans establish the Roman Empire	The Arabs establish the Arab Caliphate	The Europeans establish the European empires
An imperial culture is forged	Greco–Roman Culture	Arab–Muslim Culture	Western Culture
The imperial culture is adopted by the subject peoples	The subject peoples adopt Latin, Roman law, Roman political ideas, etc.	The subject peoples adopt Arabic, Islam, etc.	The subject peoples adopt English and French, socialism, nationalism, human rights, etc.
The subject peoples demand equal status in the name of common imperial values	Illyrians, Gauls and Punics demand equal status with the Romans in the name of common Roman values	Egyptians, Iranians and Berbers demand equal status with the Arabs in the name of common Muslim values	Indians, Chinese, and Africans demand equal status with the Europeans in the name of common Western values such as nationalism, socialism, and human rights
The empire's founders lose their dominance	Romans cease to exist as a unique ethnic group. Control of the empire passes to a new multi-ethnic elite	Arabs lose control of the Muslim world, in favor of a multi-ethnic Muslim elite	Europeans lose control of the global world, in favor of a multi-ethnic elite largely committed to Western values and ways of thinking
The imperial culture continues to flourish and develop	The Illyrians, Gauls, and Punics continue to develop their adopted Roman culture	The Egyptians, Iranians and Berbers continue to develop their adopted Muslim culture	The Indians, Chinese, and Africans continue to develop their adopted Western culture

Source: Harari, Yuval. From Animals into Gods. A Brief History of Humankind, (Israel, 2012), p. 226.

These prescriptive and descriptive distinctions emphasize chronology, but chronology is not standing alone for itself. There are profound implications to this chronological divide. As argued in the previous chapter, the history of globalization begins during the early modern period. Before the emergence of globalization, the world was not a functionally articulated unit. That condition was precisely the ongoing structuration carried on by the process of globalization. In short, the world that world historians look upon and that which

Table 8.2 Abernethy's pulses of "power-profit-proselytization" in global history

Phase	Chronology
Expansion	1415–1773
Contraction	1776–1824
Expansion	1824–1912
Unstable equilibrium	1914–1939
Contraction	1940–1980

global historians look upon are different. The world historian looks at the world as the ultimate unit of analysis from the appearance of *Homo sapiens*, if not *Australopithecus*, up to today for the sake of creating an integrated narrative of human societies or profiting from such a context for pursing any inquiry limited by a temporal, geographical, or thematic scope. The global historian looks at a world that increasingly tightens as a historically emerging functional unity in the search for worldwide connections that transform the shape of societies locally as well as enhance the articulation of a globalized world. Many of the empires performing the "Imperial Wheel" did not lead toward globalization. All of the empires belonging in "the power-profit-proselytization synergy," instead, created the globalized world.

Moreover, world and global historians look at these different worlds for different purposes. World history adopts the world as its ultimate space unit along a time span that comprehends all stages of human existence. This approach results in manifold narratives of the entire human past or some specifically defined cross-sectional issues or time period. These narratives provide the largest reservoir of possible contexts within which any historical inquiry can be conducted. World history is, then, the broadest historical approach to the human past. Global historians instead focus on the global potential of connections and their implications for clearly defined space units or subjects.

Global history

Global history adopts the interconnected world created by the process of globalization as its larger unit of analysis, which provides the ultimate context for the analysis of any historical entity, phenomenon, or process. Therefore, the first outstanding feature of global history research and publications is the interplay between a particular subject of study (for example, a society, a commodity, or an invention) and a globalizing world. The second major feature is that while the global horizon remains a constant, the particular subject of study can be defined very narrowly and specifically or very broadly and generally. The entire spectrum of scales applies for defining the subject of study. For instance, if a particular space is brought into dialogue with the globalizing world, this space might be as small as a village and as large as a continent. If the subject is a time period, its duration might be as short as one year and as long as a couple of centuries. What is crucial is the attempt to relate the specific subject of study, no matter how large or small its scale, with the globalizing world. A series of global history publications makes this point very clear.

For example, in *1688: A Global History* John Wills focuses his attention on both a very narrowly defined time period and on the lives of very few characters. However, these biographical accounts of Dom Joao Manoel Grilho, a Congolese chief, Cornelia van Nijenroode, a Netherlander-Japanese woman from Batavia, and Eusebio Chini, a missionary Jesuit in America waiting for his appointment to China, are portrayed throughout the background of an increasingly globalizing world. Through the interplay between the life trajectories of these characters, the nature of global cultural contacts are being explored. Conversely, the processes of global integration conditioned the particular fates that each of these characters confronts in their new locations.[6]

Conversely, C. A. Bayly's *The Birth of the Modern World, 1780–1914: Global Connections and Comparisons* exemplifies the adoption of a particular period as well as some prominent figures but on a far larger scale. Nevertheless, the interplay between the subject of study and the globalizing world remains a common ground between these two books. In this book, Bayly emphasizes the interconnections and worldwide interdependence in the "long nineteenth century." Although the book deals with usual nineteenth-century topics—industrialization, state building, nationalism, liberalism, socialism, and imperialism—by establishing global connections, a new perspective is offered. These connections are established in dealings with the decline of Islamic empires, rebellions in China (1850s) and India (1857–1859), the American Civil War, the European revolutions (1789, 1848), and Mexico's liberation (1867). Global connections are pursued not only in high political spheres but also in daily life in habits of dressing, eating, talking, and socializing.[7]

A similar understanding of global history as the interplay between a globalizing world and any subject on whatever scale is visualized through examples articulated by space or themes. Akira Iriye's book *China and Japan in the Global Setting* represents an early and classical example of a global history articulated through space units.[8] A more surprising example comes when the space unit under scrutiny is a tiny kingdom brought into an interplay with the wider globalizing world. In *The World and a Very Small Place in Africa* Donald Wright reconstructs the global impacts made by the great powers upon the tiny kingdom of Niumi. A 400-square-mile entity on the northern margins of the Gambia River, this tiny kingdom underwent a series of transformations since the arrival of the Europeans. Starting with the establishment of the first plantation systems during the days of Portuguese hegemony through its specialization as a peanut producer after its incorporation by Great Britain in 1891, all structural shifts are attributed to the interplay between the local and the global.[9]

The *Journal of Global History*, as the major venue for periodical publications on global history, is indicative of the specificities of this branch vis-à-vis world history. This journal concentrates, for the most part, on the modern world. Articles are monographs based on the analysis of primary sources. A predominant strategy is to entangle and contextualize whatever subject is at stake within the emergent globalized world that materialized starting in the sixteenth century. These types of subjects, research strategies, and genres observed in the *Journal of Global History* are common to those present in global history books. This consonance differs from world history's distinction between the broad accounts provided by the books and the more focalized cross-sectional articles. This difference stresses that while world history is a branch deeply committed to teaching, global history is primarily a branch devoted to research.

World history in the singular

Adopting the world as the ultimate space unit is the specific way in which world history confronts the original disciplinary assumption of studying self-enclosed units usually enclosed by political boundaries. This way of transcending boundaries is clearly different from the comparative ways of comparative history and historical sociology that maintain self-enclosed units and from civilizational analysis that creates its largest enclosed units. It is also different from contemporary connective histories as international history connects between two or more nation-states and transnational history adopts a process of transference or a transnational entity as its unit of analysis.

Moreover, the world history way of transcending boundaries is even different from global history and the history of globalization. As explained, global history's unit of analysis is the world articulated by the processes of globalization into a functional unit. As for the world-system, its world is a constructed, fixed abstraction of core, semi-peripheries, and peripheries related by their division of labor and unequal exchanges. The world of world history is not predetermined in any way, neither historically nor conceptually. It is not historically predetermined because no historical forces created an articulated world before the early modern period. It is not conceptually predetermined because world history is not a deductive enterprise with a top-down scheme for organizing and interpreting the world. This is the singularity of world history in transcending boundaries and in confronting the embedded assumption of self-enclosed units of disciplinary historiography.

However, it is in the time dimension that world history excels in its originality as well as in confronting the most basic assumption of the historical discipline: the beginning of history. History can be understood with two basic different meanings. History as a subject matter is the human past. History as a profession is a discipline with a set of methods and rules. As the academic discipline of history emerged during the last part of the nineteenth century, methods and rules predominated over the subject matter. In this way, the disciplinary requirement of basing research upon written records excluded most of human experience from the realm of history. All of human experience before the development of written records about 5000 years ago was relegated to the category of prehistory. As with the self-enclosed units assumption for the space dimension, this temporal assumption adopted at the very beginnings of the profession was never called into question, no matter how radically the discipline was transformed by economic, social, cultural, or postcolonial histories. It was only world history that shifted from privileging the disciplinary meaning of history to fully embrace history as subject matter. In this way, all of human experience became the subject of history.

These two fundamental defining premises of world history, the world as an ultimate unit of analysis and all time span of human experience, lead to the other two subsequent features of this branch of historical knowledge. First, there is the articulation of broad narratives covering the entire chronology of the human past and cross-sectional thematic accounts with similarly ambitious timeframes. Second, world history is orientated toward teaching introductory surveys at college and high school.

There are two basic forms of narratives covering all of the human past: textbooks and synthesis. The difference between these two genres is in the balance between information and interpretation. Textbooks favor information, while syntheses emphasize interpretation. Textbooks usually are collective efforts. Syntheses usually are personal visions. Textbooks provide a general survey of most prominent developments in human societies all around the world and all along the chronological time span. The evolution and migrations of hominids in general and *Homo sapiens* in particular are the common departure point. Agriculture, river valley civilizations, empires, religions, colonialism, industrialization, and modernities are the standard stages. Textbooks share similarities not only in defining these stages but also in the bulk of information provided for each of them. Nevertheless, there are particular emphases and exclusive cases and examples that generate nuances between them. Moreover, as much as textbooks are oriented toward information, they are articulated by some organizing principles in which resides their singularity.

Organizing principles are, however, the outstanding feature of world history syntheses. It is through the articulation of these principles fleshed out by selected historical examples that world historians aim to provide perspective, proportion, and context for any particular historical phenomenon. These

Table 8.3 World history in a nutshell: Major transformations by variables

- **Climate:** End of last Ice Age (9600 BCE)—Little Ice Age (1300–1850)
- **Environment:** Local human impact—Global human impact
- **Economy:** Agricultural Revolution (since ca. 12,000 BCE)—Industrial Revolution (since ca. 1800)
- **Demography:** Six million (12,000 BCE)—one billion (1800)—seven billion (today)
- **Society:** Egalitarian societies—tributary relations—capitalist relations traditional—modern—post-modern
- **Gender:** Egalitarian societies—polarization—growing equality
- **Politics:** Clan decision-making—elite politics—mass politics
- **Warfare:** Whole clan participation—warrior class—national draft—professionalization
- **Ideology (meaning):** Animism—polytheism—Axial Age—Scientific Revolution
- **Civilizations (Cultures):** Multiple regional civilizations—encompassing modern civilization and multiple modernities

three are offered by zooming out the lenses of historical observation. By doing so, major trends, patterns, and turning points are visualized across the world and along large time periods. For example, the Agricultural Revolution (about 12,000 years before the present) and the Industrial Revolution (ca. 1750 and onward) are the recurrent economic turning points related to many other major transformations in many synthetic works. Both economic transformations were preceded by an ice age (end of the last Ice Age around 9600 BCE, and end of the Little Ice Age, 1300–1850) and took place in a particularly suitable geographical settings. Agriculture took root along river valleys such as the Fertile Crescent (ranging from Mesopotamia to Egypt), and industry started along the Coal Crescent (ranging from England to Germany). Both economic turning points were also followed by a profound series of social transformations.

Demographically they resulted in an unprecedented growth in population (10 million around 6000 BCE; one billion around 1800). Socially, they established new types of social relations: tributary and capitalist, respectively. In terms of gender relations, the Agricultural Revolution resulted in a strong polarization, while the Industrial Revolution contributed to progressively eroding the gap. The first revolution created the elite politics backed by the entrenchment of a warrior class, while the second revolution resulted in the advent of mass politics, including the establishment of the national draft. In the sphere of cosmology, Axial Age schools of thought provided meaning to agricultural societies, while the Industrial Revolution is associated with the Scientific Revolution as a new mode of thinking.

As these major transformations occurred differently in different regions, world historical surveys are also articulated more or less explicitly by three major regional divergences: the "Greatest Divergence," the "Great Divergence," and the "American Divergence." The Greatest Divergence of them all is that between the development of Eurasia and America fully detached since the end of the last glacial age until 1492. In a nutshell, this Greatest Divergence refers to the lack of large mammals in America, the larger variety of plant species in Eurasia, and the geographical disposition of the continents (east-west axis for Eurasia; north-south axis for America) that enhanced or prevented, respectively, the diffusion of products and germs. These preliminary Eurasian advantages resulted from the division of labor and specialization in a huge gap between the Old and New Worlds represented by guns and steel.

The Great Divergence, coined by Kenneth Pomeranz, addressed the divergent path of development within Eurasia. In this account, Europe moved ahead due to a large series of intertwined factors that includes the legacies of the feudal past and the richness of subsoil in coal, as well as the combination of maritime trade with naval power and the collaboration between entrepreneurs and states, and, last but not least, the exploitation of African slaves and American resources.[10] To these divergences between the Old World and the New World, as well as those within Old World societies, the third major divergence concerns the huge gap that unfolded between North and Latin America starting in pre-Columbian times but enhanced and accelerated by colonization, emancipation, and entanglements between the two areas. Consideration of these three divergences is normally followed by a discussion of tendencies and attempts to converge since the twentieth century.

World history tracks these transformations and patterns worldwide no matter how connected or not world societies were. In fact, the connectivity of societies in world history studies runs along a spectrum from non-existent to tightly articulated. Under historical circumstances in which there is no connectivity between societies at all, there are four basic justifications to adopt the world as the ultimate unit of analysis. The first and simplest is that by definition a world historical survey must include all of the world regions despite the fact of disconnection. A second justification is that this disconnection is just a matter of several millennia, which viewed in perspective and proportion is but a limited parenthesis (about 10,000 years out of as much as 200,000 years) in a history that was otherwise started by human migration across the globe and continued with the encounters of these communities previously dispersed. A third justification is that even if unconnected during this parenthesis, all world regions are simultaneously impacted by shared climatic conditions.

For example, the end of both the Ice Age and the Little Ice Age had equally impacted the world at large, even though the world was completely unconnected around 9600 BCE in contrast to the globalized world of 1850. The fourth justification is that although unconnected, many societies, to some extent because of the shared climate change impacts, underwent similar evolutionary processes. The independent and relatively simultaneous emergence of agriculture worldwide is a crucial example of this type of justification. Many other evolutionary examples include the emergence of division of labor, class differentiation, cities, states, empires, Axial Age worldviews, and religions. All of these evolutionary processes shared by many societies worldwide are causally related to the advent of agriculture and temporally cover much of the 10,000 year parenthesis of world disconnection. In any event, disconnection was not absolute during the second half of this 10,000 year period.

A series of contacts were progressively unfolding since the consolidation of river valley agricultural societies. Their existence, expansion, and intensification provide a fifth justification for adopting the world as the ultimate unit of analysis. By the time that these contacts became well established interdependent relations all over the planet, the raison d'être for the world to be the ultimate unit of analysis becomes apparent. World historians share this sixth justification for the world as the ultimate unit of analysis with global historians. For global historians, though, this justification is the first one.

Besides broad narratives covering all of the chronology of the human past in the form of textbooks or syntheses, world history provides cross-sectional themes in which a particular variable, issue, or phenomenon is followed up with the world as its ultimate special context. A clear example of that is the series *Themes in World History*, edited by Peter Stearns. This series cross-sectioned world history through, by now, 26 themes in economic, political, cultural, and social issues such as agriculture and trade, wars and revolutions, religion and science, and gender and education, respectively. Most of these books present their subjects along the chronological range developed in textbooks and syntheses. Therefore, the recurrent structure in many of them includes chapters for the transition from hunters and gathers into agriculture, classical civilizations, the post-classical period (ca. 500–1500)—characterized by the preponderance of religions and Eurasian connections—European expansion and colonialism, industrialization and imperialism, and current globalization. Only the books on the United States, sport, consumerism, and poverty are exclusively modern.

This kind of historical literature provides historians from all walks of method and with different approaches with the largest repertoire of contexts to interpret any historical phenomenon or development. At the same time, the broad narratives provided by world history as well as the cross-sectional thematic accounts are indicative of its additional distinctive feature, its orientation toward teaching. The emergence and development of world history is closely associated with the development of the teaching curriculum in North American universities.

By privileging broad narratives and cross-sectional thematic accounts, world history literature is also innovative in representing a departure from one of the most cherished principles of academic historiography: the close scrutiny of primary sources. The result of enlarging time and space scales means in methodological terms that work in world history relies often times on secondary literature and/or on translated sources. This last feature represents a major divergence from the fundamental disciplinary duty of pursuing sources in their primary form and, therefore, results in strong caveats and even reluctance on the part of many historians in relation to the newer branch of world history. Nevertheless, there is an alternative way to ponder this methodological departure made by world historians from the most sacrosanct of the rules of the discipline. After more than a century of professional historiography and especially as a result of the large growth of historical publications during the last four decades, there is huge body of secondary literature. Moreover, this quantitative growth in historical publications is related to the specialization of the discipline not only in geographic units and time periods but also in specific variables, subjects, approaches, and methods. The result is a huge historiography highly fragmented in need of connection and synthesis. By pursuing this goal, world history is not only diverging methodologically from academic historiography at large but also converging with the historical discipline in its unique way.

Despite prioritizing teaching and departing from a reliance on primary sources, there is also a research dimension to world history. One of the main venues for world history research is the *Journal of World History*. Although the length of articles is unsuitable for the kind of broad narratives offered by world historians, the cross-sectional thematic accounts are good feats for this form of publication. For example, by defining a well-specified subject such as procedures of exclusion—instead of a general one as done in the above-mentioned book series edited by Peter Stears—Benjamin Z. Kedar developed a typology that matches up types of political organizations and methods of exclusion. Deportation appears as typical of empires, political exile as characteristic of city-states, and corporate expulsion as recurrent in the emergent European state system. This last particular form of exclusion, defined as the banishment of an entire category of subjects beyond the physical boundaries of a political entity, emerged from a singular conjuncture. Its origins lie in the convergence of an irrational motivation, the delimitation of the spiritual boundaries of the Christian society, a rational means of execution, and the increasing capability of secular rulers to protect their realms. Its functionality derives from conditions such as the limited size of European incipient states and their efficient machinery. From these conditions resulted the gradual replacement during the Middle Ages of massacres with corporate expulsion. Kedar's conceptualization and study of the previously neglected phenomenon of corporate expulsion offers a new perspective to the prolonged search by world history for understanding the uniqueness of the West.[11]

World history, then, is a unique historical branch distinguished by its time-space framework—the world and the whole human past as its ultimate units—as well as by its publication forms, orientation toward teaching, and singular methodology. And yet despite these singularities, world history is often times understood as the right label for all or most of the branches moving beyond the boundaries described so far. The reason for that metonymic use of the concept of world history is that world history was indeed the most widely encompassing branch until the advent of big history. These two issues, the advent of big history and all-encompassing world history, will bring this survey on the 12 branches moving toward global thinking to a close.

Big history

Big history is clearly distinctive from all other cross-boundary branches of history due to its multidisciplinary approach that studies the histories of the universe, planet Earth, life, and human societies from the beginnings of time up to the present as a unified story of growing complexity. This overall narrative is structured by eight thresholds or major turning points. The first threshold consists of the Big Bang that created the universe some 13.7 billion years ago. The second threshold is the creation of the stars, the first complex objects that started appearing around 13.1 billion years ago and that provided the source of energy and raw materials for all subsequent developments. The third threshold is the creation of the chemical elements inside of the stars or in the explosion of dying stars (supernovae). The fourth threshold focuses on the formation of the solar system, the planets, and particularly planet Earth, starting around 4.6 billion years ago. The emergence of life on Earth, around 3.5 billion years ago, represents the fifth threshold. The appearance of *Homo sapiens* and the beginning of the Paleolithic era some 250,000 years ago represent the sixth threshold. The seventh threshold was surpassed with the adventure of agriculture. The eighth threshold consists of the rise of the modern world. In order to grasp the different scales, this wide narrative is collapsed by way of illustration from 13 billion years into 13 years, resulting in the occurrence of the Big Bang 13 years ago, appearance of life on Earth four years ago, the evolution of hominids three days ago, the emergence of agriculture five minutes ago, and the Industrial Revolution six seconds ago.

Big historians are also tracking patterns, although at this largest scale the patterns under scrutiny aim to link all parts of the past through much more general phenomena such as energy consumption, increasing complexity, and potential disorder.

The adjective "big," then, qualifies history in four ways that make this branch clearly distinctive. Big means all possible scales: societal, biological, geological, and cosmological. Concomitantly, big also means fully-fledged multidisciplinarity, engaging all necessary disciplines to encompass these scales. The combination of these two meanings of the big qualifier led to the third and most fundamental. Since its emergence and up to the current wave of history writing beyond boundaries, the historical profession was a disciplinarily defined field. That is, history as the (re)construction of the past as scrutinized from written records. World history dares to redefine the profession as a subject matter rather than disciplinary enterprise. What matters is the human past as a goal, not the written records as a means. Therefore, as far as there were *Homo* species there is world history. The big qualifier of history is much more daring than that, as the anthropocentric component of history is totally removed. What makes history big is that all of the past, farther back than the emergence of hominid species, is woven into a single story. Moreover, by following cosmological principles, big also qualifies history by engaging in discussing the long-term future.

These four features make big history a clearly different historical branch. Nevertheless, big history shares some features with world history. In both cases, a powerful drive in their origins lies in curricula development. The first courses in big history that appeared in the 1970s and 1980s were taught by scholars such as Eric Chaisson and John Mears. However, it was David Christian who launched the first course under this name in 1989. His success led toward a sustained development of the branch. Subsequently, both branches are strongly geared toward teaching and the wider public. Related to that condition but also associated with their type of contents, synthetic books are a leading genre of publication. Big history is also aiming to develop textbooks to enhance the teaching of the subject, a landmark amply achieved by world history by now. As for publications beyond teaching related formats such as synthetic books and textbooks, world history launched a professional journal at an early stage as well as a series of thematic books. Big history is just taking its very first step in publishing beyond synthetic books. There are few publications associated with big history, which titles (and subjects) are not about the cosmos, the universe, space, life, evolution, or the like. A counterexample is Christian's article on the "chronometric revolution" in which he presents the radiometric dating techniques based on the breakdown of radioactive materials that allowed the reconstruction of a periodization back to the origin of the universe. Reportedly, a new genre referred to as "little big histories" is in the making and based on relating small subjects with long-term processes. Quaedackers' work-in-progress relating the history of construction and the availability of materials resulting from cosmic and geological processes is a case in point. The success of this type of project could take Big History beyond master narratives and into a research field.

Thinking history globally: Twelve paths, one metonym

A metonym is a figure of speech that refers to a whole by naming only a prominent part of it. For example, by naming the sails, we can actually refer to the ship; by saying Wall Street, we actually refer to the American economy in some cases; and by saying world history, we actually refer to histories that go beyond national, linguistic, and regional boundaries.

The H-Net webpage states at its heading

> What is World History? World history, for the purposes of H-WORLD, is defined broadly to include history beyond the national level. Thus defined, it includes comparative, interactive, transregional and planetary studies of history. It includes but is not limited to history of ancient and modern "civilizations." It includes "big history," which reaches back before human evolution, and also includes contemporary global history. World history can even be intensely local, when it focuses on global forces influencing the life of a given community, or when an individual or community is taken as a metaphor for larger issues. In any of its definitions, world history emphasizes connections among historical phenomena. Because world history is relatively new as an organized field of study, its conceptual framework and canons of presentation are in flux, so that "how to look at world history?" is as central to discussions on this list as are "what happened in world history?" and "how to teach world history?"[12]

The meaning of world history in this statement is all inclusive. All historical branches moving beyond political borders are brought under the roof of world history. That is, this particular usage of the term world history makes it a synonym of all 12 history branches presented in this book. After accomplishing the daunting task of individualizing each branch as a category, network, and historiographical project, it is worth considering the use of just one generic concept for all border crosser historiographies leading to thinking globally about history. After all, this metonymic use of world history gained enough support not only to guide such an important meeting point as H-Net but also to define the title of one of the most comprehensive and recent companions in the field, the *Companion to World History* edited by Douglas Northrop.[13]

Besides world history in its singular meaning, this Blackwell Companion also includes chapters in comparative history, big history, world-system analysis, global history, and the history of globalization. Moreover, it is very telling that the literature produced by world history defined in this generic way is structured in this companion in two main sections: one under the heading of comparisons, the other under the heading of connections. This book structure coincides precisely with one of the crucial distinctions offered in this book between those branches crossing boundaries comparatively as opposed to those doing it connectively.

Interestingly, world history is the only branch out of the 12 that is taken to represent the "spatial turn," the "new regimes of space," "global spatiality," or the "global trend." No attempts were made to designate it all using historical sociology, transnational history, or big history. More interestingly for that matter, no attempt was made to designate all 12 branches as global history, which, by the way, points once again to the fact that world history and global history are not synonyms. World history was the only concept advanced in an all-inclusive way because it indeed shares significant overlaps with all other 11 branches. World history partially overlaps with the chronology of global history and the history of globalization (ca. 1500 onward). World history partially overlaps spatially with oceanic history. World history partially overlaps with big history in both time and space: the last 3.5 million years on planet Earth. Both branches also stand out for their dedication to teaching and the publication of comprehensive narratives. World history can partially overlap, depending on the authors' approaches, with comparative history, entangled history, and the world-system approach. The building blocks of many world history textbooks and synthetic books are civilizations, a feature shared with civilizational analysis. World history shares with historical sociology the search and identification of recurrent patterns. The study of transnational transfers by transnational history falls within world history's

Table 8.4 World history overlaps with all other branches

	World history
Comparative history	Comparisons included
Civilizational analysis	Civilizations as building blocks
Historical sociology	Identification and construction of patterns
World-system approach	Application of world-system approach
Global history	Chronological overlap ca. 1500-onwards
History of globalization	Part-whole relation; focalized phenomenon
Big history	Chronological overlap ca. two million years before the present onward
	Specialization in teaching
	Master narratives and textbooks
International history	Includes international relations
Transnational history	Focus on movement and transfers
Entangled history	Entanglements included
Oceanic history	Part-whole relation; focalized area

interest in contacts and interactions between societies and cultures and so does the history of international relations.

This comprehensive series of overlaps explains why out of the 12 branches going beyond boundaries it is only world history that is offered as an umbrella term for them all.

So, are the 12 branches of history set in stone? Or rather should one generic name suffice for all the branches? In the *Companion to World History*, Barbara Weinstein describes the different shapes of the generic world by defining ten different paths that include: big history, civilizations approach, comparative history, study of bodies in movement and peripatetic lives (kin to the definition of transnational history here), oceanic area, "institutional world history," transnational history, international history, global history, and the history of globalization. This list is astonishingly similar to the list of branches presented in this book. Neither Weinstein's ten nor the 12 presented in this book are set in stone the way that the Law of the 12 Tables were in the forum of Rome. Those are just useful typologies to visualize the wide array of available tools and variety of possibilities open to us as we are willing and aiming to think globally about history.

It is time now to visualize the 12 branches altogether in a general and last rehearsal for applying global thinking to the practice of writing history.

9
All Together Now, a Last Rehearsal: Thinking Globally on Border Crossing Phenomena, the First World War

Perón's rise to power in 1943 and his presidencies during 1946–1955 unfolded within the boundaries of Argentina. As such, its history was mostly written from a national, state-based perspective. The thought experiment that begins this book added to the topical range of the historiography on Perón's Argentina—politics, foreign affairs, economics, society, gender, culture, and ideas—revealing the manifold venues opened up by moving beyond the borders of the nation-state as the unit of analysis. At the same time, by applying the 12 branches of cross-boundary history to Perón's Argentina each branch was concretely illustrated in its singularity.

Although the thought experiment performed these two tasks conveniently, there is a flip side to it as well. The point of departure for the application of all 12 branches was the history of a political regime within an enclosed nation-state. As shown in the example of Perón's Argentina, each of the 12 branches can enrich to a great extent a nation-state-based history. However, these cross-boundary branches can not only enhance nation-state-based histories but also, more fundamentally, each of them define their own writing styles and subjects of research, which usually are, as the branches themselves, border-crossing topics or border-crossing units of analysis.

Coming to the close of this journey, and having been provided with a clear conceptual framework, it is time now to visualize once again all 12 branches together in their singularities, overlaps, clusters, and manifold collaborations. Two features stand out as advantages in this final exercise in comparison with the opening thought experiment. On the one hand, by now all 12 branches have been defined, exemplified, analyzed, and classified. In this sense, the exercise provides an opportunity for review and assessment. On the other hand, this time all 12 branches are being applied to a subject that by its very definition is a cross-boundary one.

The assassination of Archduke Franz Ferdinand, the heir to the Austro-Hungarian throne, on June 28, 1914 in Sarajevo sparked the outbreak of the

158 *Thinking History Globally*

First World War. Two sets of aligned states—Britain, France, and Russia (the Triple Entente, Entente Powers, or Allies), joined by Italy, Romania, Greece, and Japan, versus Germany and Austria-Hungary (the Central Powers), joined by the Ottoman Empire and Bulgaria—were set into motion toward a military collision with a death toll of about ten million combatants. The global reach of European empires resulted in a war that spread beyond Europe and throughout Africa, Asia, the Pacific Rim, and the Indian and Atlantic oceans. The intervention of the United States tipped almost four years of stalemate in favor of the Entente. The Central Powers paid a huge price for their defeat: Austria-Hungary was carved into seven newly created states; the Ottoman Empire was dismantled from within by a nationalist revolution that created the state of Turkey and stripped from without by Britain and France from its territories in the Middle East beyond Anatolia; also Germany underwent a revolution from within that replaced the empire with a republic, while from outside it was charged as the culprit for the outbreak of the war, resulting not only in the loss of territories but also in the payment of heavy reparations to the winners. Also among members of the Triple Entente drastic transformations unfolded. Most immediate and sharply in the Russian Empire that ceased to exist by March 1917. The Soviet Union finally replaced it as a result of the Bolshevik Revolution on November 1917, loosing, however, its grip on the Baltic Rim. In the British and French empires collapse was not immediate. However, the war as observed by colonial subjects both at the front and at home put into motion increasing demands for self-determination that actualized three decades later, subsequently resulting in a global process of decolonization. It was only the United States that seemed to return to "normalcy," as incumbent President Harding referred to it, while in fact major transformations took place there too as reflected, for instance, in its transition from a debtor nation into the largest creditor state.

All of these outcomes among others set the stage for the unfolding of the twentieth century on a global scale. The First World War was a global phenomenon. That was the case because this conflagration unfolded in a world functionally articulated by the process of globalization. In such an interconnected war, soldiers from all continents in the globe fought in theaters across the world, from Pacific Islands to Africa and from Europe to the Middle East. As such, the First World War is a subject intrinsically suitable for analysis from the perspective of global history.

Thinking history globally: Contextualizing on a bigger scale

Global history

The above opening overview of the First World War can be portrayed as an outline for a global history perspective on the conflagration. A fully-fledged narrative following this outline can represent a global history of the First World War. Moreover, a global history approach can move up and down along the scale of inquiry. A move down scale would address the First World War as the ultimate context for whatever local process striving to underline the global–local connections. A move up scale, instead, would place the First World War within the context of warfare throughout the process of European internecine fighting for the sake of continental and global hegemony.

Besides providing a fully-fledged global history of the First World War, global history can also move down the scale of inquiry by offering the First World War as a meaningful global context for the study of the local. For example, in the global context of the First World War, a global history of a place named Tarkwa could be written. Tarkwa is a small town in contemporary Ghana, previously called the Gold Coast. In May 1914, the British and Australian geologists Sir Albert Ernest Kitson and Edmund Oswald Thiele discovered manganese ores about ten kilometers from Tarkwa. Manganese is a mineral used in the production of ammunitions. The mines nearby Tarkwa provided 32,000 tons of manganese during the First World War for that purpose. In conjuncture with the British war effort, this strategic finding changed the course of Tarkwa's history. The town was connected by railway to the Atlantic shore and by entering the global economy its landscape, demography, society, and culture were thoroughly transformed for years to come. The intense mining exploitation and further exploration resulted in the discovery of high quality diamond deposits by 1919. In 1934 the diamonds coming from these deposits represented a 39 percent of the global supply. In the wake of mining, the development of hydroelectric power was envisioned as early as 1915 in order to modernize exploitation. Although this project was achieved only after Ghana gained independence, it represents a long-lasting effect of the local–global conjunction between a small village in Africa and the global context provided by the First World War. Global history would apply this same type of local–global conjuncture inquiry to places of different scales, from small villages to countries, areas, and ocean basins. And not only to places but also to people, institutions, technology, commodities, fashion, and so on. What matters most is the local–global conjuncture.

Alternatively, global history can take the First World War up the scale of inquiry by placing it in the context warfare for the achievement of European and global hegemony. Such a move would lead to connecting this conflagration to several previous instances in which those goals were pursued by military means. The Revolutionary and Napoleonic wars are the obvious candidates, as these series of wars confronted the French Empire with seven different European coalitions between 1792 and 1815. Although these wars were fought in Europe and for the sake of dominating that continent, their implications were global. Napoleonic occupation of Spain led to the dismantlement of most of the Spanish Empire. The victories of the sixth and seventh coalitions against Napoleon and the French Empire established the Concert of Europe in the continent and British hegemony in the globe for a century to come, precisely until the First World War. In its turn, the Napoleonic Wars can be portrayed as a French *revanche* or second attempt following its defeat in another world war: the Seven Years' War (1756–1763). This war confronted two coalitions: the Habsburg and Bourbon dynasties in charge of the Holy Roman Empire and the French and Spanish empires, respectively, who confronted the Hanoverian and Hohenzollern dynasties ruling the British Empire and Prussia, respectively. The Prussian war effort in Europe allowed Great Britain to concentrate in prevailing at sea and establishing naval supremacy. The scope of the war was, therefore, truly global, affecting not only Europe but also the Americas, West Africa, India, and the Philippines. Great Britain made major gains in most of those locations, including eastern Canada (New France), Florida, some islands in the West Indies, Senegal, and the French trading outposts in the Indian subcontinent. The Revolutionary and Napoleonic Wars together with the Seven Years' War can be brought into a larger sequence of European wars with global outcomes in which France and Britain galvanized opposing coalitions around them. Such a sequence would include the War of the Grand Alliance (1688–1697), the French and Indian War (1689–1763), the War of the Spanish Succession (1701–1714), the War of the Austrian Succession (1742–1748), and the American Revolutionary War (1775–1783). This entire sequence was portrayed as the "Second Hundred Years War" (1688–1815).

This kind of inclusive approach to the French–English confrontation aiming for European and global hegemony can also be applied to the First World War by connecting it to the Second World War (1939–1945), seeing the two wars as an ongoing confrontation in which Germany contested British global hegemony between 1914 and 1945. In a similar way, all wars contesting Spanish and Portuguese global hegemony can be brought under the inclusive name of the "Eighty Years War" (1568–1648). Throughout this period the Hapsburg dynasty ruling the Holy Roman Empire, Spain, and Portugal (since 1580) confronted several coalitions that at different times included France, England, Dutch provinces, German principalities, Sweden, and the Ottoman Empire. As in later world wars, European and global hegemony were at stake, and war theaters included the Americas and the Indian Ocean. This conflict unfolded in tandem with the overseas expansion of the Dutch, English, and French at the expense of the defeated empires of Portugal and Spain.

Thus, moving from the First World War up the scale of inquiry into a global history of world wars, this approach offers a tour de horizon in which the articulation of the globe into an integrated economy and society emerged amid three major world wars during 1568–1648, 1688–1815, and 1914–1945. The Eighty Years War was a long-lasting campaign sustained by the laggard imperialist states that confronted and finally defeated the first global empires, Portugal and Spain. The Second Hundred Years' War was fought to fill in the power vacuum left by that defeat. Finally, the world wars brought old foes, Great Britain and France, together in dealing with Germany, the nascent contender for European and global hegemony.

World history

The brief overview on the First World War opening this chapter can serve as the core of a world history narrative on the First World War too. However, as world history narratives have teaching history as a priority, an additional genre for presenting the war is that of world history textbooks. At heart, world history textbooks structure their presentations of the First World War along similar lines of the overview offered above. This genre, however, provides more information and stands out because of its didactic style. In this way, in the short chapter allocated to the First World War, a world history textbook would explain at an entry level what were the ongoing situations within and between the contender states before the outbreak of the war, who were the leading statesmen in charge of those states, what was the overall course of the war, and what the outcomes were as reflected by the settlement agreements. To take the "before the outbreak of war" point as an example, the status of the German Empire as the rising continental power following the wars of unification would be highlighted together with the implications of this transformation. Namely, the decline of France's power as a result of being defeated by Germany in 1860 and the subordinated status of the Austro-Hungarian Empire since its defeat by Germany in 1866. These developments would be matched by Britain's growing concern with this break of the continental balance of power, a balance that since 1815 had allowed Britain to concentrate on its overseas expansion. Russia was in a shambles following its military defeats in 1856 and 1905, and because of the mounting discontent of the subjects of this absolutist monarchy, it was entering a phase of reform and modernization. A world history textbook would provide similar specifications for the opening conditions of the rest of the states, integrating the rival alliances as well as for the subsequent stages in the unfolding of the war, its course and outcomes, aiming to fulfill one of the goals of world history, teaching history to citizens of a globalized world.

For its second major goal, bringing perspectives and proportions, world history applies the cross-sectional theme approach that departs from identifying the most fundamental features underlying a phenomenon, in this case the First World War, in order to track them back in time. This exercise was already applied, in fact, by the global history of world wars. That is, in the global history of world wars sketched above the most fundamental features underlying the First World War were the outbreaks of military conflagrations between

European powers in order to achieve or maintain political and economic control both within Europe and on a global scale. Based on these primordial features, the sequence running from the Eighty Years War through the Second Hundred Years' War and up to the world wars was delineated. Moreover, these three sets of world wars not only shared primordial features but also are historically related to one another and all combined are related to a broader process, namely, the emergence of a global world.

A world history search for the occurrence of the fundamental phenomenon of which the First World War is just one occurrence would not be constrained by an interrelated sequence between the wars or by their connection to an overall process of struggle for global dominance. Therefore, both the engagement of European powers and the aim of achieving continental and global hegemony would drop from the list of primordial features. Then, a world history cross-sectional theme approach would offer a more comprehensive and ambitious way to formulate the primordial features underlying the First World War. For example, the underlying primordial feature could be defined as a military conflagration between major powers aiming to achieve or maintain political and economic control of an area as large as their logistical capabilities would allow. A cross-sectional study guided by such a definition would include or choose among, besides the three sets of world wars presented above, major wars such as the wars of Mongol conquests (1206 CE–1324 CE), the First Crusade (1096 CE–1099 CE), the wars of Muslim conquests (622 CE–732 CE), the Byzantine–Sassanid wars (502 CE–628 CE), the Punic War (264 BCE–241 BCE), the wars of Alexander the Great (335 BCE–323 BCE), the Greco-Persian Wars (499 BCE–449 BCE), and the campaigns of Ramesses II (1279 BCE–1213 BCE). These wars can be presented as worlds wars, with world in the plural as the worlds in which they were fought and the worlds that were at stake were not the planet but the restricted worlds that logistical capabilities allowed at the time. In this way, the Mongol wars of conquest represent a Eurasian world war, the First Punic wars a Mediterranean world war, and the succession of the Greco-Persian wars, the wars of Alexander the Great, and the Byzantine–Sassanid wars were East–West world wars. The plurality of the worlds can be extended to domains other than geographic ones, so that the wars of Muslim conquests and the Crusades could belong within a religious world war category, while the campaigns of Ramesses II would be part of the world wars of the ancient worlds. Those are a few examples of the many inquiring venues that a world history cross-sectional theme can open up while addressing the concept of world war. This kind of perspective can be also applied to more restricted aspects identified in the First World War and then distilled into a fundamental cross-sectional theme. For example, among many possibilities, world wars as turning points in world history, world wars and technological innovations, and logistic capacity and the range of world wars.

In dealing with a global issue such as the First World War, two overlaps between a global and world history occur: an overall synthetic narrative of the war, as outlined in the introduction to this chapter, reflects a global history as much as a world history take on the subject. Similarly, the global history upscale perspective of world wars, outlined in the global history section above, fully overlaps with a world history essay on the subject. Once again then, how do global and world histories differ while approaching a global subject such as the First World War? First, there is a chronological divide. Global history considers the globalizing world that started emerging in the modern period. World history knows neither this conceptual requisite nor its attached chronological boundary. Furthermore, for world history, the world before any global articulation is its space unit and the length of human existence its chronology. Therefore, in distinction from global history, world history is not constrained by the globalizing modern world. Second, world history has its particular venues of writing and publication, namely, books on cross-sectional themes and textbooks. Hence, besides the overlaps between global and world history in providing a synthetic overview and in approaching a global history of world wars, each of these historiographical branches has its singularities. World History strives to bring perspectives and proportions by sweeping over long periods of time and geographical scope and prioritizes teaching while relying on secondary sources. Based on primary sources, global history scrutinizes specific local–global conjunctures.

Big history

Global history and world history offer big pictures of the First World War. Both can offer a truly global coverage of this war taking place in three oceans and on three continents. World history can even add to that synthetic view the didactic components necessary for an entry-level introduction. Moreover, moving up the scale of inquiry, global history can portray the First World War as a major confrontation in a series of world wars fought for the sake of European and global dominance. World history can move beyond boundaries, tackling all wars that determined the fates of many self-contained worlds, such as the Mediterranean, the Eurasian, and the ancient worlds. And yet big history can make the First World War even bigger than that. Within its temporal range of 13 billion years, the First World War occurred, if we are to equate all this time to a single day, only two seconds ago. In other words, the First World War is only visible in the scale of modernity that encompasses the last millennium. No sign of it is perceptible in the previous six scales that include, running backward, human history, human evolution, mammalian radiations, the advent of multi-cellular organisms, and the formation of the Earth and its biosphere and the cosmos. In spite of that marginal place at first sight, the First and Second world wars taken as parts of the same sequence represent a remarkable turning point even from a big history perspective. This sequence is partially responsible for nothing less than a decisive moment in the history of the entire biosphere. Technological changes were primary forces leading toward this transformation. They account for the rise of economic global output from about $5 trillion up to the end of the world wars and around $39 trillion in the second half of the century. Such a productive economic capacity turned out to be also an environmentally destructive capacity made apparent in the contamination of fresh water and rangelands, the depletion of oceanic fisheries, deforestation, declining biodiversity, and atmospheric damage. As the world wars were decisive catalysts of the technological innovation that shaped the world since, big history offers this supplementary widest context to bring the world wars into additional perspectives and proportions.

Moreover, the environmentally destructive capacity is closely related to energy consumption. Human per capita consumption of energy has moved since pre-modern times and up to the present from 26,000 to 230,000 calories a day. This total amount includes food as well as energy use in the home, in commerce, in agricultural production, in industry, and in transport. Focusing on food consumption alone, the transition has been from 6000 to 10,000 calories per capita a day, including animal feed. These levels of energy consumption through multidisciplinary lenses may lead research into an additional direction. For example, studies of longevity have shown that low caloric intake, in comparison to either previous caloric intake by the same person or to average caloric intake for a similar body type, leads to a longer life span. Although the processes through which low caloric intake decelerates aging in a variety of species are disputed, the consistent findings indicate that caloric restriction results in longer maintenance of youthful health and in an increase of both median and maximum lifespan. A leading hypothesis sustains that low caloric intake lowers the level of activity of proteins. Organisms confronting this situation recur to autophagy, that is, cell self-eating. Autophagy allows cells to clean and recycle old or damaged cell parts while keeping the cells and the body running efficiently. The life span of the cells increases, the pace of cell replacement decreases, and the organism as a whole increases its lifespan. No clinical studies have been conducted on humans, a gap that big historians can try to fill.

The First World War provides a situation in which caloric intake dropped significantly and to different extents in the home fronts of most societies involved, while no significant modifications occurred in other societies. Concurrently, by the time of the First World War state recordkeeping had advanced enough to allow the reconstruction of life span curves in many societies. Given these two points of departure, approaching the First World War, as well as several historical occurrences of generalized falls in calorie intake, from a big history angle can serve as a huge bank of data to start assessing the effects of low caloric intake in humans. How about a counterintuitive scenario in which life expectancy rose for those that lived throughout the war? As big history stands out for its multidisciplinary approach and the sense that human societies, life, planet Earth, and the universe are all part of the same unified story of growing complexity, it encourages highly innovative multidisciplinary studies in relation to the First World War.

The history of globalization

A leading narrative on the history of globalization portrays globalization as a U-shaped scheme representing one peak of globalization during 1850–1914 named "the first globalization" and a second one from 1973 until today known as "today's globalization." Amid these two peaks lies an understudied deep valley of de-globalization opened, precisely, by the outbreak of the First World War. Therefore, looking from the angle of the history of globalization, the history of the First World War is a turning point in the history of globalization. Major shifts in the economic ties between states resulted from the outbreak of the war. To begin with, finance, trade, and migration between belligerent parties came to an abrupt halt. Second, the economic ties with third parties were affected to different degrees and in diverse ways by the war. These disruptions of the global economy resulted in two types of economic transformations: a reshuffle of the global economy at large and a restructuring of most domestic economies for each nation.

Globally, there was a transformation of the ways in which every national economy reentered the world market. Belligerent nations turned their resources inward. This turn meant that the investments, raw materials, finished products, and workers that they used to place in the world market were consumed domestically. Moreover, due to the war effort, the demand for multiple commodities and products increased while the work force decreased. The final result of these constraints was that the balance of trade of those economies was reverted. Also, financing turned the other way around for belligerent countries that were once lending economies and then became borrower ones. Conversely, non-belligerent nations found a highly demanding market for their commodities and products with steadily rising prices for them. Additionally, their former suppliers suspended or reduced exports encouraging in this way a policy of import substitution. That is, unintendedly, less developed nations were incentivized to narrow the industrial gap by establishing their own industries. Just a few examples make this complex transformation apparent: France, an economy with a solid rural sector, became dependent on Spanish goods, making the Spanish economy thrive during the war years due to a highly positive balance of trade. Britain switched from being a creditor economy into an indebted one. The United States went the other way around. Argentina, an agro-exporter economy par excellence, started industrializing in order to replace their shrinking imports as well as supply the Southern Cone with manufactured goods.

In short, the economic map of the world was redrawn in terms of rural and industrial production, balance of trade, capital investments, and indebtedness.

Domestically, each national economy pursues an adaptation to its new conditions in terms of finance, commodities supply, production, and local and foreign markets. A fundamental feature of this process of adaptation was that states stepped in aiming to adjust their national economic life to the new conditions. Simultaneously, belligerent states also coordinated their economies in order to mobilize them for waging war. It was through central planning that human and material resources were mobilized for the war effort. This new scale of state intervention in national economies on both counts paved the way for the emergence of economic central planning or command economies as a form of economic policy. This economic orientation toward state intervention, to different degrees and in many forms, became characteristic of most national economies till the emergence of neoliberalism as an alternative economic policy that became globalized starting in the 1970s. What all state interventionist policies shared was the holding of the "command heights" of the economy, that is, energy, transportation, infrastructures, and core industries under state control. Moreover, an additional common ground of these policies was the increasing replacement of the world market by a synergy of import substitution and a reinvigorated domestic market stimulated by the state. This synergy supplied the local market with local production that in turn granted wages to local workers turned into consumers. With such domestic transformation evolving rather simultaneously worldwide, it is not surprising that there were global consequences to these local reorganizations of the global economy. State interventionism as a form of national economic management had significant repercussions for the unfolding of economic globalization. In a world of more and more self-relying economies, economic globalization entered a staid curve of decline.

However, it would be paradoxical to conclude that a war fought all over the planet, by troops coming from all the continents, with states declaring war all over the world, and for the sake—ultimately—of global hegemony, brought on the demise of globalization. This paradox could be solved by refocusing the history of globalization. The study of the history of globalization has tended to focus on economic flows. Approached from this perspective, globalization goes hand-in-hand with peaceful periods in a clear-cut correlation. Looking at the history of globalization in conjunction with the First World War, however, can advance an alternative appreciation on the history of globalization. It is just a matter of recognizing that globalization can take many forms other than an economic one.

One of these additional forms has to do with acknowledging the important role that wars have played in the process of globalization. Belligerent powers usually show unparalleled interest in each other's politics, culture, and technology and go out of their way to transport men and resources to each other's territory. Allied powers from across the globe forged similarly strong links, often mobilizing and coordinating the efforts of millions of people across the world. It is plausible then to think about the First World War as a peak of globalization rather than the beginning of its end. Moreover, by applying this alternative standpoint of a history of military—rather than economic—globalization in the late modern era, a reverse U-shape curve could be offered to encapsulate the history of globalization. In sharp contrast to economic globalization, military globalization peaked during the world wars era of 1740–1815, declined in the period of 1815–1870, began to rise dramatically in the late nineteenth century, and reached another peak in the period of 1914–1945.

Thinking history globally: Conceptualizing through social sciences

Historical sociology

Global history provides synthetic overviews of the sequence of world wars that unfolded in tandem with the articulation of a globalizing world. Relying on this kind of global history, historical sociology applies the comparative method to the sequences of world wars (for example, what are the crucial similarities and differences between the Seven Years' War, the Napoleonic Wars, and the First World War?) and, based on crucial agreements between them, recognizes and formulates a recurrent pattern. Such a formulation requires the establishment of a series of necessary and sufficient conditions conducive to the phenomenon under scrutiny, in this case modern world wars. What could be the underlying conditions for the Eighty Years' War, the Second Hundred Years' War, and the world wars sequences? A close comparative scrutiny between these wars could reveal that for all of their specificities and singularities all of them share the following necessary and sufficient conditions:

1. War was preceded—and also punctuated—by colonial expansion.
2. Before the war—and also throughout it—global free trade was blocked by protectionist policies.
3. A relative decline in the power of the hegemonic state in Europe was sensible before the outbreak of war.
4. The ultimate goal of the war was to sustain or expand continental and/or world hegemony.

In a nutshell, these four conditions are observable during the Eighty Years' War, as the first major wave of European colonial expansion led by the Iberian monarchies came full circle by 1571. Back then, the establishment of Manila as a Spanish colony represented the Iberian mastering of the three oceans.

Second, this command of the seas and colonial holds in the Americas, Africa, and Asia was matched by a mercantilist policy devised to sustain a monopolistic trade between the metropolis in Iberia and the colonies abroad. This combination of a monopoly in global colonialism and the trade resulting from it reached its zenith in 1580 with the virtual unification of Spain and Portugal under Phillip II. This was the peak of power from which decline—the third condition—departed, represented by the sinking of the *Armada Invencible* (1588) as well as by four financial crises between 1557 and 1596. Finally, as North Atlantic states—England, France, and the Netherlands—started overcoming their inner problems and, galvanized by unity from within, they launched their global colonial projects, competing with and displacing Iberian hegemony and contesting Spanish hegemony in continental Europe simultaneously.

It was this second wave of European colonialism, precisely, that preceded the Second Hundred Years' War. The foundations of the Dutch, English, and French overseas empires were established back then. As these empires consolidated, they also applied mercantilist policies in order to gain monopolistic trade with their respective colonies. On the eve of the outbreak of this "second world war," French power was at its height in continental Europe. The combination of Dutch and English power, as solidified by the Glorious Revolution (1688), and the advent of William of Orange as the King of England mark the beginning of a turning point in the balance of power. In an attempt to curve French power in continental Europe, the Dutch–English merging galvanized an inter-European coalition, the Grand Alliance. The enhancement of colonial empires at the expense of the French Empire also came in tandem.

The Second Hundred Years' War ended with the British gaining the upper hand and with the establishment of a century long (1815–1914) relatively peaceful world order based on global free trade. That was the *Pax Britannica*. However, the four necessary and sufficient conditions were amassing once again toward the eruption of the world wars of 1914–1945. In the 1830s European colonialism resumed its expansion, now in Africa and Asia. Later, in the wake of the 1870s economic crisis, European states applied protectionist policies, aiming to establish monopolistic ties with their colonies once again as well as protecting their nascent industries. This same decade and since, unified Germany started emerging as a robust competitor to hegemonic Britain, whose respectability was in decline following the Boer wars (1880–1881, 1899–1902) in South Africa. As a latecomer state and colonial power, Germany aspired to match its economic and military might with its political power in the European continent and the world. For the third time in the modern world, the conditions were ripe for the outbreak of a world war.

The world-system approach

From a world-system perspective, the First World War would primarily appear as a challenge posed by imperial Germany to the global British hegemony. Since the end of the Napoleonic Wars (1815), Great Britain became the sole major global power ruling over about one-quarter of the world's population and landmass. Being the world's factory since the Industrial Revolution, Great Britain adopted, diffused, and imposed a policy of global free trade. Economic ties created an "informal empire" in Latin America besides its commonwealth and empire in Asia and Africa. Its might, power, and wealth became an inspirational model for development and progress with which nations of the world strived to become associated with and many others were willing to emulate. Unified in 1870, Germany refused to yield to free trade and embarked on an industrialization project that led the German economy to outproduce that of Great Britain. Reaching the highest economic ladder, backed by the strongest army and fastest-growing navy, Germany was ready to move from economic competition into military confrontation. This confrontation involved additional core states aligned with Great Britain (France, the United States, and Japan), semi-peripheral states (Austro-Hungary, Italy, Russia, and the Ottoman Empire), and peripheral states (Bulgaria and Romania). Germany's failed attempt to displace Great Britain as the hegemonic power of the world-system was resumed in 1939. The First and Second world wars combined resulted in the destruction and conquest of Germany and the weakening of Great Britain's hegemony in the world-system. The United States stepped into this position, resulting in a hegemonic transition of the kind that the modern world-system experienced several times since its formation.

In fact, the First World War would be placed in a longer sequence tracked by the world-system approach. Several candidates could be considered for the hegemon role throughout the existence of the modern world-system. Conversely, these hegemons are paired by counter-hegemons. The list of hegemons may include Portugal, the Netherlands, Great Britain, and the United States. The list of counter-hegemons may consist of Spain, France, Germany, and the Soviet Union. A possible sequence based on these lists would open up in the fifteenth century with a building up of Portuguese hegemony confronted by Spain and submerged by 1580. Subsequently, a defeated Spain (in 1648) paved the way for a short-lived Dutch hegemony, which by 1672 entered its own decline due to English and French harassment. More than a century later, a British hegemony finally crystallized in 1815 after a long struggle with France over world hegemony. It is within this sequential context that the German challenge to the British hegemony came to the fore, resulting not in the displacement of Britain by Germany but in facilitating the rise of the United States as the last hegemonic power, challenged without success by the Soviet Union.

Moreover, based on sequencing hegemonic and counter-hegemonic cycles, the world-system approach would also point toward a series of regularities. For example, in the sequence advanced above, what stands out is the collision between maritime (Portugal, the Netherlands, Great Britain, and the United states) and terrestrial powers (Spain, France, Germany, and the Soviet Union), with maritime powers consistently being hegemons and terrestrial powers being their challengers. Moreover, the balance of power most regularly inclined in favor of maritime powers, with the Dutch defeating Spain, Britain prevailing over France first and Germany later, and the United States overcoming the Soviet Union. While the leading strategy of the former concentrated on command of the seas, the approach of the later was the conquest of the European continent (for example, Charles I, Napoleon, and Hitler). Britain's hegemonic ascent and defense included two consecutive challenging campaigns by its adversaries: the Seven Years' War and the Revolutionary and Napoleonic Wars by the French, and the First and the Second world wars by the Germans.

In this way, the word "system" in the world-system approach can be understood in two ways. The explicit meaning is the tripartite system composed by core, semi-periphery, and peripheral regions entangled in unequal exchanges. Second, as made apparent in this brief sketch on hegemonic wars, the word "system" also denotes an attempt at systematizing the past into a series of recurrent patterns. These two meanings of the word "system" underscore the twofold contribution of the world-system approach to the understanding of the First World War. First, its contextualization within the systemic emergence of coalitions made of semi-peripheral and peripheral states articulated by hegemonic powers in the core. Second, the contextualization of the First World War in a series of sequenced patterns of hegemonic wars throughout the modern period.

Civilizational analysis

As with the Western and Eastern Fronts, comparative history can offer multiple comparisons between various aspects involved in the unfolding of the First World War. It can also look at these very same aspects in contrast to their equivalents in other wars, or it can even confront the First World War and compare it with any other war taken as a whole, where the contrast is meaningful in some respect. Civilizational analysis offers additional possibilities for comparison framed in a very singular way, that is, within the self-contained units defined as civilizations. Under this framing, the first striking feature of the First World War is its European character. Although fought all over the planet, by troops coming from all the continents, with states declaring war all over the world, and for global hegemony, the First World War was also a European war. Moreover, as the global perspective has shown, European internecine fighting was a constant feature of European civilization for about 400 years, with three world wars unfolding during 1568–1648, 1688–1815, and 1914–1945. Finally, this is a unique feature of European civilization, as no other civilization engaged in this particular type of conflict. In view of all that, civilizational analysis would raise the question of the uniqueness of the West in the context of the First World War.

The lack of a unifying empire in Europe, the way it existed in other regions (that is, the Ottoman Empire in the Middle East, the Mogul Empire in India, the Chinese Empire under the Ming and Ch'ing dynasties), and the resulting political fragmentation could be advanced as a crucial distinction of European uniqueness on several counts. For one, multiple sovereignties enabled maritime exploration, and subsequently multiple quests for global dominance were undertaken; thus, there was no monopoly on decision making, as in the case of Ming China. Second, political fragmentation resulted in endemic power struggles that recurrently reverted to warfare. Both the quest for global dominance and endemic power struggles stimulated innovation: institutional, scientific, and technological. At the same time, global dominance provided— to different extents by time and place—human and natural resources as well as markets for all the competing fragmented states of Europe. Conversely, cumulative innovations, resources, and markets accelerated the pace of military conflagration as well as its intensity, which reached a new peak in 1914 through 1918.

An alternative path of inquiry for civilizational analysis is that of inter-civilizational contacts. One way to depict the First World War in this context is as a showcase of European civilization for the rest of world civilizations and its impact on them. After four centuries of European colonialism and growing supremacy—in terms of political domination, economic exploitation, European self-perception, and colonized perceptions of Europeans—the civilizations of the world observed the European civilization at its highest military might and its lowest political and moral crisis. They could observe that firsthand because in many cases the war was brought to their doorsteps or alternatively because some of its members went to fight in Europe. They could certainly follow it up secondhand through the by then well-established world press. How were the "masters of the world" perceived anew by colonial and postcolonial subjects amid and in the wake of the war? How was cultural borrowing from the European civilization affected by that? In which ways did the war and reassessment of European civilization contribute to the reformulation of the aspirations, goals, and means of world civilizations? How similar and different were world civilizations in all these regards? Is there uniformity in them or clusters of similarity between some civilizations or unique effects and reactions? In short, the First World War European showcase can be examined as a turning point in the perception of world civilizations in regard to the European one as well as a moment of reformulation of the aims of each civilization in the shade of European carnage.

Thinking history globally: Varieties of connections

Oceanic history

Big history approaches the First World War with multidisciplinary tools. Global and world history embraced the First World War in its truly global scope. Although keeping the global framework, oceanic history would emphasize the oceans at the expense of the continents by looking at the war from docks, ships, and U-boats. In this way, oceanic history can highlight interpretations potentially overlooked while prioritizing the continental dimension. Alternative and complementary views on the First World War could emerge, right from its very beginnings. How about looking at the outbreak of the war not from Sarajevo but from Hamburg, Bremen, or Kiel? In another words, did Serbian and Pan-Slavic nationalism, Austo-Hungarian imperialism, and rival alliances suffice to result in the outbreak of the First World War? Or rather for that to happen, are the German port cities mentioned above considered to be a key component in understanding the First World War in its making? Indeed they are, because it was in these ports that the newly constructed Imperial German High Seas Fleet was stationed. After all, without that, Britain, the leading world power, would not necessarily join the Triple Entente that combined the forces of its long-lasting enemies, France and Russia. It was only the construction of the German navy that sent the British from its historical ally (Prussia) into the Entente. If Germany could gain continental hegemony with the most powerful army, global hegemony would come with a powerful navy. Britain stepped into the Entente Cordiale and later the war because the seas were at risk.

Oceanic history is key in understanding not only the outbreak of the First World War but also its course and outcome. Although most attention is attracted by the Eastern and Western Fronts in continental Europe, a simultaneous naval warfare took place literally all around the globe. During the first year of the war, British naval forces and their allies captured many of the isolated German colonies, including Samoa, Micronesia, Qingdao, German New Guinea, Togo, and Cameroon. Conversely, the German Navy raided the Indian Ocean, sinking or capturing 30 merchant ships and warships, bombarding Madras and Penang, and destroying a radio relay on the Cocos Islands. The German East Asia Squadron stormed the port of Tahiti, engaged the Royal Navy off the coast of central Chile, and was finally defeated near the Malvinas or Falkland Islands in the South Atlantic.

The inner circle of this impressive range of naval engagement, though, was in the seas around the European continent: the Black Sea, where the Ottoman and Russian fleets continuously engaged in naval battles and coastal bombardment;

the Mediterranean Sea, where, most crucially, the Triple Entente attempted to topple the Ottoman Empire by taking Istanbul via Gallipoli; the Baltic Sea defended by the Russian fleet till the collapse of the Czarists regime that led to the transformation of this sea into a German lake; and most significantly, at the very core of this inner circle, the North Atlantic and the English Channel on the one hand and the North Sea on the other hand. In both locations German and British forces, respectively, enforced naval blockades on their enemies. The British blockade on the North Sea was highly effective, cutting Germany off from overseas trade and resources. This blockade remained in place until the end of the war, despite a series of German attempts to break it, most notably in the Battle of Jutland (1916). Failure to do that led Germany to concentrate on its own blockade of the British Islands already in place since 1915. In essence, this blockade consisted of unrestricted submarine warfare since early 1917, including attacks without warning and attacks on neutrals.

While stalemate was the feature of ground battles on the Western Front, these mutual sea blockades played a pivotal role in deciding the outcome of the war. On the one hand, the British blockade on the North Sea deprived Germany of basic supplies. On the other hand, the German blockade on the North Atlantic and British Channel ended up bringing the United States into the war, tipping the balance between the rival coalitions. These outcomes of sea blockades brought the First World War to an end. By looking at the war from the sea, oceanic histories can reshape our understanding of the war by redefining it as a vast mutual sea siege. In this mutual sea siege Britain and its allies conducted an effective attrition of the Central Powers' military, economic, and political capabilities. The Germans' replication with their own submarine-based blockade on Britain, to the contrary, brought about the unintended self-inflicted defeat by recruiting the United States as its enemy.

New international history

International history is at the core of the study of the First World War. From the coalition formation and up to the concluding treaties, all diplomatic efforts entirely fall within the scope of international history. However, new international history pushes the boundaries of diplomacy into the domains of culture and society. By doing that, it stresses the input that foreign relations had upon domestic developments as well as the ways in which interstate developments influenced foreign relations. A fertile subject bringing diplomacy, society, and culture together along these lines in the context of the First World War is that of the diplomatic efforts carried out by belligerent states in order to recruit capital and manpower from those non-belligerent states where vast numbers of conational immigrants had settled.

Since 1871 and up to the time of the outbreak of the First World War, more than 42 million Europeans migrated from Europe. The pace of migration was particularly fast during the decade before the war, accounting for about a third of the above figure. Moreover, gender and age rates among European immigrants abroad made the cohorts suitable for military service disproportionally high in comparison to the overall population in their countries of origin. In the decade previous to the war, around 70 percent of all European migrants were young males. European policymakers were fully aware of this demographic situation. Therefore, in years prior to the war, they outlined courses of action in order to facilitate the repatriation of emigrant recruits from around the world if war was to erupt. From the relevant ministries—defense, foreign affairs—in the metropolises, instructions were sent to consular agents abroad to launch repatriation campaigns in the event of entering an armed conflict.

The mobilization of recruits from abroad was concomitantly easier for overseas colonial powers. Those—especially Great Britain, counting on its colonies and Commonwealth, but also France, Germany, and Belgium—could recruit soldiers among their colonial subjects without the interference of a local sovereign authority. By contrast, for countries with minor possessions overseas, the importance of repatriation was a much more pressing endeavor. The case of Italy is illuminating, with around 17 percent of its population residing overseas by the time of its entrance into the First World War. Almost a third of all European migrants during the first two decades of the twentieth century were Italians (about six million).

With these figures in mind, it is not surprising that ministries, governmental agencies, and cultural and welfare institutions run by or linked to the governments of belligerent states tried to reach out toward their citizens abroad looking for financial support and manpower for the military effort. However, those people targeted as conationals and citizens abroad were at the same time citizens or residents in their country of destination and subject to local law and regulations. Therefore, any attempt to reach out in this fashion represented an intromission in the domestic affairs of those states hosting large European communities. Basically, two ways were open for belligerent states to approach communities of conationals abroad: open negotiations with the hosting states of these conational communities to gain authorization and consent for the reach out attempts and/or secret efforts to reach out without hosting states knowing about the move or, at least, all of its details. Conversely, migratory countries in the New World were also adjusting to the situation by deciding on their policies in that matter, by sustaining diplomatic negotiations in front of the demands by belligerent states, and by scrutinizing and dealing with the extra-official initiatives carried out by belligerent states on their soil.

New international history can focus, then, on the ways in which either Germany, Austro-Hungary, the Ottoman Empire, Russia, Italy, France, or Great Britain approached either Canada, the United States, Brazil, Argentina, South Africa, Australia, or New Zealand in an effort to recruit both capital—in the form of war bonds, public debt, remittances, and donations—and manpower for the military effort during the First World War. The study of the policies adopted and measures taken by the above listed "new Europes" provides another side of this entanglement between states, revolving around the fate of a segment of their societies, that is, potential repatriates for some new subjects or others. Turning to them—as a segment of civil society with their own wills, aims, and organizations confronting the questions brought on by the outbreak of the war—is the major task of transnational history.

Transnational history

International history would deal with diplomatic engagements between belligerent and non-belligerent states concerning the recruitment of money and men from the later by the former. Transnational history, instead, would focus on these communities and their stands vis-à-vis the war, their mother countries' policies regarding them, and their hosting country's attitudes toward the multiple issues at stake derived from the war. In other words, transnational history, by replacing the state as both the basic unit of analysis and main agent, would focus on either phenomena or entities that transcend nation-states, such as transnational networks of overseas communities—either associated in institutions or related by family, friendship, or regional ties—girded for supporting the war effort of their mother countries or, contrarily, to oppose the war.

Such a project can be carried out on two different tracks. The first consists of looking at preexisting transnational networks of migrants—familial, commercial, financial, welfare, regional, political—and study their reactions and actions toward the war, the attempts made by their mother countries to recruit them for the war effort, and their host countries' responses to the war. The second track focuses on the emergence and crystallization of new transnational networks of migrants based on the affinity of their responses to the outbreak of the war, to the efforts made by their mother countries to recruit them, and to their host countries' attitudes toward the war in general and the efforts to recruit them in particular.

The first track would focus on the ways in which transnational networks operated during the war. For example, the ways in which Socialist, Communist, and Anarchist political parties and unions exchanged information, formulated their positions, learned from one another's experiences, or coordinated their actions. The history of the financial institutions that made possible the transference of funds from the expatriates to their mother countries is an additional example. A third example would be the functioning and disruption of family networks during the war years and in the aftermath in terms of communication, relocation, and remittances.

The second track would deal with the ways in which local groups and organizations with similar attitudes made efforts to transcend national boundaries in order to enhance the impact of their actions vis-à-vis the war. Tracking the collaborations between the editorial staff of migrant newspapers in several migratory hosting countries is one example for this track. The effort of patriotic leagues on the one hand and war opponent groups on the other hand establishing connections with like-minded associations in other countries provides an additional example.

In short, existing transnational networks of migrants confronted the new situation imposed by the war, and unrelated migrant groups and associations became connected and emerged as a network as a result of the challenges posed by the war. Both types of transnational networks are the subject of transnational history. Moreover, as transnational history replaces the state with intergovernmental institutions, nongovernmental organizations, and transnational non-state actors as the main units of analysis and agents, the adoption of such an organization exemplifies an additional possible research path. Possibilities, along this path, include the history of a transnational organization deeply transformed by the First World War such as the Red Cross, the history of transnational organizations emerging during the war such as transnational organized crime networks, or a transnational organization surfacing in the wake of and as a result of the war as, for instance, War Resisters' International.

Made up of conscientious objectors during the war years throughout Europe, War Resisters' International was established in 1921 and was active against warfare worldwide since. The core belief of the organization and its members is that if enough people stand in total opposition to war, governments would hesitate, or would even be unable, to make war. In other words, the organization aimed to articulate civil society within each nation-state as well as transnationally in order to counteract the belligerent policies advanced by their nation-states or any other state. The activities, publications, and finances required to advance this goal were coordinated transnationally across different continents.

War Resisters' International as a civil society-based transnational organization and a research subject for transnational history helps to highlight once more the distinction between international organizations studied by international history. War Resisters' International as well as other antiwar transnational organizations attempted to counteract not only the real politick attitude of different nation-states but also international organizations, such as the League of Nations and the international disarmament conference in the early 1930s. The emphasis on national interests within these institutions prevented quick resolutions of the atrocities and stymied the disarmament efforts. Consequently, prominent peace activists and organizations highlighted the need for a political framework that would limit the sovereignty of the nation-states and dictate non-violent solutions to international conflicts. Each of these paths of action, state-based international organizations and civil society-based transnational organizations, is approached by two cognate yet distinctive branches: International and transnational history, respectively.

Thinking history globally: Comparing and connecting

Comparative history

As comparative history seeks similarities and differences between two or more units for analytic or descriptive purposes, the First World War allows for a long list of possibilities for such contrasts. Tackling the First World War as a whole, it can be contrasted with other conflagrations on a global scale such as the 30 Years' War (1618–1648), the Seven Years' War, the Napoleonic Wars (1799–1815), or the Second World War. Looking instead at its component parts, manifold comparisons can be made between, for instance, the confronted coalitions (the Triple Entente and the Central Powers) and the strengths and weaknesses of their collaborations or between the different states involved and their respective armies, economies, technologies, and women's roles on the home front or between different battles and fronts. In this last instance, a comparative analysis of the Western and Eastern Fronts would certainly highlight the difference in their sizes and the contenders involved as a way to start making sense of their overall contrasts. The Western Front ranged from the North Sea to the French border with Switzerland, a line totaling around 700 kilometers. French, British, and later American forces were to the west of this line, Germans to its east. The Eastern Front ran from the Baltic to the Black Sea covering a distance of more than 1600 kilometers. German, Austro-Hungarian, Bulgarian, and Ottoman forces were to the west of this line, Russians and Romanians to its east.

The variation of longitude between the Western and Eastern Fronts stands out from the outset as a crucial difference between these two fronts. On top of that, the degree of economic development of the contenders on these two fronts added to the geographical one. Very simply summarized, on the Western Front industrialized nations collided. The Eastern Front, instead, was a theater of confrontation between economies developing, to different degrees, toward industrialization, except for Germany. Moreover, a synergy between these geographical and economic differences potentiated the development of a sharp disparity between the two fronts. And indeed major differences resulted from this divergent departing point. To begin with, following the halt and retreat of the German month-long penetration up to the outskirts of Paris at the Battle of Marne, the Western Front became one of trench warfare. That is, the transformation of the fighting lines into a complex of rather fixed trenches sheltering the troops from enemy fire and artillery. This fixation of the fighting lines for the sake of defensive tactics was feasible in a line about 700 kilometers long. That was not the case in a line longer than 1600 kilometers. The Eastern

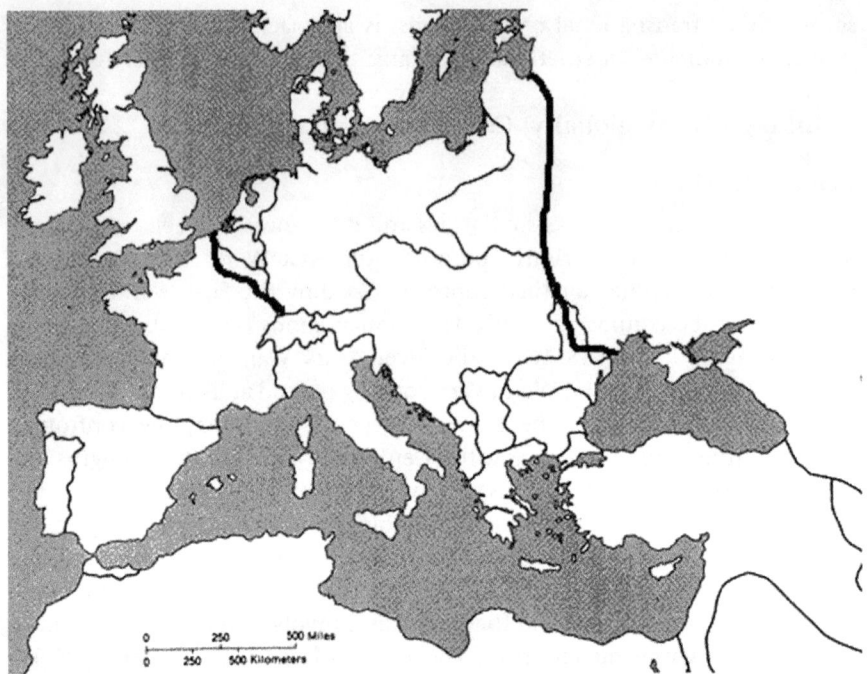

Figure 9.1 The Western and Eastern Fronts compared

Front, then, far from being a static defensive line, was one of mobile offensives and counter-offensives that since mid-1916 stabilized as an ongoing offensive of the Central Powers at the expense of Russia and Romania. These different fighting dynamics are tightly related to technological and economic considerations. Trench warfare on the Western Front was allowed by defensive devices such as mines, machine guns, and barbed wire and by regular railway supplies. These defensive devices were effective to the point of posing not just a military but also a technological and economic challenge in trying to break up the standstill that they created. The final result of this challenge is a string of technological and military developments, including aircrafts, tanks, and gas. All of these developments stemmed from the Western Front where the industrialized nations collided. None of them resulted from warfare among the industrializing nations of the Eastern Front. In this sense, the Western Front projected the specter of the future, while the Eastern Front became a phantom of the past.

Relational histories

As entangled history, a member of the relational family, shares the scale of comparative history while pursuing an entirely different goal and performing an entirely different task, it is highly illustrative to revisit the Western and

Eastern Fronts, previously brought together by way of comparison, from the perspective of entangled history. Entangling these two fronts means, instead of keeping them separate and enclosed for a clear-cut contrast, we merge their histories into one in order to underscore how the developments on one front reciprocally depended on the developments on the other front.

The First World War was first declared by Austria-Hungary on Serbia on 28 July. By the 29 July, Russia had mobilized troops along its frontiers with Germany and Austria-Hungary. Germany declared war on Russia on 1 August. Less than 48 hours later, Germany declared war on France, invading Belgium immediately after. On 7 August Russia invaded East Prussia. Within a three-day gap and 11 days since war was first declared, the two fronts were open and entangled until the end of the war.

In fact, these fronts were conceived as entangled even before the outbreak of war, as implied by the Franco-Russian Alliance and as explicitly addressed by the Schlieffen Plan. The strategic meaning of the Franco-Russian Alliance, established in 1891 and upgraded since, was precisely sandwiching Germany and imposing on her two simultaneous fronts in case of war. The chief of the German General Staff, General Count von Schlieffen, reasoned back in 1905 that this would indeed be the scenario of a future war with France. Accordingly, the German army planned on a defensive stand on the eastern border while employing the bulk of its power in a swift capture of Paris by outflanking French defenses via Holland, Belgium, and Luxemburg. Indeed, that was how the German army approached the war in August 1914, except that Holland was spared.

Hence, the fronts were entangled on paper well before coming into being, and as such they went under way in practice. Except that the devised German plan went wrong on several counts: on the east, the Russian army was able to mobilize far faster and with greater strength than expected, the defense of Berlin would demand more resources in view of that surprise. On the west, the Belgian resistance was more resilient than anticipated, the British Expeditionary Force very effective, and the French railway system proved to be decisive in bringing reserves and supplies to the theaters of battle envisioned to catch them by surprise. As a result of all that, the German advance was brought to a halt by 15 September in the wake of the Battle of the Marne and soon after the first trenches started appearing on the Western Front.

From this moment on, the entanglement intended by the Franco-Russian Alliance materialized at first, while that envisioned by the Schlieffen Plan radically departed from reality. As sought by the Franco-Russian Alliance, the German army was indeed forced to transport troops from west to east due to the mounting pressure of Russia on its border with Austria-Hungary. Contrary to that, the swift advance projected by the Schlieffen Plan for the Western Front resulted in a stalemate. By 1915 the incapability of achieving a breakthrough in the west led the German Army to strengthen its efforts in fostering conquests in the east. The Eastern Front originally envisioned by Germany as a defensive one became offensive and very dynamic. By the end of that year the forces pushed the Russian Army to a line running from Riga through Jakobstadt, Dünaburg, Baranovichi, Pinsk, Dubno and up to Ternopil. Further advances continued until the advent of the Bolshevik Revolution in November 1917, which was also associated with the entanglement of the two fronts, and even later.

Indeed, the ultimate way for Germany to bring the pincer strategy designed by the Franco-Russian Alliance to an end was by knocking Russia out of the war. That goal was fulfilled by helping the Bolshevik Party to reach power and make its "out of the war" promise good. This help was personalized by Lenin himself, who was smuggled by Germany from exile in Switzerland to Russia. Soon after the advent of the Bolsheviks to power, Germany finalized its offensive in the East in which it gained huge territories including Poland, the Baltic provinces, Ukraine, Finland, and the Caucasus and signed a peace treaty at Brest Litovsk on March 3, 1918. The entanglement of the fronts under this new circumstance meant that the German army could concentrate its efforts exclusively on the Western Front. By 21 March Germany renovated its offensives on the west that lasted until the Allies counter-offensives starting in mid-July. By 11 November the war was over.

The Western and Eastern Fronts, strategically entangled before the outbreak of the war and effectively entangled throughout the war, came to a close in an entangled way. The armistice signed on November 11, 1918, between Germany and the Allies on the Western Front invalidated the treaty of Brest Litovsk signed nine months before on the Eastern Front.

Closing conclusions

The thought experiment in the opening chapter of this book and now this chapter at its close clearly illustrate the singularity of each cross-boundary branch by applying them to the same case study, Argentina's Perón and the First World War, respectively. Interestingly enough, however, the order in which the 12 branches appear in each of these two sections is inverted. And for good reasons. Dealing with a nation-based case—Perón's Argentina—it made sense to depart from those branches closest on a space scale to national historiographies: comparative history and entangled history. Such a transition demanded just adding a second nation-state unit—Brazil for comparative history, Great Britain for entangled history—to the one under scrutiny, Argentina. Then, the methodological pathways opened by these two, comparisons and connections, paved the way into progressively bigger units, bigger scales of both space and time suitable for the other branches. Connections were applied first on states or non-state agents by international and transnational histories respectively, moving then into the larger unit of the Atlantic Basin with oceanic history. The use of comparisons led to expansion into the larger units encompassed by civilizations in civilizational analysis and into a long list of states from all over the world by historical sociology. With the world-system approach these compartmentalized states became connected into a system, an abstract model that subsequently was explored in more detail by global history and the history of globalization. World history expanded the time scale; big history expanded both time and space.

This order of presentation was reverted in this final chapter. Understandably, the most suitable historiographical branch for approaching a global phenomenon such as the First World War is global history. Its survey of the war is the entry point to the subject. Moving down the scales of time and/or place, the identification and reconstruction of connections between the local and the global constitutes a major goal. Moving up the time scale, the larger process in which the First World War is embedded—long-lasting European warfare for continental and global hegemony—becomes the major subject. The large time scale covered by this process, the entire modern period, was enormously expanded by world history, by defining a cross-sectional theme within which the First World War belongs, and even more so by big history, which placed the war as a substantial contribution to a turning point in the history of planet Earth. The application of the history of globalization to the First World War illustrated once again that what concerns it most is the articulation of the world into a single interconnected unit and its pulses since. Historical sociology and the world-system approach, instead, moved back to the larger process of long-lasting European warfare for continental and global hegemony, elaborated by global history but aiming its formalization and systemization into generalizations.

Then, from these huge and large scales a progressive shrinking of time and space scales unfolded: oceanic histories kept global coverage but concentrated on bodies of water; in a civilizational analysis sketch, it was one civilization that stood at the center for the most part. Finally, into the smaller units: the states (in the plural) and transnational non-state agents for international and transnational histories, respectively. Last but not least, the fronts: two space units enclosed and compared by comparative history, revealed through their connections by entangled history, a variety of the relational histories.

Having the 12 branches in front of us applied side by side to a nationally based case and a global one is highly instrumental in visualizing their clusters and overall classification. In terms of the scale of the units of analysis, Perón's Argentina is approached first by the smallest scale (that is, organizations), then by the medium-sized scale (that is, world region), the big scale (that is, the world), and finally the huge scale (that is, the universe). The scale of time is similarly arranged, in general, from shorter to longer time frames:

contemporary, modern, pre-modern, pre-historic, cosmic. This movement from smaller to bigger scales of space and time is associated with a transition from a more inductively oriented approach, mostly relying on primary sources, into approaches more inclined toward deductive thinking, mostly supported by secondary sources. Among the first, all branches belong within the historical profession. Within the second, history as well as the social sciences and multidisciplinarity are represented.

Table 9.1 First and last chapters contrasted: Singularities and clusters assessed (Compare with Table 2.8)

Perón's Argentina (ordered first to last)	First World War (ordered last to first)	Scale of unit of analysis	Time scope	Approach and sources	Discipline
Comparative history	Relational histories	Small	Ancient to contemporary/ mostly contemporary	Inductive/ primary	History
Relational histories	Comparative history	Small	Ancient to contemporary/ mostly contemporary	Inductive/ primary	History
International history	Transnational history	Small	Contemporary	Inductive/ primary	History
Transnational history	International history	Small	Contemporary	Inductive/ primary	History
Oceanic history	Oceanic history	Medium	Mostly modern	Inductive/ primary	History
Civilizational analysis	Civilizational analysis	Medium	Up to 5000 years	Deductive/ secondary	Sociology/ history
Historical sociology	World-system approach	Small/large	Mostly modern and contemporary/ up to 5000 years	Deductive/ secondary	Sociology
World-system approach	Historical sociology	Large/small	Mostly modern and contemporary/ up to 5000 years	Deductive/ secondary	Political economy/ sociology
Global history	History of globalization	Large	Modern onward	Deductive/ secondary	History
History of globalization	Big history	Large/huge	Modern onward/ cosmic	Deductive/ secondary	History/ multidisciplinarity
World history	World history	Large	Pre-history onward	Deductive/ secondary	History
Big history	Global history	Huge/large	Cosmic/ modern onwards	Deductive/ secondary	Multidisciplinarity/ history

The First World War as a global case study fully reverts this sequence, moving from the largest scales of space and time into the smaller ones and from the deductively oriented, secondary source-based approaches into those more inductively constructed, primary source-based approaches.

In writing the above conclusions and pulling together this last table, the final destination of this book has been reached. Thinking globally about the past is made possible by 12 major branches as exemplified in both a nation- and global-based case. These examples and their underlying conceptualization have now come full circle.

It is important to stress that definitions focused on singularity for the sake of clarity, not for building barriers between strategies. To the contrary, the existence of overlaps leading to clusters of branches and strategies was emphasized. Moreover, the focus on singularities and clusters enhanced manifold dialogues and combinations between different branches, as observed in the ways that one branch's perspective can inform several others. In practice, what matters most is not adopting one branch or the other in an exclusive way but rather to embrace inclusiveness as a way to profit from all of them. Thinking globally is an inclusive project, and thinking history globally provides a solid base for understanding our global present.

Notes

Introduction

1. Koselleck sustained a similar argument regarding the relation between the end of a global war and macro-historical writing by contextualizing the emergence of a wave of world history writing back in the second half of the eighteenth century, following the Seven Years' War. See R. Koselleck, *Futures Past: On the Semantics of Historical Time*, trans. K. Tribe (Cambridge, MA: MIT Press, 1985), 255.
2. G. Stockes, "The fates of human societies: A review of recent macrohistories," *American Historical Review* 106 (2001): 509.

1 Thinking History Globally: Theory in Practice. Argentina under Perón (1946–1955), Thinking Globally a National History

1. Laszlo Horvath, ed., *A Half Century of Peronism, 1943–1993: An International Bibliography* (Stanford: Hoover Institution, 1993).
2. R. Rein, "De los grandes relatos a los estudios de 'pequeña escala': Algunas notas acerca de la historiografía del primer peronismo," *Temas de historia argentina y americana* 14 (2009): 133–65, available at: http://bibliotecadigital.uca.edu.ar/repositorio/revistas/grandes-relatos-estudios-pequena-escala.pdf (accessed 25 May 2013).
3. Eric Hobsbawm, *The Age of Extremes, 1914–1991* (New York: Vintage Books, 1995), 96.
4. In Latin America: Justicialismo (Argentina, 1946–1955); Partido Trabalhista Brasileiro (Brazil, 1951–1954); Movimiento Nacionalista Revolucionario (Bolivia, 1952–1964); Arbenz (Guatemala, 1951–1954); Organizaciones Revolucionarias Integradas (Cuba, 1959–); Partido Revolucionario Dominicano (Dominican Republic, 1963); Frente Popular (Chile, 1970–1973). In Asia: Communist Party (Vietnam, 1945–1986); Sukarno's Indonesia (1945–1967); Indian National Congress (India, 1947–1985); Communist Party (China, 1949–1976). In the Middle East: Mosaddeq's Iran (1951–1953); "free officers" (Egypt, 1952–1970); "free officers" and Baath Party (Iraq, 1958–1979); Baath Party (Syria, 1963–); "free officers" (Libya, 1969–2011). In Africa: National Liberation Front, Algeria 1954–1988; Convention People's Party, Ghana 1957–1966; Parti Démocratique de Guinée (Guinea, 1958–1984); Union Soudanaise du Rassemblement Democratique Africain (Mali, 1960–1968); Tanganyika African National Union (Tanzania, 1964–1985); Uganda People's Congress (Uganda, 1966–1971); Avant-garde de la Révolution Malgache (Madagascar, 1975–1982).

2 Thinking History Globally: 12 Branches in Their Singularities, Overlaps, and Clusters

1. Charles Tilly, *Big Structures, Large Processes, Huge Comparisons* (New York: Russell Sage Foundation, 1984), 28–30.
2. In presenting the development of comparative history, I am following Benjamin Z. Kedar, "Outlines for Comparative History Proposed by Practicing Historians," in

New Ventures in Comparative History, ed. Benjamin Z. Kedar (Jerusalem: Magnes Press, 2009), 1–28.
3. Charles-Victor Langlois. "The Comparative History of England and France during the Middle Ages," *English Historical Review* 5 (1890): 259–63.
4. Raymond Grew, "On the Current State of Comparative Studies," in *Marc Bloch aujourd'hui. Histoire comparé et Sciences sociales*, ed. H. Atsma and A. Burguière (Paris: Editions de l'Ecole des hautes études en sciences sociales, 1990), 322–34.
5. Kedar, "Outlines for Comparative History," 27.
6. Michael Werner and Bénédicte Zimmermann, *De la comparaison à l'histoire croisée* (Paris: Seuil, 2004), 15–49. Michael Werner and Bénédicte Zimmermann, "Beyond Comparison: Histoire Croisée and the Challenge of Reflexivity," *History and Theory* 45, no. 1 (2006): 30–50.
7. Patrick Finney, "International History, Theory and the Origins of World War II," in *The History and Narrative Reader*, ed. Geoffrey Roberts (London and New York: Rutledge, 2001), 390.
8. Akira Iriye, "Culture and International History," in *Explaining the History of American Foreign Relations*, ed. Michael Hogan and Thomas Paterson (Cambridge: Cambridge University Press, 1991), 246.
9. Patrick Finney, *International History* (New York: Palgrave MacMillan, 2005), 4–10. Robert McMahon, "Toward a Pluralist Vision: The Study of American Foreign Relations as International History and National History," in *Explaining the History of American Foreign Relations*, ed. Michael Hogan and Thomas Paterson (Cambridge: Cambridge University Press, 1991), 46–48.
10. Ian Tyrell, "American Exceptionalism in an Age of International History"; Michael McGerr, "The Price of the 'New transnational History'"; Ian Tyrell, "Ian Tyrell Responds," *American Historical Review* 16, no. 4 (1991): 1031–72.
11. Marcel Mauss, "Les civilisations: Elements et formes," in *Civilisation: Le mot er l'idee*, ed. Louis Febvre et al. (Paris: La Renaissance du Livre, 1930), 89.
12. Émile Durkheim, *Les règles de la méthode sociologique* (Paris, 1895).
13. Theda Skocpol, "Sociology's Historical Imagination," in *Vision and Method in Historical Sociology*, ed. Theda Skocpol (Cambridge: Cambridge University Press, 1985), 1.
14. Available at: http://nuevomundo.revues.org/30462.
15. Bruce Mazlish, *The New Global History* (New York: Routledge, 2006).
16. *New Global Studies*, available at: http://www.degruyter.com/view/j/ngs (accessed 4 June 2013).
17. William McNeill, *Mythistory and Other Essays* (Chicago: University of Chicago Press, 1986), 71–96. J. H. Bentley, *Shapes of World History in Twentieth-Century Scholarship* (Washington, DC: American Historical Association, 1996).
18. Fred Spier, "Big History," in *A Companion to World History*, ed. Douglas Northrop (Chichester, West Sussex: Wiley-Blackwell, 2001), 171–84.
19. Dominic Sachsenmaier, *Global Perspectives on Global History: Theories and Approaches in a Connected World* (Cambridge: Cambridge University Press, 2011), 71–78, 99.

3 Thinking History Globally: Comparing or Connecting

1. C. Vann Woodward, ed., *The Comparative Approach to American History* (New York: Basic Books, 1968).
2. David Russo, *American History from a Global Perspective* (Westport: Greenwood Press, 2003).

3. Ian R. Tyrrell, *Transnational Nation: United States History in Global Perspective since 1789* (New York: Palgrave Macmillan, 2007).
4. Philip D. Morgan and Molly A. Warsh, eds., *Early North America in Global Perspective* (New York: Routledge, 2014), 4.
5. There is another branch in historiography called imperial history and dedicated precisely to the history of empires. Several practitioners of one or more of the 12 branches discussed here started their professional careers as imperial historians. Imperial history as a branch usually has a particular empire as its unit of analysis. Therefore, its methodological orientation regarding space, although different from, is also comparable to that of "methodological nationalism," except that the empire rather than the nation-state is the enclosed political unit. Methodological imperialism, then, is in contrast with the pursuit of comparing and connecting empires typical of the 12 branches of global thinking.
6. Shinu Anna Abraham, Praveena Gullapalli, Teresa P. Raczek, and Uzma Z. Rizvi, eds., *Connections and Complexity: New Approaches to the Archaeology of South Asia* (Walnut Creek: Left Coast Press, 2013), 154–55.
7. Ronald Syme, *Colonial Elites. Rome, Spain and the Americas* (Oxford: Oxford University Press, 1958); P. A. Brunt, "Reflections on British and Roman Imperialism," *Comparative Studies in Society and History* 7 (1964–65): 267–88; Frederick J. Teggart, *Rome and China: A Study of Correlations in Historical Events* (Berkeley: University of California Press, 1939); William H. McNeill, *The Rise of the West: A History of the Human Community* (New York: New American Library; London: New English Library, 1963).
8. James Lang, *Conquest and Commerce: Spain and England in the Americas* (New York: Academic Press, 1975); Anthony Pagden, *Lords of All the Worlds: Ideologies of Empire in Spain, Britain, and France, c. 1500–c. 1850* (New Haven: Yale University Press, 1995).
9. C. E. Black, *The Dynamics of Modernization: A Study in Comparative History* (New York: Harper & Row, 1966).
10. André Frank, *Capitalism and Underdevelopment in Latin America: Historical Studies of Chile and Brazil* (New York, 1969).
11. Otto Hintze, *The Historical Essays of Otto Hintze*, ed. Felix Gilbert (New York: Oxford University Press, 1975); A. A. van den Braembussche, "Historical Explanation and Comparative Method: Towards a Theory of the History of Society," *History and Theory* 28 (1989): 2–24; George M. Fredrickson, "Comparative History," in *The Past before Us: Contemporary Historical Writing in the United States*, ed. Michael Kammen (Ithaca: Cornell University Press, 1980); Victoria E. Bonnell, "The Uses of Theory, Concepts and Comparison in Historical Sociology," *Comparative Studies in Society and History* 22 (1980): 156–73; Theda Skocpol and Margaret Somers, "The Uses of Comparative History in Macrosocial Inquiry," *Comparative Studies in Society and History* 22 (1980): 174–97.
12. B. Z. Kedar, *The Changing Land: between the Jordan and the Sea: Aerial Photographs from 1917 to the Present* (Israel, 1999); John H. Elliott, *Richelieu and Olivares* (Cambridge: Cambridge University Press, 1984), 6.
13. Theda Skocpol, *States and Social Revolutions: A Comparative Analysis of France, Russia, and China* (Cambridge: Cambridge University Press, 1979).
14. John Stuart Mill, *Philosophy of Scientific Method* (New York, 1950 [1843]), Book 3, ch. 8, 211–33.
15. R. Graham, *Independence in Latin America: A Comparative Approach* (New York: McGraw-Hill, 1994).

16. Emile Durkheim, *The Rules of Sociological Method*, trans. S. Solovay and J. H. Mueller (New York and London, 1938 [1895]), ch. 6, 125–40.
17. Arnold Toynbee, *A Study of History* (London, 1934), 2, 259–61, 289–97.
18. L. Hartz, *The Founding of New Societies: Studies in the History of the United States, Latin America, South Africa, Canada, and Australia* (New York: Harcourt, Brace & World, 1964).
19. Jonathan Z. Smith, *Map Is Not Territory: Studies in the History of Religion* (Leiden, 1978), 240–64; Niall Ferguson, *Civilization The West and the Rest* (New York: Penguin Press, 2011).
20. Uri Ram, *The Globalization of Israel: McWorld in Tel Aviv, Jihad in Jerusalem* (New York: Routledge, 2008).
21. Fritz Redlich, "Toward Comparative Historiography. Background and Problems," *Kyklos: International Review of Social Sciences* 11 (1958): 362–88.
22. J. Kocka, "Comparison and Beyond," *History and Theory* 42 (2003): 39–44; J. Kocka, "The Uses of Comparative History," in *Societies Made Up of History*, ed. Bjork Ragnar and Molin Kare (Sweden, 1996), 197–209.
23. Charles Tilly, *Big Structures, Large Processes, Huge Comparisons* (New York: Russell Sage, 1984).
24. This table and many of the ideas that it summarizes were previously published in Olstein, D. "Comparative History: The Pivot of Historiography". In *New Ventures in Comparative History*, ed. Kedar, B.Z. (Jerusalem: Magnes Press, 2009), 37–52.
25. M. Paul Lewis, Gary F. Simons, and Charles D. Fennig, eds., *Ethnologue: Languages of the World, 17th edition* (Dallas: SIL International, 2013).
26. W. McNeill, *The Rise of the West: A History of the Human Community* (New York: New American Library, 1963).
27. J. McNeill and W. McNeill, *The Human Web: A Bird's-Eye View of World History* (New York: W.W. Norton, 2003).

4 Thinking History Globally: Comparing and Connecting

1. Ronald Syme, *Colonial Elites: Rome, Spain and the Americas* (Oxford: Oxford University Press, 1958); P. A. Brunt, "Reflections on British and Roman Imperialism," *Comparative Studies in Society and History* 7 (1964–65): 267–88; William H. McNeill, *The Rise of the West: A History of the Human Community* (London: New English Library, 1963).
2. C. Vann Woodward., ed., *The Comparative Approach to American History* (New York: Basic Books, 1968); David Russo, *American History from a Global Perspective* (Westport: Greenwood Press, 2003); Ian R. Tyrrell, *Transnational Nation: United States History in Global Perspective Since 1789* (Basingstoke: Palgrave Macmillan, 2007); Philip D. Morgan and Molly A. Warsh, eds., *Early North America in Global Perspective* (New York: Routledge, 2014); B. Z. Kedar, *The Changing Land: Between the Jordan and the Sea; Aerial Photographs from 1917 to the Present* (Israel, 1999); John H. Elliott, *Richelieu and Olivares* (Cambridge: Cambridge University Press, 1984), 6.
3. Alexandre Eck, "La société Jean Bodin pour l'histoire comparative des institutions," *Recueils de la Société Jean Bodin* 1 (1958): 7–9.
4. Sylvia Thrupp, "Editorial," *Comparative Studies in Society and History* 1 (1958–59): 1–4.
5. Sanjay Subrahmanyan, "Connected Histories: Notes Towards a Reconfiguration of Early Modern Eurasia," *Modern Asian Studies* 31, no. 3 (1997): 735–62.
6. Micole Seigel, "Beyond Compare: Comparative Method after the Transnational Turn," *Radical History Review* 91 (2005): 62–90.

7. Serge Gruzinski, "Les mondes mêlés de la Monarchie catholique et autres 'connected histories,'" *Annales. Histoire, Sciences Sociales* 56, no. 1 (2001): 85–117.
8. Leon Trotsky, *Revolution Betrayed: What Is the Soviet Union and Where Is It Going?*, trans. Max Eastman (North Chelmsford: Courier Dover Publications, 2004).
9. Hannah Arendt, *The Origins of Totalitarianism* (New York: Schocken Books, 2004); Hans Buchheim, *Totalitarian Rule: Its Nature and Characteristics*, trans. Ruth Hein (Middletown: Wesleyan University Press, 1968).
10. Michael Curtis, *Totalitarianism* (New Brunswick: Transaction Books, 1979); Carl J. Friedrich and Zbigniew K. Brzezinski, *Totalitarian Dictatorship and Autocracy* (Cambridge: Harvard University Press, 1956); Leonard Schapiro, *Totalitarianism* (New York: Praeger, 1972); Michael Halberstam, *Totalitarianism and the Modern Conception of Politics* (New Haven: Yale University Press, 1999).
11. Zeev Sternhell, "Fascism," in *International Fascism*, ed. Roger Griffin (London: Arnold, 1998), 34. Ian Kershaw and Moshe Lewin, *Stalinism and Nazism: Dictatorships in Comparison* (New York: Cambridge University Press, 1977).
12. Michael Kellogg, *The Russian Roots of Nazism: White Emigrés and the Making of National Socialism, 1917–1945* (Cambridge: Cambridge University Press, 2005); Michael David-Fox, Peter Holquist, and Alexander M. Martin, eds., *Fascination and Enmity: Russia and Germany as Entangled Histories, 1914–1945* (Pittsburgh: University of Pittsburgh Press, 2012).
13. Several arguments in this section were previously published in Olstein, D. "Comparative History: The Pivot of Historiography", in *New Ventures in Comparative History*, ed. B. Z. Kedar (Jerusalem, Magnes Press, 2009), 37–52.
14. J. H. Elliott, *National and Comparative History. An Inaugural Lecture Delivered before the University of Oxford on 10 May 1991* (Oxford: Oxford University Press, 1991), 1–29. For a detailed reading list on the historiographical, methodological, and theoretical contributions of comparative history see Deborah Cohen and Maura O'Connor, eds., *Comparison and History: Europe in Cross-National Perspective* (New York and London: Routledge, 2004), 181–85.
15. D. Olstein, "Comparative History: The Pivot of Historiography," 37–52.
16. Marshal Hodgson, "Conditions of Historical Comparison Among Ages and Regions," *Rethinking World History: Essays on Europe, Islam, and World History*, ed. Edmund Burke III (Cambridge: Harvard University Press, 1993), 267–87.
17. Kenneth Pomeranz, *The Great Divergence: China, Europe, and the Making of the Modern World Economy* (Princeton: Princeton University Press, 2000).
18. Philip McMichael, "Incorporating Comparison within a World-Historical Perspective: An Alternative Comparative Method," *American Sociological Review* 55 (1990): 385–97.
19. Christopher Chase-Dunn, "Cross-World-System Comparisons," *Civilizations and World Systems: Studying World-Historical Change* (Walnut Creek, 1995); Christopher Chase-Dunn and Thomas Hall, *Rise and Demise: Comparing World-Systems* (Boulder, 1997).
20. Giovanni Arrighi, "The Global Market," *Journal of World-Systems Research* 5, no. 2 (1999): 217–51; Paul Bairoch, *Economics and World History: Myths and Paradoxes* (Chicago: University of Chicago Press, 1993); Robert Feenstra, "Integration of Trade and Disintegration of Production in the Global Economy," *Journal of Economic Perspectives* 12, no. 4 (1998): 31–50; Jeffery Sachs et al., "Economic Reform and the Process of Global Integration," *Brookings Papers on Economic Activity* 1 (1995), 1–118; George Soros, "The Capitalist Threat," *Atlantic Monthly* 279, no. 2 (1997): 45–58;

George Soros, *The Crisis of Global Capitalism* (New York, 1998); Jeffery Williamson, "Globalization and Inequality Then and Now: The Late 19th and Late 20th Centuries Compared," *National Bureau of Economic Research Working Paper 5491* (Cambridge, 1996); Philip McMichael, "World-System Analysis, Globalization, and Incorporated Comparison," *Journal of World-Systems Research* 6, no. 3 (2000): 668–90.

21. Richard Baldwin and Philippe Martin, "Two Waves of Globalization: Superficial Similarities, Fundamental Differences,"*National Bureau of Economic Research Working Paper 6904* (Cambridge, 1999); Michael Bordo et al., "Is Globalization Today Really Different than Globalization a Hundred Years Ago?" *National Bureau of Economic Research Working Paper 7195* (Cambridge, 1999); Robert Chase, "The More Things Change...: Learning from Other Eras of 'Unprecedented' Globalization," *SAIS Review* 20, no. 2 (2000): 223–29.

22. Jerry Bentley, "A New Forum for Global History," *Journal of World History* 1 (1990): iii–v.

23. Stephen Hobden, *International Relations and Historical Sociology: Breaking Down Boundaries* (London and New York: Routledge, 1998); L. Snyder, *Macro-History: A Theoretical Approach to Comparative World History* (Lewiston: Edwin Mellen Press, 1999); Haupt Heinz-Gerhard and Kocka Jürgen, eds., *Comparative and Transnational History: Central European Approaches and New Perspectives* (New York: Berghahn Books, 2009); Benjamin H. Johnson and Andrew R. Graybill, eds., *Bridging National Borders in North America: Transnational and Comparative Histories* (Durham: Duke University Press, 2010).

24. Michael Geyer and Sheila Fitzpatrick, eds., *Beyond Totalitarianism: Stalinism and Nazism Compared* (Cambridge: Cambridge University Press, 2009).

5 Thinking History Globally: Varieties of Connections

1. Akira Iriye, "Culture and International History," in *Explaining the History of American Foreign Relations*, ed. Michael Hogan and Thomas Paterson (Cambridge: Cambridge University Press, 2004), 246; Patrick Finney, *International History* (Basingstoke: Palgrave MacMillan, 2005), 4–10; Robert McMahon, "Toward a Pluralist Vision: The Study of American Foreign Relations as International History and National History," in *Explaining the History of American Foreign Relations*, ed. Michael Hogan and Thomas Paterson (Cambridge: Cambridge University Press, 2004), 46–48.

2. Kristin Hoganson, *Consumers' Imperium: The Global Production of American Domesticity, 1865* (Chapel Hill: University of North Carolina Press, 2007).

3. Jessica C. E. Gienow-Hecht, *Sound Diplomacy: Music and Emotions in Transatlantic Relations, 1850–1920* (Chicago: University of Chicago Press, 2009).

4. Jessica C. E. Gienow-Hecht, *Transmission Impossible: American Journalism as Cultural Diplomacy in Postwar Germany, 1945–1955* (Los Angeles: Baton Rouge, 1999).

5. R. Kroes, R. W. Rydell, D. F. J. Bosscher, eds., *Cultural Transmissions and Receptions: American Mass Culture in Europe* (Amsterdam: VU University Press, 1993); David W. Ellwood and R. Kroes, eds., *Hollywood in Europe: Experiences of a Cultural Hegemony* (Amsterdam, 1994); R. Kroes, *If You've Seen One, You've Seen the Mall: Europeans and American Mass Culture* (Urbana: University of Illinois Press, 1996).

6. Emily S. Rosenberg, *Financial Missionaries to the World: The Politics and Culture of Dollar Diplomacy, 1900–1930* (Cambridge: Harvard University Press, 1999).

7. Additional examples of studies emphasizing the role of ideology in international history are: Frank A. Ninkovich, *Modernity and Power: A History of the Domino*

Theory in the Twentieth Century (Chicago: University of Chicago Press, 1994); Frank A. Ninkovich. *Global Dawn: The Cultural Foundation of American Internationalism, 1865–1890* (Cambridge: Harvard University Press, 2009); Michael E. Latham, *Modernization as Ideology: American Social Science and "Nation Building" in the Kennedy Era* (Chapel Hill: University of North Carolina Press, 2000).

8. Marc Gallicchio, *The African American Encounter with Japan and China: Black Internationalism in Asia, 1895–1945* (Chapel Hill: University of North Carolina Press, 2000).
9. Thomas Borstelmann, *The Cold War and the Color Line: American Race Relations in the Global Arena* (Cambridge: Harvard University Press, 2001).
10. Akira Iriye, *Global Community: The Role of International Organizations in the Making of the Contemporary World* (Berkeley: University of California Press, 2002).
11. Matthew Evangelista, *Unarmed Forces: The Transnational Movement to End the Cold War* (Ithaca, NY: Cornell University Press, 1999).
12. A. Ricardo López and Barbara Weinstein, eds., *The Making of the Middle Class: Toward a Transnational History* (Durham: Duke University Press, 2012).
13. Ibid, p.12.
14. Rodrigue, J-P et al. (2013) *The Geography of Transport Systems*, Hofstra University, Department of Global Studies & Geography, available at: http://people.hofstra.edu/geotrans.
15. David Armitage, "Three Concepts of Atlantic History," in *The British Atlantic World, 1500–1800*, eds. David Armitage and Michael J. Braddick (Basingstoke: Palgrave Macmillan, 2002), 14–15.
16. K. N. Chaudhuri, *Trade and Civilization in the Indian Ocean: An Economic History from the Rise of Islam to 1750* (Cambridge: Cambridge University Press, 1985).
17. Steven Roger Fischer, *A History of the Pacific Islands* (Basingstoke: Palgrave Macmillan, 2013).
18. J. H. Elliott, *Empires of the Atlantic World: Britain and Spain in America, 1492–1830* (New Haven: Yale University Press, 2006).

6 Thinking History Globally: Conceptualizing through Social Sciences

1. Michael Mann, *The Sources of Social Power*, vol. I (Cambridge: Cambridge University Press, 1986).
2. Shmuel Eisenstadt, *The Political System of Empire* (London and New York: Free Press of Glencoe, 1963).
3. James Mahoney, *Colonialism and Postcolonial Development: Spanish America in Comparative Perspective* (Cambridge: Cambridge University Press, 2010).
4. David Wilkinson, "Central Civilization," in *The World-System: Five Hundred Years or Five Thousand?*, ed. A. Frank and B. Gills (London: Routledge, 1993), 31–59.
5. S. N. Eisenstadt, *The Origins and Diversity of Axial Age Civilizations* (Albany: SUNY Press, 1986).
6. Samuel Huntington, *The Clash of Civilizations and the Remaking of World Order* (New York: Simon & Schuster, 1996).
7. Samuel Huntington. *Who Are We? The Challenges to America's Identity* (New York: Simon & Schuster, 2004).
8. Immanuel Wallerstein, *World-System Analysis: An Introduction* (Durham and London: Duke University Press, 2004); Giovanni Arrighi, *The Long Twentieth Century: Money,*

Power, and the Origins of Our Times (New York: Verso, 1994); Ana Margarita Cervantes-Rodriguez and Ramon Grosgoguel, eds., The *Modern/Colonial/Capitalist World-System in the Twentieth Century: Global Processes, Antisystemic Movements, and the Geopolitics of Knowledge* (Westport: Greenwood Press, 2002); Terence K. Hopkins, Immanuel Wallerstein et al., *The Age of Transition: Trajectory of the World-System, 1945–2025* (London: Zed Books, 1996); Immanuel Wallerstein, "The State and State Transformation: Will and Possibility" *Politics and Society* 1, no. 3 (May 1971): 359–64; Immanuel Wallerstein, "The States in the Institutional Vortex of the Capitalist World-Economy," *International Social Science Journal* 32, no. 4 (1980): 743–51; Immanuel Wallerstein, *The Concept of National Development, 1917–1989: Elegy and Requiem* (Binghamton: Fernand Braudel Center for the Study of Economies, Historical Systems, and Civilizations, State University of New York at Binghamton, 1991); Immanuel Wallerstein, *The Politics of the World-Economy: The States, the Movements and the Civilizations* (New York: Cambridge University Press, 1984); Immanuel Wallerstein, "Response: Declining States, Declining Rights?" *International Labor and Working-Class History* 47 (Spring 1995): 24–27; Immanuel Wallerstein, "Socialist States: Mercantilist Strategies and Revolutionary Objectives," in *Ascent and Decline in the World-System*, ed. Edward Friedman (Beverly Hills: Sage, 1982), 289–300; Immanuel Wallerstein, "States? Sovereignty? The Dilemmas of Capitalists in an Age of Transition," in *States and Sovereignty in the Global Economy*, ed. David A. Smith, Dorothy J. Solinger and Steven C. Topik (London: Routledge, 1999), 20–33; Immanuel Wallerstein, "The New World Disorder: If the States Collapse, Can the Nations Be United?," in *Between Sovereignty and Global Governance: The United Nations, the State and Civil Society*, ed. A. J. Paolini, A. P. Jarvis, and C. Reus-Smit (London: Macmillan & New York: St. Martin's Press, 1998), 171–85; William G. Martin, ed., *Semiperipheral States in the World-Economy* (New York: Greenwood Press, 1990).
9. Immanuel Wallerstein, *The Modern World-System: Capitalist Agriculture and the Origins of the European World-Economy in the Sixteenth Century* (New York: Academic Press, 1974).
10. Andreas J. W. Goldschmidt and Josef Hilbert, *Health Economy in Germany—Economical Field of the Future* [*Gesundheitswirtschaft in Deutschland—Die Zukunftsbranche*] (Germany: Wikom Publishing house, Wegscheid, 2009), 22.
11. A. Frank and B. Gills, eds., *The World-System: Five Hundred Years or Five Thousand?* (London: Routledge, 1993).
12. J. Abu-Lughod, *Before European Hegemony: The World-System A.D. 1250–1350* (New York: Oxford University Press, 1989).

7 Thinking History Globally, Thinking Globalization Historically

1. J. Bentley, "A New Forum for Global History," *Journal of World History* 1 (1990): iii–v.
2. P. Manning, *Navigating World History: Historians Create a Global Past* (New York: Palgrave, 2003), 15.
3. W. Clarence-Smith, K. Pomeranz, and P. Vries, "Editorial," *Journal of Global History* 1, no. 1 (2002): 1.
4. G. Iggers, Q. E. Wang, and S. Mukherjee, *A Global History of Modern Historiography* (New York: Pearson Longman, 2008).
5. An earlier version of this chapter has been published in Italian: Diego Olstein, Le molteplici origini della globalizzazione. Un dibattito storiografico, in "Contemporanea", 3/2006, 403–22.

6. B. Mazlish and R. Buultjens, eds., *Conceptualizing Global History* (Boulder: Westview Press, 1993); B. Mazlish, "Comparing Global History to World History," *Journal of Interdisciplinary History* 28, no. 3 (1998): 385–95.
7. R. Robertson and D. Inglis, "The Global Animus," in *Globalization and Global History*, ed. B. Gills and W. Thompson (London and New York: Routledge, 2006), 33–47.
8. D. Wilkinson, "Globalization: The First Ten, Hundred, Five Thousand, and Million Years," in *Globalization and Global History*, ed. B. Gills and W. Thompson (London and New York: Routledge, 2006), 68–78.
9. D. Flynn and A. Giráldez, "Path Dependence, Time Lags and the Birth of Globalisation: A Critique of O'Rourke and Williamson," *European Review of Economic History* 8, no. 1 (2004): 85–108.
10. D. Armitage, "Is There a Pre-History of Globalization?," in *Comparison and History: Europe in Cross-National Perspective*, ed. D. Cohen and M. O'Connor (New York and London: Routledge, 2004), 165–74.
11. G. Arrighi, "The Global Market," *Journal of World-Systems Research* 5, no. 2 (1999): 217–51; P. Bairoch, *Economics and World History: Myths and Paradoxes* (Chicago: University of Chicago Press, 1993); R. Feenstra, "Integration of Trade and Disintegration of Production in the Global Economy," *Journal of Economic Perspectives* 12, no. 4 (1998): 31–50; J. Sachs and A. Warner, "Economic Reform and the Process of Global Integration," *Brookings Papers on Economic Activity* 1 (1995): 1–118; G. Soros, "The Capitalist Threat," *Atlantic Monthly* (1997); G. Soros, *The Crisis of Global Capitalism* (New York: Pantheon, 1998); J. Williamson, "Globalization and Inequality Then and Now: The Late 19th and Late 20th Centuries Compared," *NBER Working Paper 5491* (Cambridge, 1996).
12. K. O'Rourke and J. Williamson, *Globalization and History: The Evolution of a Nineteenth-Century Atlantic Economy* (Cambridge: MIT Press, 1999).
13. K. O'Rourke and J. Williamson, "When Did Globalisation Begin?," *European Review of Economic History* 6 (2002): 23–50; M. Bordo, "Globalization in Historical Perspective," *Business Economics* (2002): 20–29.
14. C. Chase-Dunn, Y. Kawano, and B. Brewer, "Trade Globalization since 1795: Waves of Integration in the World-System," *American Sociological Review* 65, no. 1 (2002): 77–95.
15. Quoted in C. Chase-Dunn, "Globalization: A World-System Perspective," *Journal of World-Systems Research* 5, no. 2 (1999): 197.
16. C. Chase-Dunn, Y. Kawano, and B. Brewer, "Trade Globalization since 1795," 87.
17. I. Briones and A. Villela, "European Bank Penetration During the First Wave of Globalization: Lessons from Brazil and Chile, 1878–1913," *European Review of Economic History* 10, no. 3 (2006): 329–59; L. Neal and L. Davis, "The Evolution of the Structure and Performance of the London Stock Exchange in the First Global Financial Market, 1812–1914," *European Review of Economic History* 10, no. 3 (2006): 279–300; S. Battilossi, "The Determinants of Multinational Banking During the First Globalization, 1880–1914," *European Review of Economic History* 10, no. 3 (2006): 361–88.
18. R. Baldwin and P. Martin, "Two Waves of Globalization: Superficial Similarities, Fundamental Differences," *NBER Working Paper 6904* (Cambridge, 1999); J. A. Scholte, *Globalization: A Critical Introduction* (New York: Palgrave Macmillan, 2005), 117–19.
19. J. Di Leo, "Whose Theory, Which Globalism? Notes on the Double Question on Theorizing Globalism and Globalizing Theory," *Symploke* 9, no. 1 (2001): 8.
20. A. G. Hopkins, ed., *Globalization in World History* (London: Pimlico, 2002).

21. S. Amin, "Economic Globalism and Political Universalism: Conflicting Issues?," *Journal of World-Systems Research* 7, no. 3 (2000): 582–623.
22. J. Osterhammel and N. Petersson, *Globalization: A Short History*, trans. D. Geyer (Princeton and Oxford: Princeton University Press, 2005).
23. D. Held, A. McGrew, D. Goldblatt, and J. Perraton, *Global Transformations: Politics, Economics and Culture* (Cambridge: Polity Press, 1999); R. Robertson, *Globalization: Social Theory and Global Culture* (London: Sage, 1992).
24. K. O'Rourke and J. Williamson, "When Did Globalisation Begin?," 26.
25. C. Chase-Dunn, Kawano and B. Brewer, "Trade Globalization since 1795," 78; Chase-Dunn, "Globalization: A World-System Perspective," 194.
26. D. Flynn and A. Giraldez, "Path Dependence, Time Lags and the Birth of Globalisation."
27. K. O'Rourke and J. Williamson, "Once More: When Did Globalisation Begin?," *European Review of Economic History* 8, no. 1 (2004): 109–17.
28. Quoted in M. Bordo, "Globalization in Historical Perspective," 25.
29. E. Hobsbawm, *Entrevista sobre el siglo XXI* (Madrid: Ed. Crítica, 2001), 90–93.
30. C. Chase-Dunn, Kawano and B. Brewer, "Trade Globalization since 1795," 86–87.

8 Thinking History Globally: Contextualizing on a Bigger Scale

1. M. Adas, "Foreword," in *Essays on Global and Comparative History* (Washington, DC: American Historical Association, 1993).
2. B. Mazlish and R. Buultjens, eds., *Conceptualizing Global History* (Boulder: Westview Press, 1993); B. Mazlish and A. Iryie, eds., *Global History Reader* (New York: Routledge, 2004); B. Mazlish "Comparing Global History to World History," *Journal of Interdisciplinary History* 28, no. 3 (1998): 385–95.
3. Jane Burbank and Frederick Cooper, *Empires in World History: Power and the Politics of Difference* (Princeton: Princeton University Press, 2010); John Darwin, *After Tamerlane: The Rise and Fall of Global Empires, 1400–2000* (New York: Bloomsbury Press, 2008).
4. Yuval Harari, *From Animals into Gods. A Brief History of Humankind* (Israel, 2012), 211–31.
5. David Abernethy, *The Dynamics of Global Dominance: European Overseas Empires, 1415–1980* (New Haven: Yale University Press, 2000), 35–38.
6. J. Wills, *1688: A Global History* (New York: W.W. Norton, 2001).
7. C. A. Bayly, *The Birth of the Modern World, 1780–1914: Global Connections and Comparisons* (Malden, MA: Blackwell, 2004).
8. A. Iriye, *China and Japan in the Global Setting* (Cambridge: Cambridge University Press, 1992).
9. D. Wright, *The World and a Very Small Place in Africa* (New York: M. E. Sharpe, 1997).
10. K. Pomeranz, *The Great Divergence: China, Europe, and the Making of the Modern World Economy* (Princeton: Princeton University Press, 2001).
11. B. Z. Kedar, "Expulsion as an Issue of World History," *Journal of World History* 7, no. 2 (1996): 165–80.
12. Available at: http://www.h-net.org/~world/about.html (accessed on 25 February 2014).
13. Douglas Northrop, ed. *A Companion to World History* (Chichester: Wiley-Blackwell, 2012).

Analytic Bibliography

Thinking History Globally, Comparing and Connecting

Comparative History

Journals
Comparative Studies in Society and History (1958–).
Recueils de la Societé Jean Bodin (1958–).

Historiographical analysis
Atsma, H., and A. Burguière, eds. *Marc Bloch aujourd'hui: Histoire comparé et Sciences sociales*. Paris: Editions de l'Ecole des hautes études en sciences sociales, 1990.
Elliott, J. *National and Comparative History: An Inaugural Lecture Delivered before the University of Oxford on 10 May 1991*. Oxford: Oxford University Press, 1991.
Fredrickson, G. "Comparative History." In *The Past Before Us: Contemporary Historical Writing in the United States*, edited by M. Kammen. Ithaca: Cornell University Press, 1980.
Grew, R. "The Case for Comparing Histories." *American Historical Review* 85, no. 4 (1980): 763–78.
Heinz-Gerhard, H. "Comparative History." In *The International Encyclopedia of the Social and Behavioral Sciences*, vol. 4, 2397–403. Amsterdam and New York, 2001.
Hill, A., and B. Hill Jr. "Marc Bloch and Comparative History." *American Historical Review* 85 (1980): 828–57.
Hodgson, M. "Conditions of Historical Comparisons Among Ages and Regions: The Limitations of Their Validity." In *Rethinking World History: Essays on Europe, Islam, and World History* by M. Hodgson, edited with an introduction and conclusion by E. Burke, III. Cambridge: Cambridge University Press, 1993.
Kedar, B. Z. "Outlines for Comparative History Proposed by Practicing Historians." In *New Ventures in Comparative History*, edited by Benjamin Z. Kedar. Jerusalem: Magnes Press, 2009, 1–28.
Kocka, J. "Comparison and Beyond." *History and Theory* 42 (2003): 39–44.
Kocka, J. "Storia comparata." In *Enciclopedia delle scienze sociali*, vol. 8, 389–96. Rome: Istituto della Enciclopedia italiana, 1998.
Kocka, J. "The Uses of Comparative History." In *Societies Made Up of History*, edited by Bjork Ragnar and Molin Kare, 197–209. Sweden: Akademitryck AB, 1996.
Redlich, F. "Toward Comparative Historiography: Background and Problems." *Kyklos: International Review for Social Sciences* 11 (1958): 362–88.
Rossi, P., ed. *La storia comparata: Approcci e prospettive*. Milan: il Saggiatore, 1990.
Seigel, M. "Beyond Compare: Comparative Method after the Transnational Turn." *Radical History Review* 91 (Winter 2005): 62–90.
Sewell, W. Jr. "Marc Bloch and the Logic of Comparative History." *History and Theory* 6 (1967): 208–18.

Taylor, C. "Comparison, History, Truth." In *Myth and Philosophy*, edited by F. Reynolds and D. Tracey. Albany: SUNY Press, 1990.

Van den Braembussche, A. "Historical Explanation and Comparative Method: Towards a Theory of the History of Society." *History and Theory* 28 (1989): 2–24.

Selected publications

Amatori, F., and G. Jones, eds. *Business History Around the World*. Cambridge: Cambridge University Press, 2003.

Bayly, C. A., and P. F. Bang. "Introduction: Comparing Premodern Empires." *Medieval History Journal* 6, no. 2 (2003): 169–87.

Black, C. *The Dynamics of Modernization: A Study in Comparative History*. New York: Harper and Row, 1966.

Bloch, M. "Pour une histoire comparée des sociétés européennes." In *Mélanges historiques*, vol. 1, 16–40. Paris: École des Hautes Études en Sciences Sociales, 1963.

Brekke, T. *The Ethics of War in Asian Civilizations: A Comparative Perspective*. London: Routledge, 2005.

Burguière, A., and R. Grew, eds. *The Construction of Minorities: Cases for Comparison Across Time and Around the World*. Ann Arbor: University of Michigan Press, 2001.

Cantwell Smith, W. *Towards a World Theology: Faith and the Comparative History of Religion*. London: Macmillan Press, 1981.

Cohen, D., and M. O'Connor. *Comparison and History: Europe in Cross-National Perspective*. New York: Routledge, 2004.

Cole, J., ed. *Comparing Muslim Societies: Knowledge and the State in a World Civilization*. Ann Arbor: University of Michigan Press, 1992.

Dirks, N., ed. *Colonialism and Culture*. Ann Arbor: University of Michigan Press, 1992.

Earle, R., and John D. Wirth. *Identities in North America: The Search for Community*. Stanford: Stanford University Press, 1995.

Elliott, J. *Richelieu and Olivares*. Cambridge: Cambridge University Press, 1991.

Endelman, T., ed. *Comparing Jewish Societies*. Ann Arbor: University of Michigan Press, 1997.

Farmer, E., Hambly, G., Kopf, D., Marshall, B., and Taylor, R. *Comparative History of Civilizations in Asia*. Boulder: Westview Press, 1986.

Galtung, J., and S. Inayatullah, eds. *Macrohistory and Macrohistorians: Perspectives on Individual, Social, and Civilizational Change*. Westport: Praeger, 1997.

Graham, R. *Independence in Latin America: A Comparative Approach*. 2nd ed. New York: McGraw-Hill, 1994.

Grigg, D. "Regions, Models and Classes." In *Models in Geography*, edited by R. J. Chorley and P. Haggett, 461–507. London: Methuen, 1967.

Hansen, M. H., ed. *A Comparative Study of Thirty City-State Cultures*. Copenhagen: Royal Danish Academy of Sciences and Letters, 2000.

Hartz, L. *The Founding of New Societies: Studies in the History of the United States, Latin America, South Africa, Canada, and Australia*. New York: Harcourt, Brace and World, 1964.

Haupt, H. G., and J. Kocka, eds. *Comparative and Transnational History: Central European Approaches and New Perspectives*. New York: Berghahn, 2010.

Humphreys, S. C., ed. *Cultures of Scholarship*. Ann Arbor: University of Michigan Press, 1997.

International Society for the Study of European Ideas. *Turning Points in History. First International Conference of the International Society for the Study of European Ideas.* Oxford: Pergamon, 1990.
LeRoy, J. *Crafting the Third World: Theorizing Underdevelopment in Romania and Brazil.* Stanford: Stanford University Press, 1996.
Levine, D., ed. *Constructing Culture and Power in Latin America.* Ann Arbor: University of Michigan Press, 1993.
Manley, J. *The Atlas of Past Worlds: A Comparative Chronology of Human History 2000 BC—AD 1500.* London: Cassell, 1993.
Nakamura, H. *A Comparative History of Ideas.* London: Routledge, 1986.
Nakamura, H. *Parallel Developments: A Comparative History of Ideas.* Tokyo: Kodansha, 1975.
Pagden, A. *Lords of All the World: Ideologies of Empire in Spain, Britain, and France, c. 1500–c. 1800.* New Haven: Yale University Press, 1995.
Pederson, S. *Family, Dependence, and the Origins of the Welfare State: Britain and France, 1914–1945.* Cambridge: Cambridge University Press, 1993.
Reenberg Sand, E., and J. Podemann Sørensen, J., eds. *Comparative Studies in History of Religions: Their Aim, Scope, and Validity.* Copenhagen: Museum Tusculanum, University of Copenhagen, 1999.
Scharfstein, B. *A Comparative History of World Philosophy: From the Upanishads to Kant.* Albany: SUNY Press, 1998.
Smith, W. *Towards a World Theology: Faith and the Comparative History of Religion.* Basingstoke: Palgrave Macmillan, 1989.
Snyder, L. *Macro-History: A Theoretical Approach to Comparative World History.* Lewiston: Edwin Mellen Press, 1999.
Solberg, C. *The Prairies and the Pampas: Agrarian Policy in Canada and Argentina, 1880–1930.* Stanford: Stanford University Press, 1987.
Syme, R. *Colonial Elites: Rome, Spain and the Americas.* Oxford: Oxford University Press, 1958.
Tsugitaka, S., ed. *Muslim Societies: Historical and Comparative Aspects.* London: Routledge, 2004.
Vann Woodward, C., ed. *The Comparative Approach to American History.* New York: Basic Books, 1968.
Wang, Q. Edward, and Georg, G. Iggers. *Turning Points in Historiography: A Cross-Cultural Perspective.* Rochester: University of Rochester Press, 2002.
Wittfogel, K. *Oriental Despotism: A Comparative Study of Total Power.* New Haven: Yale University Press, 1967.

Relational histories: Historiographical analysis and selected publications

Conrad, Sebastian, and Shalini Randeria, eds. *Jenseits des Eurozentrismus: Postkoloniale Perspektiven in den Geschichts- und Kulturwissenschaften.* Frankfurt: Campus, 2002.
Espagne, Michel. "Sur les limites du comparatisme en histoire culturelle." *Genèses* 17 (1994): 112–21.
Gould, E. "Entangled Histories, Entangled Worlds: The English Speaking Atlantic as a Spanish Periphery." *American Historical Review* 112, no. 3 (2007): 764–86.
Gruzinski, Serge. "Les mondes mêlés de la Monarchie catholique et autres 'connected histories.'" *Annales HSS* 56, no. 1 (2001): 85–117.

Hall, Stewart. "When was the Post-Colonial? Thinking at the Limit." In *The Post-Colonial Question: Common Skies, Divided Horizons*, edited by Iain Chambers and Lidia Curtis. London: Routledge, 1996.
Islamoğlu, H., and P. Perdue. "Introduction." In *Shared Histories of Modernity: China, India, and the Ottoman Empire*, edited by H. Islamoğlu and P. Perdue, 1–20. London: Routledge, 2009.
Lepenies, W., ed. *Entangled Histories and Negotiated Universals: Centers and Peripheries in a Changing World*. Frankfurt: Campus, 2003.
Randeria, Shalini. "Entangled Histories of Uneven Modernities: Civil Society, Caste Solidarities and Legal Pluralism in Post-Colonial India." In *Unraveling Ties: From Social Cohesion to New Practices of Connectedness*, edited by Yehuda Elkana, I. Krastev, E. Macamo, and S. Randeria, 284–311. Frankfurt: Campus, 2002.
Stoler, Ann Laura, and Frederic Cooper. "Between Metropole and Colony. Rethinking a Research Agenda." In *Tensions of Empire: Colonial Cultures in a Bourgeois World*, edited by Robert W. Strayer. Berkeley: University of California Press, 1997.
Strayer, Robert, W., ed. *The Making of the Modern World. Connected Histories, Divergent Paths, 1500 to the Present*. New York: St. Martin's Press, 1989.
Subrahmanyam, Sanjay. "Connected Histories: Notes Toward a Reconfiguration of Early Modern Eurasia." *Modern Asian Studies* 31, no. 3 (1997): 735–62.
Werner, M., and B. Zimmermann. "Beyond Comparison: Histoire Corisée and the Challenge of Reflexivity." *History and Theory* 45, no. 1 (2006): 30–50.
Werner, M., and B. Zimmermann, eds. *De la comparaison à l'histoire corisée*. Paris: Seuil, 2004.

Thinking History Globally: Varieties of Connections

International history

Journals

International History Review (1979–).
Society for Historians of American Foreign Relations. Diplomatic History (1977–).
University of London, Institute of Historical Research and the School of Advanced Study. *Electronic Journal of International History* (2000–).

Historiographical analysis

Finney, Patrick, ed. *Palgrave Advances in International History*. Basingstoke: Palgrave Macmillan, 2005.
Manela, Erez. "The United States in the World," in Eric Foner and Lisa McGirr, eds., American History Now. Philadelphia, Temple University Press, 2011.
Trachtenberg, Marc. *The Craft of International History: A Guide to Method*. Princeton: Princeton University Press, 2005.

Selected publications

Atwood, Mark Lawrence, and Fredrik Logevall, eds. *The First Vietnam War: Colonial Conflict and Cold War Crisis*. Cambridge: Harvard University Press, 2007.
Borstelmann, Thomas. *The Cold War and the Color Line: American Race Relations in the Global Arena*. Cambridge: Harvard University Press, 2001.

Bradley, Mark Philip. *Imagining Vietnam and America: The Making of Postcolonial Vietnam, 1919–1950*. Chapel Hill: University of North Carolina Press, 2000.

Campbell, Craig, and Fredrik Logevall. *America's Cold War: The Politics of Insecurity*. Cambridge: Belknap Press of Harvard University Press, 2009.

Cobbs, Elizabeth Hoffman. *All You Need Is Love: The Peace Corps and the Spirit of the 1960s*. Cambridge: Harvard University Press, 1998.

Connelly, Mathew. *A Diplomatic Revolution: Algeria's Fight for Independence and the Origins of the Post-Cold War Era*. Oxford and New York: Oxford University Press, 2002.

Connelly, Mathew. *Fatal Misconception: The Struggle to Control World Population*. Cambridge, MA: Harvard University Press, 2008.

Cullather, Nick. *The Hungry World: America's Cold War Battle Against Poverty in Asia*. Harvard, 2010. Cambridge, MA: Harvard University Press, 2010.

Dudziak, Mary L. *Cold War Civil Rights: Race and the Image of American Democracy*. Princeton: Princeton University Press, 2000.

Ellwood, David W., and R. Kroes, eds. *Hollywood in Europe. Experiences of a Cultural Hegemony*. Amsterdam: VU University Press, 1994.

Engerman, David. *Modernization from the Other Shore: American Intellectuals and the Romance of Russian Development*. Cambridge, MA: Harvard University Press, 2003.

Engerman, David. *Know Your Enemy: The Rise and Fall of America's Soviet Experts*. Oxford: Oxford University Press, 2009.

Eschen, Penny M. Von. *Race Against Empire: Black Americans and Anticolonialism, 1937–1957*. Ithaca: Cornell University Press, 1997.

Fineman, Daniel. *A Special Relationship: The United States and Military Government in Thailand, 1947–1958*. University of Hawai'i Press: Honolulu, 1997.

Foglesong, David S. *America's Secret War against Bolshevism: U.S. Intervention in the Russian Civil War, 1917–1920*. Chapel Hill: University of North Carolina Press, 1995.

Foglesong, David S. *The American Mission and the "Evil Empire": The Crusade for a "Free Russia" Since 1881*. New York: Cambridge University Press, 2007.

Fursenko, Aleksandr, and Timothy Naftali. *One Hell of a Gamble: Khrushchev, Castro, and Kennedy, 1958–1964*. New York: W. W. Norton, 1997.

Gallicchio, Marc. *The African American Encounter With Japan and China: Black Internationalism in Asia, 1895–1945*. Chapel Hill: University of North Carolina Press, 2000.

Gallicchio, Marc. *The Scramble for Asia: U.S. Military Power in the Aftermath of the Pacific War*. Lanham: Rowman and Littlefield, 2008.

Gienow-Hecht, Jessica C. E. *Sound Diplomacy: Music and Emotions in Transatlantic Relations, 1850–1920*. Chicago: University of Chicago Press, 2009.

Gienow-Hecht, Jessica C. E. *Transmission Impossible: American Journalism as Cultural Diplomacy in Postwar Germany, 1945–1955*. Los Angeles: Baton Rouge, 1999.

Hoganson, Kristin. *Consumers' Imperium: The Global Production of American Domesticity, 1865*. Chapel Hill: University of North Carolina Press, 2007.

Hoganson, Kristin. *Fighting for American Manhood: How Gender Politics Provoked the Spanish-American and Philippine-American Wars*. New Haven: Yale University Press, 2000.

Jian, Chen. *China's Road to the Korean War: The Making of the Sino-American Confrontation*. Columbia University Press: New York, 1994.

Jian, Chen. *Mao's China and the Cold War*. Chapel Hill: University of North Carolina Press, 2000.

Kedar, Claudia. *The International Monetary Fund and Latin America: The Argentine Puzzle in Context*. Philadelphia: Temple University Press, 2013.

Koshiro, Yukiko. *Transpacific Racisms and the U.S. Occupation of Japan*. New York: Columbia University Press, 1999.
Kroes, R. *If You've Seen One, You've Seen the Mall: Europeans and American Mass Culture*. University of Illinois Press: Urbana, 1996.
Kroes, R., R. W. Rydell, and D. F. J. Bosscher, eds. *Cultural Transmissions and Receptions: American Mass Culture in Europe*. Amsterdam: VU University Press, 1993.
Langley, Lester D. *The Americas in the Age of Revolution, 1750–1850*. New Haven: Yale University Press, 1996
Langley, Lester D. *The Americas in the Modern Age*. New Haven: Yale University Press, 2003.
Langley, Lester D. and Thomas Schoonover. *The Banana Men: American Mercenaries and Entrepreneurs in Central America, 1880–1930*. Lexington: University Press of Kentucky, 1995.
Latham, Michael E. *Modernization as Ideology: American Social Science and "Nation Building" in the Kennedy Era*. Chapel Hill: University of North Carolina Press, 2000.
Latham, M. *The Right Kind of Revolution: Modernization, Development, and U.S. Foreign Policy from the Cold War to the Present*. Ithaca: Cornell University Press, 2011.
Logevall, Fredrik. *Choosing War: The Lost Chance for Peace and the Escalation of War in Vietnam*. Berkeley: University of California Press, 1999.
Manela, Erez. *The Wilsonian Moment: Self-Determination and the International Origins of Anticolonial Nationalism*. New York: Oxford University Press, 2007.
Mitchell, Nancy. *The Danger of Dreams: German and American Imperialism in Latin America*. Chapel Hill: University of North Carolina Press, 1999.
Naftali, Timothy J. *Blind Spot: The Secret History of American Counterterrorism*. New York: Basic Books, 2005.
Ninkovich, Frank A. *Global Dawn: The Cultural Foundation of American Internationalism, 1865–1890*. Cambridge: Harvard University Press, 2009.
Ninkovich, Frank A. *Modernity and Power: A History of the Domino Theory in the Twentieth Century*. Chicago: University of Chicago Press, 1994.
Plummer, Brenda Gayle. *Rising Wind: Black Americans and U.S. Foreign Affairs, 1935–1960*. Chapel Hill: University of North Carolina Press, 1996.
Roorda, Eric Paul. *The Dictator Next Door: The Good Neighbor Policy and the Trujillo Regime in the Dominican Republic, 1930–1945*. Durham: Duke University Press, 1998.
Rosenberg, Emily S. *Financial Missionaries to the World: The Politics and Culture of Dollar Diplomacy, 1900–1930*. Cambridge: Harvard University Press, 1999.
Rotter, Andrew J. *Comrades at Odds: The United States and India, 1947–1964*. Ithaca: Cornell University Press, 2000.
Rydell, Robert W., and Rob Kroes. *Buffalo Bill in Bologna: The Americanization of the World, 1869–1922*. Chicago: University of Chicago Press, 2005.
Saul, Norman E. *Concord and Conflict: The United States and Russia, 1867–1914*. Lawrence: University Press of Kansas, 1996.
Saul, Norman E. *Friends or Foes? The United States and Soviet Russia, 1921–1941*. Lawrence: University Press of Kansas, 2006.
Saul, Norman E. *War and Revolution: The United States and Russia, 1914–1921*. Lawrence: University Press of Kansas, 2001.
Schoonover, Thomas. *The United States in Central America, 1860–1911: Episodes of Social Imperialism and Imperial Rivalry in the World-System*. Durham, NC: Duke University Press, 1991.
Schwartz, Thomas. *America's Germany: John J. McCloy and the Federal Republic of Germany*. Cambridge: Harvard University Press, 1991.

Stueck, William, ed. *The Korean War in World History.* Lexington: University Press of Kentucky, 2004.
Stueck, William. *Rethinking the Korean War: A New Diplomatic and Strategic History.* Princeton: Princeton University Press, 2002.
Stueck, William. *The Korean War: An International History.* Princeton: Princeton University Press, 1995.
Suri, Jeremy. *Power and Protest.* Cambridge, MA: Harvard University Press, 2003.
Suri, Jeremy. *Liberty's Surest Guardian: American Nation-Building from the Founders to Obama.* New York: Free Press, 2011.
Trachtenberg, Marc. *A Constructed Peace: The Making of the European Settlement, 1945–1963.* Princeton: Princeton University Press, 1999.
Trachtenberg, Marc, ed. *Between Empire and Alliance: America and Europe During the Cold War.* Lanham: Rowman and Littlefield Publishers, 2003.
Wagnleitner, Reinhold. *Coca Colonization and the Cold War: The Cultural Mission of the United States in Austria after the Second World War.* Translated by Diana M. Wolf. Chapel Hill: University of North Carolina Press, 1994.
Westad, Odd. *The Global Cold War: Third World Interventions and the Making of Our Times.* Cambridge, Cambridge University Press, 2006.
Westad, Odd. *Restless Empire: China and the World since 1750.* New York: Basic Books, 2012.

Transnational history

Historiographical analysis
Adam, Thomas. *Intercultural Transfers and the Making of the Modern World. Sources and Contexts.* Houndmills, Basingstoke, Hampshire, New York: Palgrave Macmillan, 2012.
"AHR Conversation: On Transnational History" (Participants: C.A. Bayly, Sven Beckert, Matthew Connelly, Isabel Hofmeyr, Wendy Kozol, and Patricia Seed). *American Historical Review* (December 2006): 1441–64.
Iriye, Akira. *Global and Transnational History: The Past, Present, and Future.* Basingstoke: Palgrave Macmillan, 2012.
Lake, Marilyn, and Ann Curthoys, eds. *Connected Worlds: History in Transnational Perspective.* Canberra: ANU e-Press, 2006.
Saunier, Pierre-Yves. *Transnational History.* Houndmills, Basingstoke, Hampshire; New York, NY: Palgrave Macmillan, 2013.

Selected publications

Feldman, Christine Jacqueline. *"We Are the Mods": A Transnational History of a Youth Subculture.* New York: Peter Lang, 2009.
Gerd-Rainer, Horn, and Kenney Padraic, eds. *Transnational Moments of Change: Europe 1945, 1968, 1989.* Lanham: Rowman and Littlefield, 2004.
Geyer, M. "The New Consensus." In *Transnational Geschichte* [Transnational Praxis], edited by M. Middell. Gottingen: Vendenhoeck and Ruprecht, 2012.
Grace, Nancy M., and Jennie Skerl, eds. *The Transnational Beat Generation.* New York: Palgrave Macmillan, 2012.
Hilmes, Michele. *Network Nations: A Transnational History of British and American Broadcasting.* New York: Routledge, 2012.
Iriye, Akira. *Cultural Internationalism and World Order.* Baltimore: Johns Hopkins University Press, 1997.

Iriye, Akira. *Global Community: The Role of International Organizations in the Making of the Contemporary World*. Berkeley: University of California Press, 2002.
Iriye, Akira, and Pierre-Yves Saunier, eds. *The Palgrave Dictionary of Transnational History: From the Mid 19th Century to the Present Day*. Basingstoke: Palgrave Macmillan, 2009.
López, A. Ricardo, and Barbara Weinstein, eds. *The Making of the Middle Class: Toward a Transnational History*. Durham: Duke University Press, 2012.
López, Kathleen. *Chinese Cubans: A Transnational History*. Chapell Hill: The University of North Carolina Press, 2013.
McCarthy, Dennis M. P. *An Economic History of Organized Crime: A National and Transnational Approach*. New York: Routledge, 2011.
Owen, John. *The Clash of Ideas in World Politics: Transnational Networks, States, and Regime Change, 1510–2010*. Princeton: Princeton University Press, 2010.
Putnam, Lara. *Radical Moves: Caribbean Migrants and the Politics of Race in the Jazz Age*. Chapel Hill: University of North Carolina Press, 2013.
Riordan-Goncalves, Julia, and Patricia Swier, eds. *Dictatorships in the Hispanic World: Transatlantic and Transnational Perspectives*. Madison: Fairleigh Dickinson University Press, 2013.
Rodríguez, Ana Patricia. *Dividing the Isthmus: Central American Transnational Histories, Literatures, and Cultures*. Austin: University of Texas Press, 2009.
Snyder, Sarah B. *Human Rights Activism and the End of the Cold War: A Transnational History of the Helsinki Network*. New York: Cambridge University Press, 2011.
Tyrrell, Ian R. *Transnational Nation: United States History in Global Perspective Since 1789*. Basingstoke; New York: Palgrave Macmillan, 2007.
Van der Linden, Marcel. *Transnational Labour History: Explorations*. Burlington, VT: Ashgate, 2002.
Van der Vleuten, Erik. "Toward a Transnational History of Technology: Meanings, Promises, Pitfalls." *Technology and Culture* 49, no. 4, (October 2008): 974–94.
Van Lente, Dick, ed. *The Nuclear Age in Popular Media: A Transnational History, 1945–1965*. New York: Palgrave Macmillan, 2012.

Oceanic histories

Journals

Atlantic Studies (2004–).
International Journal of Maritime History (1988–).
Journal of Pacific History (1977–).
Pacific Historical Review (1933–).

Historiographical analysis

Armitage, David. "Three Concepts of Atlantic History." In *The British Atlantic World, 1500–1800*, edited by David Armitage and Michael J. Braddick. Basingstoke: Palgrave Macmillian, 2002.
Bailyn, Bernard. "The Idea of Atlantic History," *Itinerario* 20, no. 1 (1996): 19–44.
Finamore, Daniel, ed. *Maritime History as World History*. Gainesville: University of Florida Press, 2004.
O'Reilly. "Genealogies of Atlantic History," *Atlantic Studies* 1 (2004): 66–84.
Polónia, Amélia. "Maritime History: A Gateway to Global History?" In *Maritime History as Global History,* edited by Maria Fusaro and Amélia Polónia. New York: St. John's, 2010.

Selected books

Arasaratnam, Sinnappah. "Recent Trends in the Historiography of the Indian Ocean, 1500–1800." *Journal of World History* 1, no. 2 (1990): 225–48.
Bailyn, Bernard. *Atlantic History: Concept and Contours*. Cambridge: Cambridge University Press, 2005.
Benjamin, T. *The Atlantic world: Europeans, Africans, Indians and Their Shared History, 1400–1900*. New York: Cambridge University Press, 2009.
Benjamin, T., T. Hall, and D Rutherford. *The Atlantic World in the Age of Empire*. Belmont, CA: Wadsworth, 2000.
Borsa, Giorgio, ed. *Trade and Politics in the Indian Ocean: Historical and Contemporary Perspectives*. New Delhi: Manohar, 1990.
Bose, Sugata. *A Hundred Horizons: The Indian Ocean in the Age of Global Empire*. Cambridge: Harvard University Press, 2006.
Braudel, Fernand. *The Mediterranean and the Mediterranean World in the Age of Philip II*. 2 vols. Translated by Sian Reynolds. Berkeley: University of California Press, 1995.
Chandra, Satish, ed. *The Indian Ocean: Explorations in History, Commerce and Politics*. New Delhi and Newbury Park: Sage Publications, 1987.
Chaudhuri, K. N. *Asia Before Europe: Economy and Civilisation of the Indian Ocean from the Rise of Islam to 1750*. Cambridge: Cambridge University Press, 1990.
Chaudhuri, K. N. "The Unity and Disunity of Indian Ocean History from the Rise of Islam to 1750: The Outline of a Theory and Historical Discourse." *Journal of World History* 4, no. 1 (1993): 1–7.
Chaudhuri, K. N. *Trade and Civilization in the Indian Ocean from the Rise of Islam to 1750*. London: Cambridge University Press, 1985.
Corbin, Alain. *The Lure of the Sea: The Discovery of the Seaside in the Western World, 1750–1840*. Berkeley: University of California Press, 1994.
Cunliffe, Barry. *Facing the Ocean: The Atlantic and Its Peoples*. Oxford; New York: Oxford University Press, 2001.
Curtin, Philip D. *The Atlantic Slave Trade: A Census*. Madison: University of Wisconsin Press, 1969.
Das Gupta, Ashin, and Michael Pearson, eds. *India and the Indian Ocean, 1500–1800*. Calcutta and New York: Oxford University Press, 1987.
Das Gupta, Uma, ed. *The World of the Indian Ocean Merchant 1500–1800: Collected Essays of Ashin Das Gupta*. New Delhi and New York: Oxford University Press, 2001.
Dening, Greg. *Mr. Bligh's Bad Language: Passion, Power and Theatre on the Bounty*. Cambridge; New York: Cambridge University Press, 1992.
Dirlik, Arif, ed. *What Is in a Rim? Critical Perspectives on the Pacific Region Idea*. Boulder: Westview, 1993.
Elliott, J. H. *Empires of the Atlantic World: Britain and Spain in America, 1492–1830*. New Haven: Yale University Press, 2006.
Ellis, Richard. *The Empty Ocean*. Washington, DC: Island Press/Shearwater Books, 2003.
Falola, T. *The Atlantic World, 1450–2000*. Bloomington: Indiana University Press, 2008.
Finamore, Daniel, ed. *Maritime History as World History*. Salem, MA: Peabody Essex Museum; Gainesville: University Press of Florida, 2004.
Gabaccia, Donna. "A Long Atlantic in a Wider World." *Atlantic Studies* 1 (2004): 1–27.
Gillis, John. *Islands of the Mind: How the Human Imagination Created the Atlantic World*. New York: Palgrave Macmillan, 2004.
Gilroy, Paul. *The Black Atlantic: Modernity and Double Consciousness*. Cambridge: Cambridge University Press, 1993.

Gordon, John Steele. *A Thread Across the Ocean: The Heroic Story of the Transatlantic Cable*. New York: Walker & Co., 2003.

Gould, Eliga, and Peter S. Onuf, eds. *Empire and Nation: The American Revolution in the Atlantic World*. Baltimore: Johns Hopkins University Press, 2004.

Greene, Jack P., and Philip D. Morgan, eds. *Atlantic History: A Critical Appraisal*. Oxford: Oxford University Press, 2009.

Greer, A., and K. Mills. 2007. "A Catholic Atlantic." In *The Atlantic In Global History, 1500–2000*, edited by J. Cañizares-Esguerra and E. R. Seenan, 3–19. Upper Saddle River, NJ: Prentice Hall, 2007.

Grove, Richard H. *Green Imperialism: Colonial Expansion, Tropical Island Edens and the Origins of Environmentalism, 1600–1868*. Cambridge: Cambridge University Press, 1996.

Hall, Richard. *Empires of the Monsoon: A History of the Indian Ocean and Its Invaders*. London: HarperCollins, 1996.

Housley, Rupert A., and Geraint Coles, eds. *Atlantic Connections and Adaptations: Economies, Environments and Subsistence in Lands Bordering the North Atlantic*. Oxford: Oxbow, 2001.

Huguette, and Pierre Chaunu, *Séville et l'Atlantique, 1504–1650*. 9 vols., 1955–1960.

Jones, E., Frost, L., and White, C. *Coming Full Circle: An Economic History of the Pacific Rim*. Boulder: Westview Press, 1993.

Karras, Alan L., and J. R. McNeill, eds. *Atlantic American Societies: From Columbus through Abolition, 1492–1888*. London and New York: Routledge, 2002.

Kearney, Milo. *The Indian Ocean in World History*. New York: Routledge, 2004.

Klein, Bernard, and Gesa Mackenthune, eds. *Sea Changes: Historicizing the Ocean*. New York: Routledge, 2004.

Kurlansky, Mike. *Cod: A Biography of the Fish That Changed the World*. New York: Walker and Co., 1998.

Linebaugh, Peter, and Marcus Rediker. *The Many-Headed Hydra: The Hidden History of the Revolutionary Atlantic*. Boston, 2001.

Lombard, Denys, and Jean Aubin, eds. *Marchands et hommes d'affaires asiatiques dans l'Océan Indien et la Mer de Chine, 13e-20e siécles*. Paris: EHESS, 1988 (republished in English as *Asian Merchants and Businessmen in the Indian Ocean and the China Sea*. New Delhi and New York: Oxford University Press, 2000).

Mancke, Elizabeth, and Carole Shammas, eds. *The Creation of the British Atlantic World*. Baltimore: Johns Hopkins University Press, 2005.

Matsuda, Matt K. *Pacific Worlds: A History of Seas, Peoples, and Cultures*. New York: Cambridge University Press, 2012.

McPherson, Kenneth. *The Indian Ocean: A History of People and the Sea*. Delhi and New York: Oxford University Press, 1993.

Milo, Kearney. *The Indian Ocean in World History*. New York: Routledge, 2004.

Mukherjee, Rudrangshu, and Lakshmi Subramanian, eds. *Politics and Trade in the Indian Ocean: Essays In Honour of Ashin Das Gupta*. Delhi and Oxford: Oxford University Press, 1999.

Pearson, Michael N. *The Indian Ocean*. London: Routledge, 2003.

Pearson, Michael. *The World of the Indian Ocean, 1500–1800: Studies in Economic, Social and Cultural History*. Burlington: Ashgate, 2005.

Pirenne, Jacques. *The Tides of History*. 2 vols. Translated by Lovett Edwards. London: George Allen & Unwin, 1962.

Reade, Julian. *The Indian Ocean in Antiquity*. London: Kegan Paul International and the British Museum, 1996.

Rediker, Marcus. *Between the Devil and the Deep Blue Sea: Merchant Seamen, Pirates and the Anglo-American Maritime World, 1700–1750.* Cambridge: Cambridge University Press, 1989.

Risso, Patricia. *Merchants and Faith: Muslim Commerce and Culture in the Indian Ocean.* Boulder: Westview Press, 1995.

Rozwadowski, Helen M. *Fathoming the Ocean: The Discovery and Exploration of the Deep Sea.* Cambridge: Harvard University Press, 2005.

Rozwadowski, Helen M., and David, K. Van Keuren, eds. *The Machine in Neptune's Garden: Historical Perspectives on Technology and the Marine Environment.* Sagamore Beach: Science History Publications/USA, 2004.

Steinberg, Philip. *The Social Construction of the Ocean.* Cambridge: Cambridge University Press, 2001.

Thornton, J. *Africa and the Africans in the Making of the Atlantic World, 1400–1680.* New York, London: Cambridge University Press, 1992.

Vink, Marcus P. M. "Indian Ocean Studies and the 'New Thalassology.'" *Journal of Global History* 2 (2007): 41–62.

Wills, John, Jr. "Maritime Asia, 1500–1800: The Interactive Emergence of European Domination." *American Historical Review* 98, no. 1 (1993): 83–105.

Thinking History Globally: Conceptualizing through Social Sciences

Historical sociology

Journals
Journal of Historical Sociology (1988–).
Thesis Eleven (1980–).

Historiographical analysis

Abbot, A. "History and Sociology: The Lost Synthesis." In *Engaging the Past: The Uses of History Across the Social Sciences*, edited by E. Monkkonen. Durham, NC: Duke University Press, 1994.

Abrams, P. *Historical Sociology*. Ithaca: Cornell University Press, 1982.

Bates, R., Greif, A., Levi, M. Rosenthal, J., and Weingast, B. *Analytic Narratives*. Princeton: Princeton University Press, 1999.

Bendix, R. *Force, Fate, and Freedom: On Historical Sociology*. Berkeley: University of California Press, 1984.

Bryant, J. M. "Evidence and Explanation in History and Sociology: Critical Reflections on Goldthorpe's Critique of Historical Sociology." *British Journal of Sociology* 45, no. (1994): 3–19.

Burke, P. *History and Social Theory*. Cambridge: Polity Press, 1992.

Delanty, G., and E. Isin, eds. *Handbook of Historical Sociology*. London; Thousand Oaks: Sage, 2003.

Gaudemet, J. *Sociologie Historique: les maîtres du pouvoir.* Paris: Montchrestien, 1994.

Hobden, S. *International Relations and Historical Sociology: Breaking Down Boundaries.* New York: Routledge, 1998.

Hobden, S., and J. Hobson, eds. *Historical Sociology of International Relations.* Cambridge; New York: Cambridge University Press, 2002.

Lachman, Richard. *What Is Historical Sociology?* Cambridge: Polity Press, 2013.
MacRaild, D., and A. Taylor. *Social Theory and Social History.* Basingstoke: Palgrave Macmillan, 2004.
Siemens, R. *Introduction to Cultural Historical Sociology.* Lewiston: The Edwin Mellen Press, 1998.
Skocpol, T., ed. *Vision and Method in Historical Sociology.* Cambridge: Cambridge University Press, 1985.
Smith, D. *The Rise of Historical Sociology.* Philadelphia: Temple University Press, 1991.
Szakolczai, Á. *Reflexive Historical Sociology.* London; New York: Routledge, 2000.
Tilly, C. *As Sociology Meets History.* New York: Academic Press, 1981.
Tilly, C. *Big Structures, Large Processes, Huge Comparisons.* New York: Russell Sage Foundation, 1984.

Selected publications

Anderson, P. *Lineages of the Absolutist State.* London: NLB, 1974.
Anderson, P. *Passages From Antiquity to Feudalism.* London: Verso, 1978.
Bendix, R. *Kings or People: Power and Mandate to Rule.* Berkeley: University of California Press, 1978.
Bendix, R. *Nation-Building and Citizenship: Studies of Our Changing Social Order.* New York: John Wiley & Sons, 1964.
Bryant, J. M. "The West and the Rest Revised: Debiting Capital Origins, European Colonialism, and the Advent of Modernity." *Canadian Journal of Sociology* 31, no. 4 (2006): 403–44.
Collins, R. *Macrohistory: Essays in Sociology of the Long Run.* Stanford: Stanford University Press, 1999.
Eisenstadt, S. N. *The Political System of Empires.* New York: Free Press of Glencoe, 1963.
Gellner, E. *Plough, Sword, and Book: The Structure of Human History.* Chicago: University of Chicago Press, 1989.
Mann, M. *The Sources of Social Power.* Cambridge: Cambridge University Press, 1987–1993.
Markoff, John. *The Abolition of Feudalism: Peasants, Lords, and Legislators in the French Revolution.* University Park: Pennsylvania State University Press, 1996.
Moore, B., Jr. *Moral Purity and Persecution in History.* Princeton: Princeton University Press, 2000.
Moore, B., Jr. *Social Origins of Dictatorship and Democracy: Lord and Peasant in the Making of the Modern World.* Harmondsworth: Penguin Books, 1966.
Runciman, W. *A Treatise on Social Theory.* Cambridge: Cambridge University Press, 1983–1997.
Sanderson, S. K. *Social Transformations: A General Theory of Historical Development.* Lanham, MD: Rowman & Littlefield Publishers, 1999.
Sanderson, S. K., and A. S. Alderson. *World Societies: The Evolution of Human Social Life.* Boston: Allyn & Bacon, 2005.
Skocpol, T. *Social Revolutions in the Modern World.* Cambridge: Cambridge University Press, 1994.
Skocpol, T. *States and Social Revolutions: A Comparative Analysis of France, Russia, and China.* Cambridge; New York: Cambridge University Press, 1979.
Snooks, G. *Global Transition: A General Theory of Economic Development.* Basingstoke: Macmillan, 1999.

Snooks, G. *Longrun Dynamics: A General Economic and Political Theory.* Basingstoke: Macmillan Press, 1998.
Snooks, G. *The Dynamic Society: Exploring the Sources of Global Change.* New York: Routledge, 1996.
Snooks, G. *The Ephemeral Civilization. Exploding the Myth of Social Evolution.* London; New York: Routledge, 1998.
Snooks, G. *The Laws of History.* London, New York: Routledge, 1998.
Therborn, G. *European Modernity and Beyond: The Trajectory of European Societies, 1945–2000.* London: Sage, 1995.
Tilly, C. *Coercion, Capital, and European States, AD 990–1990.* Oxford: Basil Blackwell, 1990.
Tilly, C. *Contention and Democracy in Europe, 1650–2000.* Cambridge, UK; New York: Cambridge University Press, 2004.
Tilly, C. *Social Movements, 1768–2004.* Boulder: Paradigm Publishers, 2004.

Civilizational analysis

Journal

Comparative Civilizations Reviews (1979–).

Historiographical analysis

Arjomand, S., and Tiryakian, E., eds. *Rethinking Civilizational Analysis.* Summer: Sage Publications, 2004.
Sanderson, S. K. *Civilizations and World-Systems: Studying World-Historical Change.* Walnut Creek: Altamira, 1995.
Segesvary, V. *Dialogue of Civilizations: An Introduction to Civilizational Analysis.* Lanham: University Press of America, 2000.

Selected publications

Bagby, P. *Culture and History: Prolegomena to the Comparative Study of Civilizations.* Westport: Greenwood Press, 1976.
Braudel, F. *Civilisation matérielle et capitalisme, XVe-XVIIIe siècle.* Paris: A. Colin, 1967.
Braudel, F. *Grammaire des civilisations.* Paris: Arthaud-Flammarion, 1987.
Eckhardt, W. *Civilizations, Empires, and Wars: A Quantitative History of War.* Jefferson, NC: McFarland, 1992.
Eisenstadt, S. N., ed. *The Origins and Diversity of Axial Age Civilization.* Albany, NY: State University of New York Press, 1986.
Fernández-Armesto, F. *Civilizations: Culture, Ambition, and the Transformation of Nature.* New York: Free Press, 2001.
Fernández-Armesto, F. *Civilizations.* London: Macmillan, 2000.
Huntington, S. *The Clash of Civilizations and the Remaking of World Order.* New York: Simon & Schuster, 1996.
Krishna, D. *Prolegomena to Any Future Historiography of Cultures and Civilizations.* Delhi: Project of History of Indian Science, Philosophy, and Culture; New Delhi: Distributed by Munshiram Manoharlal Publishers, 1997.
Melko, M. *The Nature of Civilizations.* Boston: Porter Sargent, 1969.

Melko, M., and Scott, L., eds. *The Boundaries of Civilizations in Space and Time*. Lanham, MD: University Press of America, 1987.

Pollock, S. "Axialism and Empire". In *Axial Civilizations and the World History*, edited by J. Arnason, S. Eisenstadt, and B. Wittrock, 397–450. Leiden: Brill, 2005.

Wengrow, D. *What Makes a Civilization? The Ancient Near Future of the West*. Oxford: Oxford University Press, 2010.

World-system approach

Journals

Journal of World-Systems Research (1995–).
Review (1977–).

Historiographical analysis

Babones, S., and Chase-Dunn, C., eds. *Routledge Handbook of World-System Analysis*. London; New York: Routledge, 2012.

Denemark, R., Friedman, J., Gills, B., and Modelski, G. eds. *World-System History: The Social Science of Long-Term Change*. London; New York: Routledge, 2000.

Hall, T., ed. *A World-Systems Reader: New Perspectives on Gender, Urbanism, Cultures, Indigenous Peoples, and Ecology*. Lanham, MD: Rowman & Littlefield, 2000.

Sanderson, S. K. *Civilizations and World-Systems: Studying World-Historical Change*. Walnut Creek, CA: Altamira, 1995.

Shannon, T. *An Introduction to the World-System Perspective*. Boulder: Westview Press, 1989.

Voros, J. "Marco-Perspectives Beyond the World-System." *Journal of Future Studies* 11, no. 3 (2007): 1–28.

Wallerstein, I. *World-Systems Analysis: An Introduction*. Durham: Duke University Press, 2004.

Selected publications

Abu-Lughod, J. *Before European Hegemony: The World-System A.D. 1250–1350*. New York: Oxford University Press, 1989.

Arrighi, G. *The Long Twentieth Century: Money, Power, and the Origins of Our Times*. London, New York: Verso, 1994.

Chase-Dunn, C. *Global Formation: Structure of the World Economy*. Lanham, MD: Rowman & Littlefield Publishers, 1998.

Chase-Dunn, C., and Bruce Lerro. *Social Change. Globalization from the Stone Age to the Present*. Boulder and London: Paradigm Publishers, 2014.

Chase-Dunn, C., and T. Hall. *Rise and Demise: Comparing World-Systems. Cross-World-System Comparisons*. Boulder: Westview Press, 1997.

Chase-Dunn, C., Manning, S., and Hall, T. "Rise and Fall, East-West Synchronicity and Indic Exceptionalism Revisited." *Social Science History* 24 (2000): 727–54.

Frank, A., and B. Gills, eds. *The World-System: Five Hundred Years or Five Thousand?* London: Routledge, 1993.

Grosfoguel, R., and Cervantes-Rodríguez, A., eds. *The Modern/Colonial/Capitalist World-System in the Twentieth Century: Global Processes, Antisystemic Movements, and the Geopolitics of Knowledge*. Westport, CT: Greenwood Press, 2002.

Herkenrath, M., C. König, H. Scholtz, and T. Volken. "Divergence and Convergence in the Contemporary World-System: An Introduction." *International Journal of Comparative Sociology* 46, nos. 5–6 (2005): 363–82.
Hopkins, T., and I. Wallerstein, eds. *Processes of the World-System*. Beverly Hills, CA: Sage Publications, 1980.
Hopkins, T., Wallerstein, I., and Associates. *World-Systems Analysis: Theory and Methodology*. Beverly Hills, CA: Sage Publications, 1982.
Kohl, P. "The Use and Abuse of World-Systems Theory." In *Archaeological Thought in America*, edited by C.C. Lamberg-Karlovsky, 218–240. Cambridge: Cambridge University Press, 1989.
Preyer, G., and M. Bös, eds. *Borderlines in a Globalized World: New Perspectives in a Sociology of the World-System*. Boston; London: Kluwer Academic, 2002.
Wallerstein, I. *Historical Capitalism*. London: Verso, 1984.
Wallerstein, I., and Lee, R. *Overcoming the Two Cultures: Science Versus the Humanities in the Modern World-System*. Boulder, CO: Paradigm Publishers, 2004.
Wallerstein, I. *The End of the World as We Know It: Social Science for the Twenty-First Century*. Minneapolis, MN: University of Minnesota Press, 1999.
Wallerstein, I. *The Modern World-System: Capitalist Agriculture and the Origins of the European World-Economy in the Sixteenth Century*. New York: Academic Press, 1976.
Wallerstein, I. *The Modern World-System: Mercantilism and the Consolidation of the European World-Economy, 1600–1750*. New York: Academic Press, 1976.
Wallerstein, I. *The Modern World-System: The Second Era of Great Expansion of the Capitalist World-Economy, 1730–1840s*. New York: Academic Press, 1989.
Wallerstein, I. *The Uncertainties of Knowledge*. Philadelphia: Temple University Press, 2004.
Wallerstein, I. *Unthinking Social Science: The Limits of Nineteenth-Century Paradigms*. Philadelphia: Temple University Press, 2001.

Thinking History Globally: Contextualizing on a Bigger Scale

History of globalization

Journals
Itinerario. International Journal on the History of European Expansion and Global Interaction (1977–).
New Global Studies (2007–).

Historiographical analysis
Olstein, D. "Le molteplici origini della globalizzazione. Un dibattito storiografico". *Contemporanea* 3 (2006): 403–22.

Selected publications
Armitage, D. "Is There a Pre-History of Globalization?" In *Comparison and History: Europe in Cross-National Perspective,* edited by D. Cohen, and M. O'Connor, 165–74. New York and London: Routledge, 2004.
Baldwin, R., and P. Martin. "Two Waves of Globalization: Superficial Similarities, Fundamental Differences." *NBER Working Paper 6904*. Cambridge, 1999.

Battilossi, S. "The Determinants of Multinational Banking During the First Globalization, 1880–1914," *European Review of Economic History* 10, no. 3 (2006): 361–88.

Bordo, M., B. Eichengreen, and D. Irwin. "Is Globalization Today Really Different than Globalization a Hundred Years Ago?" *NBER Working Paper 7195*. Cambridge, 1999.

Bordo, M. "Globalization in Historical Perspective." *Business Economics* (2002): 20–29.

Briones, I., and A. Villela, "European Bank Penetration During the First Wave of Globalization: Lessons from Brazil and Chile, 1878–1913," *European Review of Economic History* 10, no. 3 (2006): 329–59.

Chase-Dunn, C., Y. Kawano, and B. Brewer. "Trade Globalization since 1795: Waves of Integration in the World-System." *American Sociological Review* 65, no. 1 (2002): 77–95.

Erlichman, H. J. *Conquest, Tribute, and Trade: The Quest for Precious Metals and the Birth of Globalization.* Amherst, NY: Prometheus, 2010.

Flynn, D., and A. Giráldez. "Path Dependence, Time Lags and the Birth of Globalisation: A Critique of O'Rourke and Williamson." *European Review of Economic History.* 8, no. 1 (2004): 85–108.

Gills, B., and W. Thompson, eds. *Globalization and Global History.* London and New York: Routledge, 2006.

Hopkins, A. G., ed. *Globalization in World History.* London: Pimlico, 2002.

James, H. *The End of Globalization: Lessons from the Great Depression.* Cambridge, MA: Harvard University Press, 2001.

McKeown, A. M. "Periodizing Globalization." *History Workshop Journal* 63, no. 1 (2007): 218–230.

Neal, L., and L. Davis. "The Evolution of the Structure and Performance of the London Stock Exchange in the First Global Financial Market, 1812–1914." *European Review of Economic History* 10, no. 3 (2006): 279–300.

O'Rourke, K., and J. Williamson. *Globalization and History: The Evolution of a Nineteenth-Century Atlantic Economy.* Cambridge: MIT Press, 1999.

O'Rourke, K., and J. Williamson. "Once More: When did Globalisation Begin?" *European Review of Economic History* 8, no. 1 (2004): 109–17.

O'Rourke, K., and J. Williamson. "When Did Globalisation Begin?" *European Review of Economic History* 6 (2002): 23–50.

Osterhammel, J., and N. Petersson. *Globalization. A Short History.* Translated by D. Geyer. Princeton and Oxford: Princeton University Press, 2005.

Steger, Manfred B. *Globalization: A Very Short Introduction.* Oxford: Oxford University Press, 2003.

Williamson, J. "Globalization and Inequality Then and Now: The Late 19th and Late 20th Centuries Compared." *NBER Working Paper 5491,* Cambridge, 1996.

Global history

Journals

Comparativ. Zeitschrift für Globalgeschichte und vergleichende Gesellschaftsforschung (1991–).
Journal of Global History (2006–).

Historiographical analysis

Berg, Maxine, ed. *Writing the History of the Global: Challenges for the 21st Century.* Oxford: Oxford University Press for the British Academy, 2013.

Crossley, Pamela Kyle. *What Is Global History?* Cambridge: Polity, 2008.

Hopkins, A. G., ed. *Global History: Interactions Between the Universal and the Local.* Basingstoke [England]; New York: Palgrave-Macmillan, 2006.
Mazlish, B. *The New Global History.* London: Routledge, 2006.
Mazlish, B., and Akira Iriye, eds. *The Global History Reader.* New York: Routledge, 2005.
Mazlish, B., and R. Buultjens, eds. *Conceptualizing Global History.* Boulder, CO: Westview Press, 1993.
Sachsenmaier, D. *Global Perspectives on Global History: Theories and Approaches in a Connected World.* New York: Cambridge University Press, 2011.

Selected publications

Abernethy, D. *The Dynamics of Global Dominance. European Overseas Empires, 1415–1980.* New Haven: Yale University Press, 2000.
Adas, M. "From Settler Colony to Global Hegemon: Integrating the Exceptionalist Narrative of the American Experience into World History." *American Historical Review* 106 (2001): 1692–720.
Adas, M. *Machines as the Measure of Men: Science, Technology, and Ideologies of Western Dominance.* Ithaca: Cornell University Press, 1989.
Amsden, A. *The Rise of "the Rest": Challenges to the West From Late-Industrializing Economies.* Oxford; New York: Oxford University Press, 2001.
Bayly, C. *Imperial Meridian: The British Empire and the World, 1780–1830.* London, New York: Longman, 1989.
Bayly, C. *The Birth of the Modern World, 1780–1914: Global Connections and Comparisons.* Malden: Blackwell, 2004.
Black, Jeremy. *Introduction to Global Military History: 1775 to the Present Day.* London; New York: Routledge, 2005.
Bodley, J. *The Power of Scale: A Global History Approach.* Armonk, NY: M.E. Sharpe, 2003.
Boswell, T., and C. Chase-Dunn. *The Spiral of Socialism and Capitalism: Towards Global Democracy.* Boulder: Lynne Rienner, 2000.
Bright, C., and M. Geyer. "Regimes of World Order: Global Integration and the Production of Difference in Twentieth-Century World History." In *Interactions: Transregional Perspectives On World History*, edited by J.cH. Bentley, R. Bridenthal, and A. A. Yang. Honolulu: University of Hawai'i Press, 2005.
Chase, K. W. *Firearms: A Global History to 1700.* Cambridge; New York: Cambridge University Press, 2003.
Clarence-Smith, W. *The Global Coffee Economy in Africa, Asia, and Latin America, 1500–1989.* New York: Cambridge University Press, 2003.
Conrad, S., A. Eckert, and U. Freitag, eds. *Globalgeschichte. Theorien, Ansätze und Themen.* Frankfurt am main: Campus, 2007.
Darwin, J. *After Tamerlane: The Rise and Fall of Global Empires, 1400–2000.* New York: Bloomsbury Press: Distributed to the trade by Macmillan, 2008.
Darwin, J. *The Empire Project: Rise and Fall of the British World-System 1830–1970.* Cambridge, UK; New York: Cambridge University Press, 2009.
David, J., T. David, and B. Lüthi, eds. "Globalgeschichte/Histoire Globale/Global History," Special Issue, *Traverse: zeitschrift für Geschichte/Revue d'histoire* 14 (Zurich), no. 3 (2007).
Frank, A. *ReOrient: Global Economy in the Asian Age.* Berkeley: University of California Press, 1998.

Getz, T., and H. Streets-Salter. *Modern Imperialism and Colonialism: A Global Perspective*. Harlow: Pearson Longman, 2010.
Goldstone, J. *Revolution and Rebellion in the Early Modern World*. Berkeley: University of California Press, 1990.
Goldstone, J. *Why Europe? The Rise of the West in World History, 1500–1850*. Boston: McGraw-hill, 2008.
Gran, P. *Beyond Eurocentrism: A New View of Modern World History*. Syracuse: Syracuse University Press, 1996.
Guha, R. *Environmentalism: A Global History*. New York: Longman, 2000.
Gungwu, W., ed. *Global History and Migrations*. Boulder: Westview, 1997.
Headrick, D. *The Invisible Weapon: Telecommunications and International Politics, 1851–1945*. New York: Oxford University Press, 1991.
Headrick, D. *The Tentacles of Progress: Technology Transfer in the Age of Imperialism, 1850–1940*. New York: Oxford University Press, 1988.
Headrick, D. *When Information Came of Age: Technologies of Knowledge in the Age of Reason and Revolution, 1700–1850*. Oxford, New York: Oxford University Press, 2000.
Iriye, A. *China and Japan in the Global Setting*. Cambridge, MA: Harvard University Press, 1992.
Lim, J., and K. Petrone, eds. *Gender Politics and Mass Dictatorship: Global Perspectives*. Basingstoke: Palgrave Macmillan, 2011.
Lucassen, J., and L. Lucassen. "The Mobility Transition Revisited, 1500–1900: What the Case of Europe Can Offer to Global History." *Journal of Global History* 4, no. 3 (2009): 347–77.
Maier, C. S. "Transformations of Territoriality, 1600–2000." In *Transnational. Geschichte: Themen, Trendenzen und Theorien*, edited by G. Budde, S. Conrad, and O. Janz, 32–55. Gottingen: Vendenhoeck & Ruprecht.
Manning, P. *The African Diaspora: A History through Culture*. New York: Columbia University Press, 2009.
Markovits, C. *The Global World of Indian Merchants, 1750–1947: Traders of Sind from Bukhara to Panama*. Cambridge, NY: Cambridge University Press, 2000.
Marks, R. B. *The Origins of the Modern World: A Global and Ecological Narrative From the Fifteenth to the Twenty-First Century*. 2nd ed. New York: Rowman & Littlefield, 2007.
Marks, R. *The Origins of the Modern World: A Global and Ecological Narrative*. Lanham, MD: Rowman & Littlefield, 2002.
McKeown, A. *Melancholy Order: Asian Migration and the Globalization of Borders*. New York: Columbia University Press, 2008.
McNeill, J. R., and Erin Stewart Mauldin, eds. *A Companion to Global Environmental History*. West Sussex: Wiley-Blackwell, 2012.
McNeill, J. *Something New Under the Sun: An Environmental History of the Twentieth-Century World*. New York: W.W. Norton, 2002.
Middell, M., and K. Naumann. "Global History 2008–2010. empirische erträge, konzeptionelle Debatten, neue synthesen." In *Die Verwandlung der weltgeschichtssechreibung*. Issue of comparative 20 6, edited by M. Middell, 93–133, 2010.
Pomeranz, K. *The Great Divergence: China, Europe and the Making of the Modern World Economy*. Princeton, Oxford: Princeton University Press, 2000.
Pomeranz, K., and S. Topik. *The World that Trade Created: Society, Culture, and the World Economy, 1400–the Present*. Armonk: M.E. Sharpe, 1999.
Riley, J. *Rising Life Expectancy: A Global History*. Cambridge, NY: Cambridge University Press, 2001.

Russo, D. *American History From a Global Perspective: An Interpretation*. Westport: Praeger, 2000.
Thompson, W. *The Emergence of the Global Political Economy*. London; New York: Routledge, 2000.
Vanhaute, E. "Who Is Afraid of Global History? Ambition, Pitfalls and Limits of Learning Global History." *Österreichishche Zeitschrift für Geschichtswissenschaften* 20, no. 2 (2009): 22–39.
Wills, J. *1688: A Global History*. New York: W.W. Norton, 2001.
Wright, D. *The World and a Very Small Place in Africa*. New York: M. E. Sharpe, 1997.

World history

Journals
Asian Review of World Histories (2013–).
Journal of World History (1990–).
Monde(s). Histoire, Espaces, Relations (2012–).
World History Bulletin (1983–).
World History Connected (e-Journal) (2003–).
Zeitschrift für Weltgeschichte (2000–).

Historiographical analysis
Adams, S., M. Adas, and K. Reilly, eds. *World History: Selected Course Outlines and Reading Lists From American Colleges and Universities*. Princeton: Markus Wiener Publishers, 1998.
Bentley, J. H., ed. *The Oxford Handbook of World History*. Oxford; New York: Oxford University Press, 2011.
Bentley, J. H. *Shapes of World History in Twentieth-Century Scholarship*. Washington, D.C.: American Historical Association, 1996.
Bentley, J. H. "The Journal of World History." In *Global Practices in World History: Advances Worldwide*, edited by P. Manning, 129–40. Princeton: Markus Wiener Publishers, 2008.
Burbank, J., and F. Cooper. *Empires in World History*. Princeton, NJ: Princeton University Press, 2010.
Costello, P. *World Historians and Their Goals: Twentieth-Century Answers to Modernism*. DeKalb, IL: Northern Illinois University Press, 1993.
Dirlink, A. "Confounding Metaphors, Inventions of the World: What Is World History For?" In *Writing World History, 1800–2000*, edited by B. Stuchtey and E. Fuch, 91–133. Oxford: Oxford University Press, 2003.
Drilink, A. "Performing the World: Reality and Representation in the Making of World Histories." *Journal of World History* 16, no. 4 (2005): 319–410.
Dunn, R., ed. *The New World History: A Teacher's Companion*. Boston: Bedford/St. Martin's, 2000.
Geyer, M., and Bright, Ch. "World History in a Global Age." *American Historical Review*, 100 (1995): 1030–1060.
Hughes-Warrington, M., ed. *Palgrave Advances in World History*. New York: Palgrave Macmillan, 2004.
Manning, P. *Navigating World History. Historians Create a Global Past*. New York: Palgrave Mcmillan, 2003.

Mazlish, B. "Comparing Global History to World History." *Journal of Interdisciplinary History* 28, no. 3 (1998): 385–95.

McNeill, W. *Mythistory and Other Essays*. Chicago: University of Chicago Press, 1986.

Northrop, D., ed. *A Companion to World History*. Chichester, West Sussex: Wiley-Blackwell, 2012.

Pomper, P., R. Elphick, and R. Vann, eds. "World Historians and Their Critics," *Special Issue History and Theory* 34, no. 2 (1995).

Seigel, M. "World History's Narrative Problem." *Hispanic American Historical Review* 84, no. 3 (2004): 431–46.

Stearns, P. *World History: The Basics*. New York: Routledge, 2011.

Stockes, G. "The Fates of Human Societies: A Review of Recent Macrohistories." *American Historical Review* 106 (2001): 508–525.

Stuchtey, B. and E. Fuchs, eds. *Writing World History, 1800–2000*. Oxford: Oxford University Press, 2003.

Tortarolo, E. "World Histories in Twentieth Century and Beyond." *Storia Della Storiografia* 38 (2000): 129–37.

Waters, N., ed. *Beyond the Area Studies War: Toward a New International Studies*. Hanover, NH: University Press of New England, 2000.

Textbooks

Adams, P., Langer, E., Hwa, L., Stearns, P., and Wiesner-Hansk, M. *Experiencing World History*. New York & London: New York University Press, 2000.

Bentley, J., and H. Ziegler. *Traditions & Encounters. A Global Perspective on the Past*. Boston: McGraw Hill, 2000.

Brummett, P., Jewsbury, G., and Lewis, C. *Civilization. Past and Present*. New York: Longman, 2000.

Bulliet, R. W., Crossley, P., Headrick, D., Hirsch, S., and Johnson, L. *The Earth and Its Peoples: A Global History*. Brief Edition. Boston: Houghton Mifflin Company, 2000.

Chodorow, S., Gatzke, H., and Schirokauer, C. *A History of the World*. San Diego, CA: Harcourt Brace Jovanovich, 1986.

Craig, A., Graham, W., Kagan, D., Ozmet, S., and Turner, F. *The Heritage of World Civilizations*. 5th ed. Upper Saddle River, NJ: Prentice Hall, 2000.

Duiker, W., and J. Spielvogel. *World History*. 3rd ed. Belmont, CA: Wadsworth/Thomson Learning, 2001.

Esler, A., ed. *The Human Venture. A World History: From the Prehistory to the Present*. Upper Saddle River, NJ: Prentice Hall, 2000.

Greaves, R., Zaller, R., Cannistrato, P., and Murphy, R. *Civilizations of the World. The Human Adventure*. 3rd ed. New York: Longman, 1997.

McGaughey, W. *Five Epochs of Civilization*. Minneapolis, MN: Thistlerose Pub, 2000.

McKay, J., Hill, B., Buckler, J., Buckley Ebrey, P., Beck, R., Haru Crowston, C., and Wiesner-Hansk, M. *A History of World Societies*. Boston & New York: Houghton Mifflin Company, 2000.

Morillo, S. *Frameworks of World History. Networks, Hierarchies, Culture*. New York: Oxford University Press, 2013.

Stearns, R., Adas, M., and Schwarts, S. *World Civilizations. The Global Experience*. 3rd ed. New York: Longman, 2001.

Tignor, R., et al. *Worlds Together, Worlds Apart*. New York: W. W. Norton & Company, Inc., 2002.

Upshur, J. L., et al. *World History: Comprehensive Volume*. Belmont, CA: Wadsworth, 1999.

World history synthesis

Blainey, G. *A Very Short History of the World.* London; New York: Penguin Books, 2004.
Clark, R. *The Global Imperative: An Interpretive History of the Spread of Humankind.* Boulder, CO: Westview Press, 1997.
Davis, J. *The Human Story: Our History, From the Stone Age to Today.* New York: HarperCollins, 2004.
Diamond, J. *Collapse. How Societies Choose to Fail or Survive.* Victoria: McPerson's Printing Group, 2005.
Diamond, J. *Guns, Germs, and Steel: The Fates of Human Societies.* London: Vintage Random House, 1998.
Dirlik, A., V. Bahl, and P. Gran, eds. *History After the Three Worlds: Post-Eurocentric Historiographies.* Lanham, MD: Rowman & Littlefield, 2000.
Fernández-Armesto, F. *Humankind: A Brief History.* Oxford; New York: Oxford University Press, 2004.
Fernández-Armesto, F. *So You Think You're Human?: A Brief History of Humankind.* Oxford: Oxford University Press, 2004.
Fromkin, D. *The Way of the World: From the Dawn of Civilization to the Eve of the Twenty-First Century.* New York: Knopf, 1999.
Hodgson, M. *Rethinking World History: Essays on Europe, Islam, and World History,* edited, with an introduction and conclusion by Burke, E. III. Cambridge; New York: Cambridge University Press, 1993.
Kishlansky, M., P. Geary, P. O'Brien, and R. Wong. *Societies and Cultures in World History.* New York: Harper Collins, 1995.
McNeill, W. H. *A World History.* 4th ed. New York: Oxford University Press, 1999.
McNeill, W. *The Rise of the West: A History of the Human Community.* New York: New American Library; London: New English Library, 1963.
McNeill, J., and W. McNeill. *The Human Web: A Bird's-Eye View of World History.* New York: W. W. Norton & Company, 2003.
Ponting, C. *World History: A New Perspective.* London: Chatto & Windus, 2000.
Stavrianos, L. S. *Lifelines From Our Past: A New World History.* Armonk, NY: M.E. Sharpe, 1997.
Stearns, P. N. *World History: Patterns of Change and Continuity.* New York: Harper & Row, 1987.

Selected publications by variables

Temporal units

Bernier, R. *The World in 1800.* New York: John Wiley & Sons, 2000.
Fernández-Armesto, F. *Millenium: A History of the Last Thousand Years.* New York: Scribner, 1995.
Grenville, J. A. S. *A History of the World From the 20th to the 21st Century.* London; New York: Routledge, 2005.
Hichens, M. *The Troubled Century: British and World History 1914–1993.* Edinburgh: Pentland Press, 1994.
Keylor, W. *The Twentieth Century World.* New York: Oxford University Press, 2001.
Keys, D. *Catastrophe: An Investigation into the Origins of the Modern World.* New York: Ballantine Pub., 2000.
Ponting, C. *The Twentieth Century: A World History.* New York: Henry Holt, 1999.
Roberts, J. *Twentieth Century: The History of the World, 1901 to 2000.* New York: Viking, 1999.

Space units

Adshead, S. *Central Asia in World History*. New York: St. Martin's Press, 1993.

Adshead, S. *China in World History*. New York: St. Martin's Press, 1995.

Christian, D. "The Silk Road or Steppe Roads? The Silk Roads in World History." *Journal of World History* 11 (2000): 1–26.

Cohen, W. *East Asia at the Center: Four Thousand Years of Engagements with the World*. New York: Columbia University Press, 2000.

Curtin, P. *The World and the West: The European Challenge and the Overseas Response in the Age of Empire*. New York: Cambridge University Press, 2000.

Eaton, R. *Islamic History as Global History*. Washington, DC: American Historical Association.

Embree, A., and C. Gluck, eds. *Asia in Western and World History: A Guide for Teaching*. Armonk: M.E. Sharpe.

Frank, A. *The Centrality of Central Asia*. Amsterdam: VU University Press, 1992.

Hodgson, M. *The Venture of Islam: A Short History of Islamic Civilization*. Chicago: University of Chicago Press, 1974.

Lieberman, V., ed. *Beyond Binary Histories: Re-Imagining Eurasia to c. 1830*, Ann Arbor: University of Michigan Press, 1999.

Pagden, A. *Peoples and Empires: A Short History of European Migration, Exploration, and Conquest, From Greece to the Present*. New York: Modern Library, 2003.

Prazniak, R. *Dialogues Across Civilizations: Sketches in World History From the Chinese and European Experiences*. Boulder, CO: Westview Press, 1996.

Russell-Wood, A. *A World on the Move: The Portuguese in Africa, Asia, and America, 1415–1808*. New York: St. Martin's Press, 1993.

Russell-Wood, A., ed. *An Expanding World: The European Impact on World History, 1450–1800*. 31 vols. Aldershot: Ashgate, 1995–2000.

So, A. *The South China Silk District: Local Historical Transformation and World-System Theory*. Albany: State University of New York Press., 1986.

Stearns, P. *Western Civilization in World History*. New York: Routledge, 2003.

Wong, R. *China Transformed: Historical Change and the Limits of European Experience*. Ithaca, NY: Cornell University Press, 1997.

Xinru, L. *The Silk Road: Borderland Trade and Cultural Interactions in Eurasia*. Washington, D.C.: American Historical Association, 1988.

Economy

Adas, M., ed. *Agricultural and Pastoral Societies in Ancient and Classical History*. American Historical Association. Philadelphia: Temple University Press, 2001.

Adshead, S. *Salt and Civilization*. Houndmills, Basingstoke, Hampshire: Macmillan, 1992.

Asakura, Hironori. *World History of the Customs and Tariffs*. Brussels: World Customs Organization, 2004.

Bairoch, P. *Economics and World History: Myths and Paradoxes*. Chicago: University of Chicago Press, 1993.

Cameron, R. *A Concise Economic History of the World: From Paleolithic Times to the Present*. New York: Oxford University Press, 1993.

Campbell, J., and Pryce, W. *Brick: A World History*. London: Thames & Hudson, 2003.

Curtin, P. *Cross-Cultural Trade in World History*. Cambridge: Cambridge University Press, 1984.

Curtin, P. D. *Cross-Cultural Trade in World History*. London: Cambridge University Press, 1984.

Grew, R., ed. *Food in Global History*. Boulder, CO: Westview Press, 1999.

Jones, E. *Growth Recurring: Economic Change in World History.* Oxford: Clarendon Press, 1988.
Kurlansky, M. *Cod: A Biography of the Fish that Changed the World.* Toronto: A.A. Knopf Canada, 1997.
Kurlansky, M. *Salt: A World History.* New York: Walker and Co., 2002.
Landes, D. *The Wealth and Poverty of Nations: Why Some Are So Rich and Some So Poor.* London: Little, Brown, 1998.
Maddison, A. *The World Economy: A Millennial Perspective.* Paris: Development Centre of the Organisation for Economic Co-operation and Development, 2001.
Moore, K., and D. Lewis. *Birth of the Multinational: 2000 Years of Ancient Business History-From Ashur to Augustus.* Copenhagen: Copenhagen Business School Press, 1999.
Smil, V. *Energy in World History.* Boulder: Westview Press, 1994.
Smith, A. *Creating a World Economy: Merchant Capital, Colonialism, and World Trade, 1400–1825.* Boulder: Westview Press, 1991.
Southall, A. *The City in Time and Space: From Birth to Apocalypse.* Cambridge, NY: Cambridge University Press, 1998.
Stearns, P. *Consumerism in World History: The Global Transformation of Desire.* New York: Routledge, 2001.
Stearns, P. *The Industrial Revolution in World History.* Boulder, CO: Westview Press, 2001.
Tracy, J., ed. *The Rise of Merchant Empires: Long-Distance Trade in The Early Modern World, 1350–1750.* Cambridge, New York: Cambridge University Press, 2001.
Tracy, J. *The Political Economy of Merchant Empires: State Power and World Trade, 1350–1750.* Cambridge, NY: Cambridge University Press, 1991.
Vasey, D. *An Ecological History of Agriculture.* Ames: Iowa State University Press, 1992.

Environment

Caras, R. *A Perfect Harmony: The Intertwining Lives of Animals and Humans Throughout History.* New York: Simon & Schuster, 1996.
Crosby, A. *Ecological Imperialism: The Biological Expansion of Europe, 900–1900.* Cambridge: Cambridge University Press, 1986.
Crosby, A. *Germs, Seeds & Animals: Studies in Ecological History.* Armonk, NY: M.E. Sharpe, 1994.
Hughes, J., ed. *The Face of the Earth: Environment and World History.* Armonk, NY: M.E. Sharpe, 1999.
O'Connor, J. *Natural Causes: Essays in Ecological Marxism.* New York: Guilford Press, 1998.
Ponting, C. *A Green History of the World: The Environment and the Collapse of Great Civilizations.* New York: Penguin Books, 1991.

Demography

Cohen, E. *Global Diasporas.* Seattle, Washington, DC: University of Washington, 1997.
De Pauw, L. *Battle Cries and Lullabies: Woman in War from Prehistory to the Present.* Norman: University of Oklahoma Press, 1998.
Kenneth, F. Kiple, ed. *The Cambridge World History of Human Disease.* Cambridge, NY: Cambridge University Press, 1993.
Manning, P., dir. *Migration in Modern World History, 1500–2000* [CD-ROM]. Belmont, CA: Wadsworth, produced by the World History Center.
Peter, N. Stearns. *Childhood in World History.* New York: Taylor & Francis, 2005.

Quale, G. *Families in Context: A World History of Population.* New York: Greenwood Press, 1992.
Quale, R. *A History of Marriage Systems.* New York: Greenwood Press, 1988.
Sowell, T. *Migrations and Cultures: A Worldview.* New York: BasicBooks, 1996.

Gender

Stearns, P. *Gender in World History.* New York: Routledge, 2000.
Strobel, M. *Gender, Sex, and Empire.* Washington, DC: American Historical Association, 1993.

Culture

Del Testa, D., Lemoine, F., Strickland, J., eds. *Global History: Cultural Encounters From Antiquity to the Present.* Armonk, NY: Sharpe Reference, 2004.
Hastings, Adrian, ed. *A World History of Christianity.* Grand Rapids, MI: W.B. Eerdmans, 1999.
Mangan, J. A., ed. *Europe, Sport, World: Shaping Global Societies.* London: Frank Cass, 2001.
McClellan, J. III, and Dorn, H. *Science and Technology in World History: An Introduction.* Baltimore: The Johns Hopkins University Press, 1999.
McComb, D. *Sports in World History.* New York: Routledge, 2004.
Mokyr, Y. *Twenty-Five Centuries of Technological Change: An Historical Survey.* New York: Harwood Academic Publishers, 1990.
Pacey, A. *Technology in World Civilization: A Thousand-Years History.* Cambridge, MA: MIT Press, 1996.
Rehbock, P. "Globalizing the History of Science". *Journal of World History.* 12 (2001): 183–92.

Politics

Adas, M., ed. *Islamic & European Expansion: The Forging of a Global Order.* American Historical Association. Philadelphia: Temple University Press, 1993.
Benedictow, O. J. *The Black Death, 1346–1353: The Complete History.* Woodbridge, UK: Boydell.
Benton, L. *Law and Colonial Cultures: Legal Regimes in World History, 1400–1900.* Cambridge: Cambridge University Press, 2002.
Benton, L. "No Longer Odd Region Out: Repositioning Latin America in World History." *Hispanic American Historical Review* 84, no. 3 (2004): 423–30.
Burg, D. F. *A World History of Tax Rebellions: An Encyclopedia of Tax Rebels, Revolts, and Riots From Antiquity to the Present.* New York: Routledge, 2004.
Buzan, B., and R. Little. *International Systems in World History: Remaking the Study of International Relations.* Oxford: Oxford University Press, 2000.
Crosby, A. *Throwing Fire: Projectile Technology Through History.* Cambridge, NY: Cambridge University Press, 2000.
Geyer, M., and C. Bright. "For a Unified History of the World in the Twentieth Century." *Radical History Review* 39 (1987): 69–91.
Geyer, M., and C. Bright. "World History in a Global Age." *American Historical Review* 100 (1995): 1034–60.
Gran, P. *The Rise of the Rich: A New View of Modern World History.* Syracuse, NY: Syracuse University Press, 2009.

Grosses, P. "l'histoire mondiale/globale. Une jeunesse exubérante mais difficile." *Vingtième siècle* 110 (Apr.–June): 3–18
Knutsen, T. *The Rise and Fall of World Orders*. Manchester, NY: Manchester University Press, 1999.
Lal, V. "Much Ado About Something: The New Malaise of World History." *Radical History Review* 91 (Winter 2005): 124–30.
Lal, V. Provincializing the West: World History from Perspective of Indian History. In *Writing World History* 1800–2000, edited by B. Stuchtey and E. Fuchs, 271–89. Oxford: Oxford University Press.
Lange, E. "Introduction: Placing Latin America in World History." *Hispanic American Historical Review* 84, no. 3 (July 30): 393–98.
Mair, V., ed. *Contact and Exchange in the Ancient World*. Honolulu: University of Hawai'i Press, 2006.
Spellman, W. M. *Monarchies 1000–2000*. London: Reaktion Books, 2001.

Big history: Selected publications

Benjamin, C. G. R., ed. "Introduction to Forum on Big History." *World History Connected* 6, no. 3 (Oct. 2009), available at: http://worldhistoryconnected.press.illinois.edu/6.3/index.html (accessed Feb. 2012).
Brown, C. S. *Big History: From the Big Bang to the Present*. New York: New Press, 2007.
Christian, David. *Maps of Time: An Introduction to Big History*. Berkeley: University of California Press, 2004.
Christian, D. "Big History: The Big Bang, Life on Earth, and the Rise of Humanity." *The Teaching Company*, Course No. 8050, 2004, available at: http://www.teach12.com/ttcx/CourseDescLong 2.aspx?cid=8050 (accessed Feb. 2012).
Christian, D. "The Case for 'Big History.'" *Journal of World History* 2, no. 2 (1991): 223–28.
Christian, D. *This Fleeting World: A Short History of Humanity*. Great Barrington, MA: Berkshire, 2008.
Christian, D. "World History in Context." *Journal of World History* 14, no. 4 (2003): 437–58.
Spier, F. *The Structure of Big History: From the Big Bang Until Today*. Amsterdam: University of Amsterdam Press, 1996.

Index

Abernethy, David, 142–4
Abu-Lughod, Janet, 123–4
Academic history/disciplinary history, 36, 39, 46
African Network in Global History, 43, 48
Agricultural revolution, 80, 148
American divergence, 62, 66–7, 115, 118
American Historical Review, 37, 95
American imperialism, 102–3
Amin, Samir, 131–2
Ancient Greece, tyrants, 27
Anderson, Perry, 113
Annales School, 37–8, 41
Argentina, 9–32
Arias, Arnulfo, 20
Armitage, David, 110, 127
Arnason, Johann, 113
Arrighi, Giovanni, 129
Asian Association of World Historians, 43, 48
Asian Review of World Histories, 43, 48–9
Atlantic history, 38, 111
Atlantic Studies, 38, 47
Augustine, 45
Axial Age, 117–19, 148–50

Bailyn, Bernard, 38
Bairoch, Paul, 134
Bendix, Reinhard, 40, 113
Bentley, Jerry, 125
Betancourt, Rómulo, 20
Big history, 28, 46–7, 152–3, 163–5, 218
Bloch, Marc, 34
Bonnell, Victoria, 68
Bordo, Michael, 44, 129
Borkenau, Franz, 39
Bossuet, Jacques Bénigne, 45
Braudel, Fernand, 37, 42, 113
Brazil, 11–12
Brazil and United States, compared and connected, 85
British and Spanish empires, compared, connected, and conceptualized, 64–6, 115
Burbank, Jane, 142

Cardenas, Lázaro, 20, 25
category, 33–4, 47–8
causation, endogenous, 65–8, 91, 116
causation, exogenous, 65–8, 78, 124
Chaisson, Eric J., 46
Chambers, Robert, 46
Chase-Dunn, Christopher, 92, 129, 133
Chauduri, Kirti N., 38, 110
Chaunu, Pierre, 38
Chiang Kai-shek, 103
China and Rome, connected, 65, 138
Christian, David, 46, 153
circum-oceanic, 110
cis-oceanic, 110
Cistercian order, 77
civilizational analysis, 19–21, 39–40, 113, 116–19, 170–2, 206–7
climate, 2, 27, 76, 84, 122, 148–50
closed-boundaries histories, 4–5, 9–10
Cold war, 6, 10, 61, 102–6
communications, 75, 86, 127, 130
Comparative Civilizations Review, 40, 48
comparative designs
  asymmetrical comparisons, 73
  contrast-oriented, 69
  incorporated comparison, 91–2
  macro-analytic, 69
  mutual comparisons, 94–5
  parallel comparisons, 70–1
comparative history, 11, 34–5, 87–90, 177–9, 194–6
comparative method, 68–73
  method of concomitant variations, 24, 70, 89
  method of crucial agreement, 69–70, 84, 128, 138, 167
  method of crucial difference, 63–4, 66, 69–71, 82, 91, 96, 138, 177

219

Comparative Studies in Society and
    History, 35, 47
Comparativ—Zeitschrift für
    Globalgeschichte und vergleichende
    Gesellschaftsforschung, 42, 48
comparing, 11–13, 29–32, 59–60
comparison and conceptualization,
    synergy, 29
comparisons and connections,
    complimentarily, 90–7
comparisons and connections,
    contradictions, 68, 83–7
conceptualizing, 19, 113
Condorcet, Marquis de, 45
connected histories, 13–14, 51, 84–6, 98
connecting, 11, 14, 29–32, 59–60
connections as method, 15, 74–9
conquests, 27, 59, 65, 76, 122, 138, 162,
    169–70
consumerism, 101, 150
contextualizing, 24, 30
Cooper, Frederick, 142
cross-boundaries histories, 5–6, 31, 33, 37,
    98–100
culturalist turn, 100–1

Darwin, John, 142
dependency theory, 41–2, 66–7
diachronic time, 63–8, 77, 91, 114, 116
diasporas, 110–11
Diplomatic History, 36, 47
Durkheim, Émile, 40, 70, 89, 113

East Asia and Europe, compared and
    connected, 83–5
Egypt, 12–13
Eisenstadt, Shmuel Noah, 113–18
Elliott, John H., 35, 111
empires, Spanish and British compared,
    connected, and conceptualized,
    64–6, 115
empires of the classical age, compared,
    connected and conceptualized, 2, 65,
    71, 78, 114–15
empires in world and global history, 142–4
ENIUGH, European Network in Universal
    and Global History, 43, 48
entangled history (*histoire croisée*), 13–14,
    35–6, 85–6, 98, 178–80

environment, 2, 27, 61, 70, 76, 105, 125,
    134, 148, 164
Espagne, Michelle, 37
Eurasia, compared and connected, 83–4
Evangelista, Matthew, 105–6

Ferguson, Niall, 71
Fernández Armesto, Felipe, 127
First World War, 157–83
Fischer, Steven R., 110
Fitzpatrick, Sheila, 96
Flynn, Dennis, 44
Frank, Andre Gunder, 120
Fredrickson, George, 68

Gallicchio, Marc, 103
Gambia, 145–6
Germany and United States connected,
    85, 101–2
geschichte.transnational, 37, 47
Geyer, Michael, 96
Ghana, 159
Gienow-Hecht, Jessica C. E., 101–2
Gills, Barry, 44
Giraldez, Arturo, 44
global history, 24–6, 42–3, 125–6, 140–6,
    158–61, 209–12
global history, up and down scales, 144–6,
    158–61
globalization, definition, 136–9
globalization, "first", 26, 30, 131, 133, 165
globalization, history of, 26–7, 43–4,
    126–3, 165–7, 208–9
globalization, "today," contemporary, or
    current, 3–4, 6, 26, 30–1, 36, 80, 104,
    126, 128, 133
global spatiality, 50, 56, 155
global trend, 50, 56, 155
global turn, 50, 56, 155
global village, 3–4
Great Britain, 14–16, 134, 169–70
great divergence, 28, 91, 149
Grew, Raymond, 35
Gruzinski, Serge, 35, 98

Harari, Yuval, 142–3
Hartz, Louis, 70
Hegel, Georg Wilhelm Friedrich, 46
hegemonic cycles, 89, 170
hegemony, 119–20, 123, 135, 159

hegemony, American and British compared, 129
Herder, Johann Gottfried von, 39
Herodotus, 45
Hintze, Otto, 68
historical connections, 74–5
historical sociology, 6, 21–2, 40–1, 114–16, 167–8, 204–6
Hodgson, Marshal G. S., 44, 91
Hoganson, Kristin, 101
Hopkins, Antony, 44
Humboldt, Alexander von, 46
Huntington, Samuel, 113, 118–19
H-WORLD, 154

Ibn Khaldun, 45
Ibn Rušd, 77
Iggers, Georg, 125
imperial history, 62–4, 123
inclusiveness, comparisons and connections, 90–7
Indian Ocean history, 38–9, 99, 107–8
Industrial Revolution, 71, 113, 148, 152
The International History Review, 36, 47
International Journal of Maritime History, 39, 47
international organizations, 37, 176
Iriye, Akira, 37, 105, 140, 145
İslamoğlu-İnan, Huri, 98
Itinerario: International Journal on the History of European Expansion and Global Interaction, 44

Jastrow, Robert, 46
Journal of Global History, 42, 48
Journal of Historical Sociology, 40, 48
Journal of Pacific History, 38, 47
Journal of World History, 45, 49, 95
Journal of World-System Research, 42, 48

Kedar, B. Z., 69, 82, 151
Kocka, Jürgen, 72–3
Kondratiev waves, 89, 120

Lang, James, 66
Langlois, Charles-Victor, 34
Latin America and North America, compared, connected and conceptualized, 62, 66–7, 70–1, 115–16, 118–19
Latin America, wars of independence, compared, 70
Lieberman, Victor, 83–4
Lipset, Seymour Martin, 40, 113
long nineteenth century (1789–1914), 28, 145

Mahoney, James, 115
Maimonides, 78
Manning, Patrick, 125
Mann, Michael, 114–15
Maritime History, 39, 47
Marx, Karl, 40
Mazlish, Bruce, 42–4, 140–1
McMichael, Philip, 91
McNeill, John Robert, 81
McNeill, William H., 44, 65, 80–1
Mediterranean Sea, 1, 18, 77, 99, 173
Mesopotamia and Ancient Egypt, compared, connected and conceptualized, 62–4, 93, 111, 114, 117, 122–3
Metahistories, 5
methodological nationalism, 4–5, 50, 88
Migration, 10, 27, 37, 59–61, 64–5, 71, 76, 111, 118, 128, 130–1, 147, 173–4
Mill, John Stuart, 69
modernization theory, 66–7
Monde(s). Histoire, espaces, relations, 49
Mongol Empire, 80, 123, 138, 142, 162
Montesquieu, 39, 113
More, Barrington, 113
Mukherjee, Supriya, 125
multidisciplinarity, 153, 182
multinational corporations, 37, 104, 127, 140
Mumford, Lewis, 5

Nasser, Gamal Abdel, 12
nation-state based history, 3–4, 9–10
Nazi Germany and Soviet Russia, compared, connected, and conceptualized, 86–7, 96
Nehru, Jawaharlal, 21–2
Nelson, Benjamin, 113
neoliberal policies, 71
network, 33–4

network, transnational, 75–7, 79
New Global Studies, 43, 48
new international history, 15–16, 36, 99–104, 173–5, 197–200
new regimes of space, 50, 155
Nkrumah, Kwame, 21–2
NOGWHISTO, Network of Global and World History Organizations, 43, 48
nomadic societies, 45, 65, 80
nongovernmental organizations, 4, 16, 17–18, 37, 104, 176
Northrop, Douglas, 154
Nuevo Mundo Mundos Nuevos, 43, 48

oceanic histories, 18–19, 37–9, 106–12, 172–3, 201–4
oceanic and land base histories, complementary, 107–10
O'Rourke, Kevin, 44
Osterhammel, Jürgen, 44, 132

Pacific Historical Review, 38, 47
Pacific history, 39
Pagden, Anthony, 66
Perdue, Peter, 98
Perón, Eva, 10, 17–18
Perón, Juan Domingo, 9–32, 157, 180–2
Petersson, Niels, 44, 132
Pirenne, Henri, 34
plagues, 27, 123
Pomeranz, Kenneth, 91, 149
populist regimes, 20–1
Prebisch, Raúl, 41

Radhanites, 77
Rashid al-din Fadl Allah, 45
Recueils de la Société Jean Bodin pour l'histoire comparative des institutions, 35, 47, 83
Red Latinoamericana de Historia Global, 43, 48
Redlich, Fritz, 72
relational histories, 11, 13–14, 35–6, 85–7, 98–9, 178–82, 196–7
religion, 77–8, 113, 117–18
Review, 42, 48
revolutions, 25, 33, 41, 69, 85–7, 145, 158, 167–8, 180
Roman Empire, 1–2

Roman Empire, compared, connected, and conceptualized, 64–5, 114, 143
Rome and China, connected, 65, 138
Rosenberg, Emily S., 102

Sachs, Jeffrey, 134
Sagan, Carl, 46
Scale, 50–2
Scientific revolution, 62, 148
shared histories, 13–14, 86, 98
short twentieth century (1914–1989), 28–31
Silk Road, 108–9
Sima Qian, 45
Skocpol, Theda, 68–9
Smelser, Neil, 40, 113
Smith, Jonathan, 71–2, 94
social sciences, 19, 39, 68–9, 113
Somers, Margaret, 68–9
Soviet Union and Nazi Germany, compared, connected, and conceptualized, 86–7, 97
Spanish and British empires, compared, connected, and conceptualized, 64–6, 115
spatial turn, 50, 56, 155
Spengler, Oswald, 39, 113
Spice Road, 108–9
Stavrianos, Leften, 44
Stearns, Peter, 150
Subrahmanyam, Sanjay, 35, 83–4, 98
Sukarno, 21–2
Sun Yat-Sen, 25
synchronic time, 2, 64–8, 77–8, 84, 101, 108, 114, 124
synergies between branches, 29–32, 95–7, 183

Taylor, Alan, 44
Thomas Aquinas, 78
Thompson, William, 44
Tilly, Charles, 73, 113
time scope, 52–3
Tocqueville, Alexis de, 40
Toynbee, Arnold, 39, 70, 113
trade, 14, 18, 27, 41, 61–7, 76, 77
transfers, 16–17, 29, 37, 61, 86, 110, 155
transnational history, 16–18, 36–7, 104–6, 175–7, 200–1

trans-oceanic, 110–12
transportation, 3, 14, 18, 74, 108, 130, 134, 166
typology, 47–8

United States and Germany connected, 85, 101–2
United States and Latin American histories, compared, connected, and conceptualized, 62, 66–7, 70–1, 85, 115–16, 118–19
United States history, compared and connected, 60–1
   Civil War compared to War of Paraguay, 67
   race relations compared and connected, 103–4
units of analysis, 50–2
universal history, 45–7

Van den Braembussche A. A., 68, 73
Vargas, Getulio, 11–12
Velasco Ibarra, José María, 20
Vico, Giambattista, 39
Vikings and Polynesians compared, 91
Voltaire, 45

Wallesrtein, Immanuel, 41, 121

Wang, Q. Edward, 125
Weber, Max, 40, 113
Weinstein, Barbara, 156
Wells, H. G., 5
Werner, Michael, 35, 98
Wilkinson, David, 117, 119, 127
Williamson, Jeffrey, 44
Wittrock, Björn, 113
world history, 27–8, 44–6, 140–4, 146–52, 155–6, 161–3, 212–18
World History Association, 43, 48
World History Bulletin, 45, 49
World History Connected, 45, 49
world history, cross-sectional themes, 27, 150–2, 161–3
World history survey, compared and connected, 80–1, 96, 147–50
world history, synthesis, 80–1, 147–50
world history, teaching, 96, 147–50
world history, textbooks, 96, 147–50
world-system approach, 22–4, 40–2, 80, 119–24, 169–70, 207–8
World Wars, in global and world histories, 158–62
writing systems, compared, 93–5

Zimmermann, Bénédicte, 35

CPSIA information can be obtained
at www.ICGtesting.com
Printed in the USA
LVHW081528130721
692566LV00004B/267